PCHS MEDIA CENTER
GRANT, NEBRASKA

DATE DUE			

Assisted Suicide

Karen F. Balkin, *Book Editor*

Bruce Glassman, *Vice President*
Bonnie Szumski, *Publisher*
Helen Cothran, *Managing Editor*

GREENHAVEN PRESS
An imprint of Thomson Gale, a part of The Thomson Corporation

Detroit • New York • San Francisco • San Diego • New Haven, Conn.
Waterville, Maine • London • Munich

LIBRARY OF CONGRESS CATALOGING-IN-PUBLICATION DATA

Assisted suicide / Karen F. Balkin, book editor.
   p. cm. — (Current controversies)
Includes bibliographical references and index.
ISBN 0-7377-2198-7 (lib. : alk. paper) — ISBN 0-7377-2199-5 (pbk. : alk. paper)
   1. Assisted suicide. 2. Assisted suicide—Moral and ethical aspects. 3. Assisted suicide—Social aspects. 4. Right to die—Social aspects. 5. Euthanasia—Social aspects. I. Balkin, Karen F., 1949– . II. Series.
R726.A852 2005
179.7—dc22
                                                             2004047375

Printed in the United States of America

Contents

Chapter 1: Is Assisted Suicide Ethical?

Yes: Assisted Suicide Is Ethical

No: Assisted Suicide Is Not Ethical

Chapter 2: Should Assisted-Suicide Decisions Be Made by the States?

Yes: Assisted-Suicide Decisions Should Be Made by the States

No: Assisted-Suicide Decisions Should Not Be Made by the States

Chapter 3: Would Legalizing Assisted Suicide Harm America's Health Care?

Yes: Legalizing Assisted Suicide Would Harm America's Health Care

Foreword

By definition, controversies are "discussions of questions in which opposing opinions clash" (Webster's Twentieth Century Dictionary Unabridged). Few would deny that controversies are a pervasive part of the human condition and exist on virtually every level of human enterprise. Controversies transpire between individuals and among groups, within nations and between nations. Controversies supply the grist necessary for progress by providing challenges and challengers to the status quo. They also create atmospheres where strife and warfare can flourish. A world without controversies would be a peaceful world; but it also would be, by and large, static and prosaic.

The Series' Purpose

The purpose of the Current Controversies series is to explore many of the social, political, and economic controversies dominating the national and international scenes today. Titles selected for inclusion in the series are highly focused and specific. For example, from the larger category of criminal justice, Current Controversies deals with specific topics such as police brutality, gun control, white collar crime, and others. The debates in Current Controversies also are presented in a useful, timeless fashion. Articles and book excerpts included in each title are selected if they contribute valuable, long-range ideas to the overall debate. And wherever possible, current information is enhanced with historical documents and other relevant materials. Thus, while individual titles are current in focus, every effort is made to ensure that they will not become quickly outdated. Books in the Current Controversies series will remain important resources for librarians, teachers, and students for many years.

In addition to keeping the titles focused and specific, great care is taken in the editorial format of each book in the series. Book introductions and chapter prefaces are offered to provide background material for readers. Chapters are organized around several key questions that are answered with diverse opinions representing all points on the political spectrum. Materials in each chapter include opinions in which authors clearly disagree as well as alternative opinions in which authors may agree on a broader issue but disagree on the possible solutions. In this way, the content of each volume in Current Controversies mirrors the mosaic of opinions encountered in society. Readers will quickly realize that there are many viable answers to these complex issues. By questioning each author's conclusions, students and casual readers can begin to develop the critical thinking skills so important to evaluating opinionated material.

Current Controversies is also ideal for controlled research. Each anthology in the series is composed of primary sources taken from a wide gamut of informational categories including periodicals, newspapers, books, United States and foreign government documents, and the publications of private and public organizations. Readers will find factual support for reports, debates, and research papers covering all areas of important issues. In addition, an annotated table of contents, an index, a book and periodical bibliography, and a list of organizations to contact are included in each book to expedite further research.

Perhaps more than ever before in history, people are confronted with diverse and contradictory information. During the Persian Gulf War, for example, the public was not only treated to minute-to-minute coverage of the war, it was also inundated with critiques of the coverage and countless analyses of the factors motivating U.S. involvement. Being able to sort through the plethora of opinions accompanying today's major issues, and to draw one's own conclusions, can be a complicated and frustrating struggle. It is the editors' hope that Current Controversies will help readers with this struggle.

Greenhaven Press anthologies primarily consist of previously published material taken from a variety of sources, including periodicals, books, scholarly journals, newspapers, government documents, and position papers from private and public organizations. These original sources are often edited for length and to ensure their accessibility for a young adult audience. The anthology editors also change the original titles of these works in order to clearly present the main thesis of each viewpoint and to explicitly indicate the opinion presented in the viewpoint. These alterations are made in consideration of both the reading and comprehension levels of a young adult audience. Every effort is made to ensure that Greenhaven Press accurately reflects the original intent of the authors included in this anthology.

> *"Euthanasia should be voluntary, legal, and rare."*
> —Derek Humphry, founder of the Hemlock Society

Introduction

In 1975 British journalist Derek Humphry helped his terminally ill wife, Jean, commit suicide in England. He knew he was breaking the law and risking a fourteen-year prison sentence when he obtained barbiturates from a London doctor, mixed them into a cup of milky coffee, and gave the mixture to his 42-year-old wife. After struggling with breast and bone cancer for more than two years, she was dead in less than an hour. Humphry was investigated but never prosecuted for his wife's death.

Jean's Way, Humphry's book detailing his wife's fight against cancer, her decision to choose the time, place, and method of her death, and his role in helping her, was published in March 1978 in England. The book caused a worldwide sensation and was eventually translated into most major languages. It ran through sixteen printings in England, and was published in the United States in 1979. Humphry, who had come to California for a job with the *Los Angeles Times*, was unprepared for America's response to his book—people began approaching him to help them help their loved ones die. He quickly realized the need for an organization devoted to educating the public about physician-assisted suicide (PAS) and working to change U.S. laws so that the practice would be legal. Humphry maintained, "My motive is to achieve a democratic change in the law to permit physician-assisted dying for the terminally and hopelessly ill." In 1980, with the help of Ann Wickett, Gerald A. Larue, and Richard S. Scott, Humphry founded the Hemlock Society—now the oldest, largest, and most politically powerful right-to-die organization in the United States. The Hemlock Society changed forever debates about assisted suicide and helped improve end-of-life care.

Humphry used royalties from *Jean's Way* to fund the fledgling organization. However, the book that would prove to be the Hemlock Society's philosophical and financial foundation would not be published until the following year. In 1981 Humphrey's *Let Me Die Before I Wake*, the first book describing how a patient could end his or her own life, was published for Hemlock Society members only. It was released publicly in 1982 and sold over twenty-five thousand copies a year over the next ten years. However, *Let Me Die Before I Wake* was outstripped by Humphry's next book, the controversial *Final Exit: The Practicalities of Self-Deliverance and Assisted Suicide for the Dying*, which has sold over one million copies to date.

With Humphry as executive director and president from 1988 to 1990, the Hemlock Society grew rapidly. It swelled to over fifty thousand members with ninety chapters throughout the United States and became an international presence in the World Federation of Right-to-Die Societies. True to its original mission of education and political activism, in 1984 the Hemlock Society began a national campaign to promote knowledge and awareness of advance directives—legal documents detailing the extent of life support measures a person desires in the event of a terminal illness or life-threatening accident. As a direct result of the Hemlock Society's efforts, many states began passing laws governing the use of advance directives, and in 1991 the U.S. Congress passed the Patient Self-Determination Act, which requires nursing homes, hospitals, home health agencies, and health maintenance organizations (HMOs) to provide patients with information on laws in their state regarding advance directives.

The Hemlock Society continued its grassroots political activism, sending a draft of the Humane and Dignified Death Act to state legislators all over the United States in 1986. The act was intended to be a template that states could use if they ever decided to try to legalize assisted suicide. Well funded by its large membership and substantial book royalties, the Hemlock Society backed physician-assisted suicide citizens' ballot measures in 1988 (California) and 1991 (Washington), both of which ultimately failed, and the successful Death with Dignity Act in Oregon in 1994. The society has also helped defeat repeated challenges to Oregon's law permitting physician-assisted suicide.

For the first ten years of its existence, the Hemlock Society was at the forefront of the assisted-suicide movement in the United States. Humphry and others in leadership positions maintained that assisted suicide should be available to the terminally ill, the hopelessly ill—such as patients with multiple sclerosis—and the elderly with severe health problems. However, as the organization became more powerful and active in state politics and the push for legalization of physician-assisted suicide became more intense, the Hemlock Society moved away from this broad advocacy and concentrated its attention on winning the right to PAS for the "advanced terminally ill." Focusing on terminal illness was a political expediency—there was greater general support for laws allowing physician-assisted suicide for those already doomed to death. Humphry, however, disagreed with the society's change in focus, insisting that assisted suicide should be more widely available and that the Hemlock Society should continue to advocate for laws that applied to broader groups. Humphry maintained an association with the Hemlock Society but retired from active participation in 1992 to pursue writing and lecturing. Eventually he formed a new group, the Euthanasia Research and Guidance Organization (ERGO).

While some consider the Hemlock Society radical by the very nature of its intent, it has provided a moderate voice within the right-to-die movement. Its continued insistence that only the terminally ill should be allowed assistance in dying and that universal access to physician-assisted methods of suicide should not be legal reflects a more conservative approach than that taken by other U.S. right-to-die organizations. According to the Hemlock Society's current president, David F. Walker, the organization "only supports hastened death in those cases in which all medical options have been exhausted and the patient has been diagnosed as terminal." He emphasizes that the Hemlock Society's priority continues to be to help pass legislation that would "guarantee control over medical treatment to terminal patients in consultation and with the support of the treating physicians."

To further these political goals and to express a new association with broader, end-of-life issues, the Hemlock Society changed its name in 2003 to End-of-Life Choices. Faye Girsh, the organization's senior vice president, explains the name change in greater detail: "The goal of the name change is to increase membership, to accelerate name recognition and approval, and work with legislators sympathetic to our mission, who find the name Hemlock offensive and difficult to explain." According to Girsh, polls show that the majority of the public supports physician aid in dying for the terminally ill but do not identify with the name Hemlock.

The organization continues to evolve and expand its political and financial support base. In February 2004 End-of-Life Choices merged with Compassion in Dying, a national organization that promotes care and choice at the end of life, providing education, advocacy, and service programs. David Brand, executive director of End-of-Life Choices, contends that "leaders of Choices and Compassion believe unification is in the best interests of the movement, and represents the best opportunity to realize twin goals of excellent care and optimal choice for all Americans at the end of life." Hemlock Society founder Humphry chose to disassociate himself from End-of-Life Choices when the decision was made to merge with Compassion in Dying. He cited philosophical differences and continues to write and work with his new organization, ERGO.

The Hemlock Society has had a substantial impact on the debate surrounding the legalization of physician-assisted suicide and the improvement of end-of-life care in the United States. Authors in *Current Controversies: Assisted Suicide* examine the question of whether PAS should be legalized, whether states should have the authority to decide assisted suicide legality, whether acceptance of PAS would harm America's health care, and how the world views assisted suicide.

Chapter 1

Is Assisted Suicide Ethical?

Chapter Preface

One of the strongest ethical arguments against physician-assisted suicide (PAS) is that vulnerable groups will not be adequately protected. Opponents of physician-assisted suicide argue that even the most restrictive laws can not safeguard the poor, the elderly, or the physically and mentally disabled from coerced suicide or even murder. This line of reasoning is often referred to as the slippery slope argument, suggesting that one step toward legalizing PAS will inevitably lead to other steps in the same direction until people are put to death without their consent.

Many disabled people maintain that this slippery slope is significantly steeper and riskier for them than it is for able-bodied people. Their greatest fear is not that they will accidentally slide down the incline toward assisted suicide, but that they will be pushed toward involuntary euthanasia by a culture that neither understands nor values them. For this reason, disabled advocacy groups opposing physician-assisted suicide, such as Not Dead Yet (NDY) and American Disabled for Attendant Programs Today (ADAPT), maintain that physician-assisted suicide is unethical and should not be legalized.

These groups insist that a double standard exists regarding value of life: A person who is not disabled is valued whereas a person who is disabled is not. According to Diane Coleman, founder and president of NDY, society's prejudice against people with disabilities results in a devaluation of the lives of disabled people. Many lay people as well as those in the medical establishment cannot understand why disabled people do not welcome suicide as an opportunity to free themselves from the pain and indignity of their disability. Harriet McBryde Johnson, a disabled disability rights attorney and supporter of NDY, says, "What we confront usually isn't homicidal hate, it's that pervasive assumption that our lives are inherently bad." Moreover, disabled people suffer additional pressure from a health care system that increasingly regards them as a long-term liability. Colman contends that

> Assisted suicide has been marketed to the American public as a step toward
> increasing individual freedom, but choice is an empty slogan in a world full of
> pressures on people with chronic illnesses and disabilities. Now is not the time
> to establish a public policy securing the profits of a health care system that
> abandons those most in need and would bury the evidence.

Julie G. Madorsky, clinical professor of rehabilitation medicine at Western University of Health Sciences in Pomona, California, acknowledges that many disabled people worry that PAS may become "a convenient rationing tool" and "that it may become easier to dispose of disabled people than to meet their needs for living fulfilling and meaningful lives."

This is what frightens disabled people most—that physicians and other able-bodied people who consider disabled lives worthless and expendable and insurance carriers who want to deny expensive treatment options to disabled people will decide that PAS is in the best interest of the disabled. After that, disabled advocacy groups opposing assisted suicide insist, it is just a short slide to involuntary euthanasia. For these reasons, many disabled advocacy groups are ethically opposed to physician-assisted suicide. They argue that discrimination against disabled people puts them at greater risk for abuse if this practice is legalized. Authors in the following chapter debate what implications the legalization of physician-assisted suicide would have on all Americans, including the disabled, the poor, and the elderly.

Allowing Competent People to Commit Suicide Is Ethical

by Robert Young

About the author: *Robert Young is a member of the faculty of Humanities and Social Sciences at La Trobe University in Victoria, Australia.*

When a person commits an act of euthanasia he brings about the death of another person because he believes the latter's present existence is so bad that she would be better off dead, or believes that unless he intervenes and ends her life, it will become so bad that she would be better off dead. The motive of the person who commits an act of euthanasia is to benefit the one whose death is brought about. (Though what was just said also holds for many instances of physician-assisted suicide, some wish to restrict the use of the latter term to forms of assistance which stop short of the physician 'bringing about the death' of the patient, such as those involving mechanical means which have to be activated by the patient.)

Our concern will be with *voluntary* euthanasia—that is, with those instances of euthanasia in which a clearly competent person makes a voluntary and enduring request to be helped to die. There shall be occasion to mention *non-voluntary euthanasia*—instances of euthanasia where a person is either not competent to, or unable to, express a wish about euthanasia, and there is no one authorised to make a substituted judgement (wherein a proxy chooses as the no longer competent patient would have chosen had she remained competent)—in the context of considering the claim that permitting voluntary euthanasia will lead via a slippery slope to permitting non-voluntary euthanasia. Nothing will be said here about *involuntary euthanasia*, where a competent person's life is brought to an end despite an explicit expression of opposition to euthanasia, beyond saying that, no matter how honourable the perpetrator's motive, such a death is, and ought to be, unlawful.

Morality of Assisted Suicide

Debate about the morality and legality of voluntary euthanasia is, for the most part, a phenomenon of the second half of the twentieth century. Certainly, the ancient Greeks and Romans did not consider life needed to be preserved at any cost and were, in consequence, tolerant of suicide in cases where no relief could be offered to the dying or, in the case of the Stoics and Epicureans, where a person no longer cared for his life. In the sixteenth century, Thomas More, in describing a utopian community, envisaged such a community as one that would facilitate the death of those whose lives had become burdensome as a result of 'torturing and lingering pain'. But it has only been in the last hundred years that there have been concerted efforts to make legal provision for voluntary euthanasia. Until quite recently there had been no success in obtaining such legal provision (though assisted suicide has been legally tolerated in Switzerland for many years). However, in the nineteen seventies and eighties a series of court cases in The Netherlands culminated in agreement being reached between the legal and medical authorities to ensure that no physician would be prosecuted for assisting a patient to die as long as certain guidelines were strictly adhered to. In brief, the guidelines were established to permit physicians to practise voluntary euthanasia in instances where a competent patient had made a voluntary and informed decision to die, the patient's suffering was unbearable, there was no way of making that suffering bearable which was acceptable to the patient, and the physician's judgements as to diagnosis and prognosis were confirmed after consultation with another physician.

In the nineteen nineties the first legislative approval for voluntary euthanasia was achieved with the passage of a bill in the parliament of Australia's Northern Territory to enable physicians to practise voluntary euthanasia. Subsequent to the Act's proclamation in 1996 it faced a series of legal challenges from opponents of voluntary euthanasia. In 1997 the challenges culminated in the Australian National Parliament overturning the legislation when it prohibited Australian Territories (the Australian Capital Territory and the Northern Territory) from enacting legislation to permit euthanasia. In Oregon in the United States legislation was introduced in 1997 to permit physician-assisted suicide when a second referendum clearly endorsed the proposed legislation. Later in 1997 the Supreme Court of the United States ruled that there is no constitutional right to physician-assisted suicide. However, the Court

> *"Normal adults are presumed to choose voluntarily unless the presence of defeating considerations can be established."*

did not preclude individual States from legislating in favour of physician-assisted suicide. The Oregon legislation has, in consequence, remained operative and has been successfully utilised by a number of people. In November 2000 The Netherlands passed legislation to legalise the practice of voluntary euthanasia. The legislation passed through all the parliamentary stages early in 2001 and so became law. The Belgian parliament passed similar legislation in May 2002.

With that brief sketch of the historical background in place, we now proceed to set out the conditions which those who have advocated making voluntary euthanasia legally permissible have wished to insist should be satisfied. The conditions are stated with some care so as to focus the moral debate about legislation. Second, we shall go on to outline the positive moral case underpinning the push to make voluntary euthanasia legally permissible. Third, we shall then consider the more important of the morally grounded objections which have been advanced by those opposed to the legalisation of voluntary euthanasia.

Conditions for Assisted Suicide

Advocates of voluntary euthanasia contend that if a person is

(a) suffering from a terminal illness;

(b) unlikely to benefit from the discovery of a cure for that illness during what remains of her life expectancy;

(c) as a direct result of the illness, either suffering intolerable pain, or only has available a life that is unacceptably burdensome (because the illness has to be treated in ways which lead to her being unacceptably dependent on others or on technological means of life support);

> *"The onus of establishing . . . lack of competence is on those who refuse to accept the person's choice."*

(d) has an enduring, voluntary and competent wish to die (or has, prior to losing the competence to do so, expressed a wish to die in the event that conditions (a)–(c) are satisfied); and

(e) unable without assistance to commit suicide,

then there should be legal and medical provision to enable her to be allowed to die or assisted to die.

It should be acknowledged that these conditions are quite restrictive, indeed more restrictive than some would think appropriate. In particular, the conditions concern access only to voluntary euthanasia for those who are *terminally ill*. While that expression is not free of all ambiguity, for present purposes it can be agreed that it does not include the bringing about of the death of, say, victims of accidents who are rendered quadriplegic or victims of early Alzheimer's Disease. Those who consider that such cases show the first condition to be too restrictive may nonetheless accept that including them would, at least for the time being, make it far harder to obtain legal protection for helping those terminally ill persons who wish to die. The fifth condition further restricts access to voluntary euthanasia by excluding those capable of ending their own lives, and so will not only be thought unduly restrictive by those who think physician-assisted suicide a better course to follow, but will be considered morally much harder to justify by those who think health care practitioners may never justifiably kill their patients. More on this anon.

The second condition is intended simply to reflect the fact that we normally are able to say that someone's health status is incurable. So-called 'miracle' cures may be spoken of by sensationalist journalists, but progress toward medical breakthroughs is typically painstaking. If there are miracles wrought by God that will be quite another matter entirely, but it is

> *"The central ethical argument for voluntary euthanasia . . . is directly connected with . . . competence because autonomy presupposes competence."*

at least clear that not everyone's death is thus to be staved off.

The third condition recognises what many who oppose the legalisation of voluntary euthanasia do not, namely that it is not only release from pain that leads people to want to be helped to die. In The Netherlands, for example, it has been found to be a less significant reason for requesting assistance with dying than other forms of suffering and frustration with loss of independence. Sufferers from some terminal conditions may have their pain relieved but have to endure side effects that for them make life unbearable. Others may not have to cope with pain but instead be incapable, as with motor neurone disease, of living without life supports which at the same time rob their lives of quality.

A final preliminary point is that the fourth condition requires that the choice to die not only be voluntary but that it be made in an enduring (not merely a one-off) way and be competent. The choice is one that will require discussion and time for reflection and so should not be settled in a moment. As in other decisions affecting matters of importance, normal adults are presumed to choose voluntarily unless the presence of defeating considerations can be established. The onus of establishing lack of voluntariness or lack of competence is on those who refuse to accept the person's choice. There is no need to deny that it can sometimes be met (e.g. by pointing to the person's being in a state of clinical depression). The claim is only that the onus falls on those who deny that a normal adult's choice is not competent.

The Ethical Case for Assisted Suicide

The central ethical argument for voluntary euthanasia—that respect for persons demands respect for their autonomous choices as long as those choices do not result in harm to others—is directly connected with this issue of competence because autonomy presupposes competence. People have an interest in making important decisions about their lives in accordance with their own conception of how they want their lives to go. In exercising autonomy or self-determination people take responsibility for their lives and, since dying is a part of life, choices about the manner of their dying and the timing of their death are, for many people, part of what is involved in taking responsibility for their lives. Most people are concerned about what the last phase of their lives will be like, not merely because of fears that their dying might involve them in great suffering, but also because of the desire to retain their dignity and as much control over their lives as possible during this phase.

The technological interventions of modern medicine have had an effect on how drawn out the dying phase may be. Sometimes this added life is an occasion for rejoicing, sometimes it may serve to stretch out the period of significant physical and intellectual decline in such a way as to impair and burden the end of life so that life comes to be no longer worth living. There is no single, objectively correct answer, which has application to everyone, as to when, if at all, life becomes a burden and unwanted. But that simply points up the importance of individuals being able to decide autonomously for themselves whether their own lives retain sufficient quality and dignity. In making such decisions individuals decide about the mix between their self-determination and their well-being that suits them. Given that a critically ill person is typically in a severely compromised and debilitated state it is, other things being equal, the patient's judgement of whether continued life is a benefit that must carry the greatest weight, provided always that the patient is competent.

Suppose it is agreed that a person's exercise of her autonomy warrants our respect. If medical assistance is to be provided to help a person achieve her autonomously chosen goal of an easeful death (because she cannot end her own life), the autonomy of the assisting professional(s) also has to be respected. The value (or right) of self-determination does not entitle a patient to compel a medical professional to act contrary to her own moral or professional values. If voluntary euthanasia is to be legally permitted it must be against a backdrop of respect for professional autonomy.

> *"The patient's judgement of whether continued life is a benefit . . . must carry the greatest weight, provided always that the patient is competent."*

Thus, if a doctor's view of her moral or professional responsibilities is at odds with the request of her patient for euthanasia, provision must be made for the transfer of the patient's care to another who faces no such conflict.

Opponents of voluntary euthanasia have endeavoured to counter this very straightforward moral case for the practice in a variety of ways. Some of the counter-arguments are concerned only with whether the moral case warrants making the practice of voluntary euthanasia legal, others are concerned with trying to undermine the moral case itself. . . .

It is often said that it is not necessary nowadays for anyone to die while suffering from intolerable or overwhelming pain. We are getting better at providing effective palliative care and hospice care is available. Given these considerations it is urged that voluntary euthanasia is unnecessary.

There are several flaws in this counter-argument. First, while both good palliative care and hospice care make important contributions to the care of the dying neither is a panacea. To get the best palliative care for an individual involves trial and error with some consequent suffering in the process. But, far more importantly, even high quality palliative care commonly exacts a price in the form of side effects such as nausea, incontinence, loss of awareness because of semi-permanent drowsiness, and so on. A rosy picture is often painted as to how palliative care can transform the plight of the dying. Such a picture is misleading according to those who have closely observed the effect of extended courses of treatment with drugs like morphine, a point acknowledged as well by many skilled palliative care specialists. Second, though the sort of care provided through hospices is to be applauded, it is care that is available only to a small proportion of the terminally ill and then usually only in the very last stages of the illness (typically a matter of a few weeks). Third, the point of greatest significance is that not everyone wishes to avail themselves of either palliative care or hospice care. For those who prefer to die in their own way and in their own time neither palliative care nor hospice care may be attractive. For many dying patients it is having their autonomous wishes frustrated that is a source of the deepest distress. Fourth, as indicated earlier when the conditions under which voluntary euthanasia is advocated were outlined, not everyone who is dying is suffering because of the pain occasioned by their illness. For those for whom what is intolerable is their dependence on others or on machinery, the availability of effective pain control will be quite irrelevant.

> *"What is really at issue ... is whether anyone can ever form a competent, enduring and voluntary wish about being better off dead rather than continuing to suffer."*

A Competent Wish to Be Dead

A second, related objection to permitting the legalisation of voluntary euthanasia is to the effect that we never have sufficient evidence to be justified in believing that a dying person's request to be helped to die is competent, enduring and genuinely voluntary.

Notice first that a request to die may not reflect an enduring desire to die (cf. some attempts to commit suicide may similarly reflect temporary despair). That is why advocates of voluntary euthanasia have argued that normally a cooling off period should be allowed. But that said, the objection claims we can *never* be justified in believing someone's request to die reflects a settled preference for death. This goes too far. If someone discusses the issue with others on different occasions, or reflects on the issue over an extended period, and does not waver in her conviction, her wish to die is surely an enduring one.

But, it might be said, what if a person is racked with pain, or befuddled because of the measures taken to relieve her pain, and so not able to think clearly and rationally about the alternatives? It has to be agreed that a person in those circumstances who wants to die cannot be assumed to have a competent, enduring and genuinely voluntary desire to die. However, there are at least two important points to make about those in such circumstances. First, they do not account for all of the terminally ill, so even if it is acknowledged that such people are incapable of agreeing to voluntary euthanasia that does not show that no one can ever voluntarily

> *[Physicians] should not be prohibited . . . from lending their professional assistance to those competent, terminally ill persons . . . who wish for an easy death."*

request help to die. Second, it is possible for a person to indicate in advance of losing the capacity to give competent, enduring and voluntary consent, how she would wish to be treated should she become terminally ill and be suffering intolerably from pain or from loss of control over her life. 'Living wills' or 'advance declarations' are legally useful instruments for giving voice to people's wishes while they are capable of giving competent, enduring and voluntary consent, including to their wanting help to die. As long as they are easily revocable in the event of a change of mind (just as ordinary wills are), they should be respected as evidence of a well thought out conviction. It should be noted, though, that any request for voluntary euthanasia or physician-assisted suicide will not be able lawfully to be implemented (outside of The Netherlands, Belgium and Oregon).

Perhaps, though, what is really at issue in this objection is whether anyone can ever form a competent, enduring and voluntary wish about being better off dead rather than continuing to suffer from an illness *before actually suffering the illness*. If this is what underlies the objection it is surely too paternalistic to be acceptable. Why cannot a person have sufficient inductive evidence (e.g. based on the experience of the deaths of friends or family) to know her own mind and act accordingly?

The Double Effect

According to one interpretation of the traditional 'doctrine of double effect' it is permissible to act in ways which it is foreseen will have bad consequences provided only that

    (a) this occurs as a side effect (or indirectly) to the achievement of the act which is directly aimed at or intended;

    (b) the act directly aimed at is itself morally good or, at least, morally neutral;

    (c) the good effect is not achieved by way of the bad, that is, the bad must not be a means to the good; and

    (d) the bad consequences must not be so serious as to outweigh the good effect.

In line with the doctrine of double effect it is, for example, held to be permissible to alleviate pain by administering drugs like morphine which it is foreseen will shorten life, whereas to give an overdose or injection with the direct intention of terminating a patient's life (whether at her request or not) is considered morally indefensible. This is not the appropriate forum to give full consideration to this doctrine. However, there is one vital criticism to be made of the doctrine concerning its relevance to the issue of voluntary euthanasia. . . .

The criticism of the relevance of the doctrine of double effect to any critique of voluntary euthanasia, at least on what seems to me to be a defensible reading of that doctrine, is simply this: the doctrine can only be relevant where a person's death is an evil or, to put it another way, a *harm*. Sometimes 'harm' is understood simply as damage to a person's interest whether consented to or not. At other times it is more strictly understood as wrongfully inflicted damage. On either account, if the death of a person who wishes to die is not harmful (because from that person's standpoint it is, in fact, beneficial), the doctrine of double effect can have no relevance to the debate about the permissibility of voluntary euthanasia. . . .

Respect for Personal Autonomy Is Key

Legal permission for doctors to perform voluntary euthanasia cannot simply be grounded in the right of self-determination of patients. . . . The law does not presently permit an individual to consent to her own death. Nevertheless, the very same fundamental basis of the right to decide about life-sustaining treatment—respect for a person's autonomy—underpins voluntary euthanasia as well. Extending the right of self-determination to cover cases of voluntary euthanasia would not, therefore, amount to a dramatic shift in legal policy. No novel legal values or principles need to be invoked. Indeed, the fact that suicide and attempted suicide are no longer criminal offences in many jurisdictions indicates that the central importance of individual self-determination in a closely analogous setting has been accepted. The fact that assisted suicide and voluntary euthanasia have not yet been widely decriminalised is probably best explained along the lines that have frequently been offered for excluding consent of the victim as a justification for an act of killing, namely the difficulties thought to exist in establishing the genuineness of the consent. The establishment of suitable procedures for giving consent to assisted suicide and voluntary euthanasia would seem to be no harder than establishing procedures for competently refusing burdensome or otherwise unwanted medical treatment. The latter has already been accomplished in many jurisdictions, so the former should be capable of establishment as well.

Suppose that the moral case for legalising voluntary euthanasia does come to be judged as stronger than the case against (as the drift of this article would imply), and voluntary euthanasia is made legally permissible. Should doctors take part in the practice? Should only doctors perform voluntary euthanasia? The proper administration of medical care is not at odds with an understanding of medical care that both promotes patients' welfare interests and respects their self-determination. It is these twin values which should guide medical care, not a commitment to preserving life at all costs, or preserving life without regard to whether patients want their lives prolonged when they judge that life is no longer of benefit or value to themselves. Many doctors in The Netherlands and, to judge from available survey evidence, in other Western countries as well, see the practice of (voluntary) euthanasia as not only compatible with their professional commitments but also with their conception of the best medical care for the dying. That being so, they should not be prohibited by law from lending their professional assistance to those competent, terminally ill persons for whom no cure is possible and who wish for an easy death.

Assisted Suicide Is Compassionate

by Richard T. Hull

About the author: *Richard T. Hull is professor emeritus of philosophy at the State University of New York at Buffalo.*

In early 1997, the medical community awaited the U.S. Supreme Court's decision in *Vacco v. Quill.* Ultimately, the high court would overturn this suit, in which doctors and patients had sought to overturn New York's law prohibiting physician-assisted suicide. But it was fascinating to see how much attention physicians suddenly paid to the question of pain management while they were waiting.

Politicians and physicians alike felt shaken by the fact that the suit had made it as far as the Supreme Court. Medical schools scrutinized their curricula to see how, if at all, effective pain management was taught. The possibility that physician-assisted suicide would be declared as much a patient's right as the withdrawal of life-sustaining technology was a clarion call that medicine needed to "houseclean" its attitudes toward providing adequate narcotics for managing pain.

The ability to demand physician aid in dying is the only resource dying patients have with which to "send a message" (as our public rhetoric is so fond of putting it) to physicians, insurers, and politicians that end-of-life care is inadequate. Far too many patients spend their last days without adequate palliation of pain. Physicians sensitive to their cries hesitate to order adequate narcotics, for fear of scrutiny by state health departments and federal drug agents. Further, many physicians view imminent death as a sign of failure in the eyes of their colleagues, or just refuse to recognize that the seemingly endless variety of tests and procedures available to them can simply translate into a seemingly endless period of dying badly. Faced with all this, the ability to demand—and receive— physician aid in dying may be severely compromised patients' only way to tell caregivers that something inhumane stalks them: the inhumanity of neglect and despair.

Physician-Assisted Suicide Gives Power to Patients

Many physicians tell me that they feel it is an affront to suppose that their duty to care extends to a duty to kill or assist in suicide. If so, is it not even more an affront, as dying patients and their families tell me, to have to beg for increases in pain medication, only to be told that "We don't want to make you an addict, do we?" or that "Doctor's orders are being followed, and Doctor can't be reached to revise them." If apologists for the status quo fear that a slippery slope will lead to voluntary euthanasia, then nonvoluntary euthanasia, the proponents of change already know that we've been on a slippery slope of inadequate management of suffering for decades.

Let's examine some of the stronger arguments against physician-assisted suicide—while keeping in mind that these arguments may not be the deepest reasons some people oppose it. My lingering sense is that the unspoken problem with physician-assisted suicide is that it puts power where opponents don't want it: in the hands of patients and their loved ones. I want to see if there are ways of sorting out who holds the power to choose the time and manner of dying that make sense.

1. Many severely compromised individuals, in their depression, loneliness, loss of normal life, and despair, have asked their physicians to assist them in dying. Yet later (after physicians resisted their requests and others awakened them to alternative opportunities) they have returned to meaningful lives.

No sane advocate of physician-assisted suicide would deny the importance of meeting the demand to die with reluctance and a reflective, thorough examination of alternative options. The likelihood of profound mood swings during therapy makes it imperative to distinguish between a patient's acute anguish of loss and his or her rational dismay at the prospect of long-term descent into the tubes and machines of intensive care.

But note that, in stories like the above, it is the very possibility of legal physician-assisted suicide that empowers patients to draw attention to their suffering and command the resources they need to live on. Patients who cannot demand to die can find their complaints more easily dismissed as "the disease talking" or as weakness of character.

> *"It is the very possibility of legal physician-assisted suicide that empowers patients to draw attention to their suffering and command the resources they need to live on."*

2. Medicine would be transformed for the worse if doctors could legally help patients end their lives. The public would become distrustful, wondering whether physicians were truly committed to saving lives, or if they would stop striving as soon as it became inconvenient.

Doubtless there are physicians who, by want of training or some psychological or moral defect, lack the compassionate sensitivity to hear a demand for aid in dying and act on it with reluctance, only after thorough investigation of the patient's situation. Such physicians should not be empowered to assist patients to die. I would propose that this power be restricted to physicians whose primary training and profession is in pain management and palliation: they are best equipped to ensure that reasonable alternatives to euthanasia and suicide are exhausted. Further, patients' appeals for assisted suicide should be scrutinized by the same institutional ethics committees that already review requests for the suspension of life-sustaining technology as a protection against patient confusion and relatives' greed.

Assisted Suicide and Self-Sacrifice

3. Euthanasia and physician-assisted suicide are incompatible with our obligations to respect the human spirit and human life.

When I hear all motives for euthanasia and physician-assisted suicide swept so cavalierly into the dustbin labeled Failure to Respect Human Life, I'm prompted to say, "Really? *Always?*" Those same opponents who find physician-assisted suicide appalling will typically excuse, even acclaim, self-sacrifice on behalf of others. A soldier throws himself on a grenade to save his fellows. A pedestrian leaps into the path of a truck to save a child. Firefighters remain in a collapsing building rather than abandon trapped victims. These, too, are decisions to embrace death, yet we leave them to the conscience of the agent. Why tar all examples of euthanasia and physician-assisted suicide with a common brush? Given

> *"Why withhold from individuals who clearly perceive the financial and emotional burdens their dying imposes on loved ones the power to lessen . . . those burdens?"*

that we do not have the power to ameliorate every disease and never will, why withhold from individuals who clearly perceive the financial and emotional burdens their dying imposes on loved ones the power to lessen the duration and extent of those burdens, in pursuit of the values they have worked to support throughout their lives?

Consider also that some suffering cannot be relieved by any means while maintaining consciousness. There are individuals, like myself, who regard conscious life as essential to personal identity. I find it nonsensical to maintain that it is profoundly morally *preferable* to be rendered comatose by drugs while awaiting life's "natural end," than to hasten death's arrival while still consciously able to embrace and welcome one's release. If I am irreversibly comatose, "I" am dead; prolongation of "my life" at that point is ghoulish, and I should not be required to undergo such indignity.

Finally, the question, "What kind of life is worth living?" is highly personal. There are good reasons patients diagnosed with a wide range of conditions might not wish to live to the natural end of their diseases. How dare politicians and moralists presume to make these final judgments if they don't have to live with the results? Of course, every demand for physician-assisted suicide must be scrutinized, and determined to be fully informed. To withhold aid in dying beyond that point is, first, barbarically cruel. Second, it only increases the risk that individuals determined to end their lives will attempt to do so by nonmedical means, possibly endangering others or further magnifying their own suffering.

> *"Every demand for physician-assisted suicide must be scrutinized."*

4. The time-honored doctrine of double effect permits administering pain-relieving drugs that have the effect of shortening life, provided the intent of the physician is the relief of the pain and not the (foreseen) death of the patient. Isn't that sufficient?

Others may find comfort in the notion that the intention of the agent, not the consequences of his or her action, is the measure of morality. I do not. In any case, preferences among ethical theories are like preferences among religious persuasions: no such preference should be legislated for all citizens. For the thinker who focuses on consequences rather than intentions, the fact that we permit terminal care regimens to shorten life *in any context* shows that the line has already been crossed. The fact that physicians must, at the insistence of the competent patient or the incompetent patient's duly appointed surrogate, withdraw life-sustaining technology shows that physicians *can* assist patient suicides and can perform euthanasia on those fortunate enough to be dependent on machines. It becomes a matter of simple justice—equal protection before the law—to permit the same privileges to other terminal patients. That the U.S. Supreme Court has ruled against this argument did not dissuade the citizens of the State of Oregon from embracing it. States like New York that have turned back such initiatives must bear the shame of having imposed religious majorities' philosophies on all who suffer.

Assisted Suicide Promotes Personal Autonomy

by Betty Rollin

About the author: *Betty Rollin is a board member of the Death with Dignity National Center and author of* Last Wish.

There's a big anniversary in Oregon [in October 2002], and those of us in the other 49 states should take note. It's the fifth year that Oregon's Death With Dignity Act, which allows physician-assisted dying, has been in place, and it has resulted in one major surprise: At last count, only about 91 terminally ill people have taken advantage of the law. In addition, all of the deaths went without a hitch. With two exceptions, there was no nausea or vomiting as a result of the large doses of medication required to end life. And few of those who chose a physician's help in dying died alone.

Proponents of the initiative never thought there'd be a stampede of people rushing to die, although opponents predicted one. Most people cling to life, even if they're suffering. But if that is so, what's the point? Why fight so hard for legislation, why spend so much time and money to benefit so few?

The answer can be found among those who chose not to die with assistance, like Ray Frank, a 56-year-old computer programmer who suffered from terminal kidney and lung cancer. When his pain became intolerable, Frank asked doctors if he would qualify legally (Oregon's law has many safeguards) for assistance in dying. When his doctors said that even if he were eligible they would not help him (which is their right), Frank panicked and asked a friend to buy him a shotgun, planning to use it as soon as he got home from the hospital. Instead, the friend contacted Compassion in Dying, an organization that helps terminally ill people who want a hastened death, and it referred Frank to a doctor who treated his symptoms and helped him apply to die with assistance.

Frank's anxiety was so relieved that he never bought the gun, never spoke of assisted suicide again and died naturally within the two-week waiting period the law requires.

Peace of Mind vs. Terror

There's no way to statistically measure peace of mind or quantify the death of terror. But here's a guess: For every one of the 91 terminally ill patients in Oregon who died with assistance from a physician, thousands have had their fears quieted just knowing such assistance would be there.

Studies have shown that, when asked, people express far more fear of suffering at the end of life than they do about dying with reason. Medical technology, dazzling though it is, often prolongs life cruelly. Many physicians hate to "give up" on a patient and often continue to "fight" the disease mindlessly, without regard for the patient's suffering or wishes. Often patients feel locked in life. They don't necessarily want out, but they want to know where the key is.

> *"What mattered most was knowing [my mother] could die. She was calling the shots again; her death would be like her life."*

I saw this about the time I helped my mother die. When she knew I had found a way out for her, a calm came over her that was almost weird. Her sister, who didn't know she was plotting to die, thought she was recovering from her illness. "Your mother seems so well," she said. "Can she be getting better?"

In a way, yes, I could have replied. Because she had become herself again. With terror gone, despite her suffering, she was her old, in-control self. I could tell because she immediately began bossing me around.

"Go into my closet," she said, hours before she swallowed a lethal dose of barbiturates. "There's a hat from Bloomingdale's I forgot to return. So don't forget to return it."

In Control

I had no idea of what to make of this. I remember thinking, "She's so alive; how could she want to die?" As she began to count the pills, I asked her, my voice trembling, if she was sure she wanted to go through with it. She looked at me as if I had lost my mind. "Next to the happiness of my children," she said, "I want to die more than anything else in the world."

My mother died peacefully, gracefully, gratefully. But I know that what mattered most was knowing she could die. She was calling the shots again; her death would be like her life. It was her last wish, and she got it.

Have we Americans ever felt less in control than we do now? But in Oregon, people have a small amount of control over one aspect of their lives: their deaths. Not a small thing.

The Elderly View Assisted Suicide as a Way to Protect Their Dignity

by Prem S. Fry

About the author: *Prem S. Fry is a research associate at Trinity Western University in Langley, British Columbia, Canada. He is editor in chief of* Ageing International, *the journal of the International Federation on Ageing.*

The growth of sophisticated life-sustaining medical technology, combined with a greater focus on medical care at the end of life, has resulted in a longer life for an increasing number of older adults in Canada and the United States. However, the increasing attention being given to prolonging life has resulted in insufficient attention to protecting the quality of life of this population. Thus, for most older adults, the promise of longevity presents serious concerns about the future quality of a life that has been prolonged by medical advances.

As a result, for older adults quality of life is becoming much more than a rating of physical health status as reflected in illness, disease, physical and functional decline, and infirmity. It now includes an assessment of the way that individuals feel not only about medical and physical health aspects of their lives but also about their social, emotional and economic health. In order to explore what constitutes quality of life for most elderly people and what, in their view, needs to be done to protect this quality of life, my research associates and I conducted a mail survey of 331 Canadian seniors (181 men and 150 women) between the ages of 60 and 85. Additionally, we conducted interviews with over 100 older men and women in various walks of life in order to acquire an in-depth, first-hand understanding of their quality-of-life-related concerns and what factors contribute to morale and provide the basis for health and psychological well-being in late life. Respondents to the mail survey and interviews were invited to comment also on anxieties and concerns regarding their present and future well-being.

We identified a number of factors that reflect older adults' major concerns about their quality of life and what courses of action they feel are necessary to protect it against deterioration. . . . Respondents had strong convictions about their inherent right to full control over end-of-life decision making. For example, they believed they should have an uncontested right to decide when they want to terminate life. Many respondents expressed the view that they were the best judges of whether or not their quality of life was at an acceptable level. They felt that if they were dissatisfied with their quality of life, their right to terminate life should be recognized and respected by society. In this context, many respondents to our survey expressed a need for a guaranteed right to physician-assisted suicide (PAS) at any time they feel that the emotional, intellectual or physical health-related quality of life has deteriorated to an unacceptable level.

Although a majority of respondents favored a living will or an advance directive that would allow them to specify in writing their preference for medical treatment, most respondents were doubtful about the effectiveness of this self-determining mechanism if a family member were designated to make medical decisions for them. Many felt that the proxy naming procedure was not practical for them, given their family circumstances and lack of contact with their adult children, and many were doubtful that their advance directives would be honored by health care providers or their proxy. These concerns appeared to be pervasive among our sample and also to be very similar to concerns noted in other earlier studies. The respondents expressed the view that highly qualified court-appointed health care professionals, lawyers and heads of religious foundations should be called upon to implement older adults' medical directives in ways consistent with individual needs and preferences. Many suggested that community-appointed ombudsmen should be entrusted with the task of implementing advance directives.

Respondents' uppermost aspirations were for empowerment and self-determination. When asked what constitutes protection of a good quality of life, many respondents asked for legal assurance of long-term employability, guarantees of good medical care, economic security and safe living environments. In addition to wanting complete autonomy and control over personal decision mak-

> *"Many [elderly adults] . . . expressed a need for a guaranteed right to physician-assisted suicide . . . any time . . . quality of life has deteriorated to an unacceptable level."*

ing, they wished for assurances of a guaranteed income and of ethical conduct by medical practitioners, legal advisors and government bodies.

With respect to fears and anxieties for future quality of life, many respondents worried that with increasing age they may become victims of violence and abuse. Indeed, many admitted to several such experiences, both from outsiders and from within the families of their adult children. For many respondents, par-

ticularly those who were economically disadvantaged, the greatest threat to
their quality of life was the absence of protection against such threats.

Many elderly people worry about abandonment in late life; they fear that the
social system, through sheer negligence, will allow them to die alone, without
social support or adequate physical or emotional care. These fears persist
notwithstanding the fact that many of the respondents acknowledged firm religious commitments and affiliation with church groups.

Physicians Should Provide PAS Information

More dialogue between practitioners and the elderly people they serve is the
first step toward helping elderly clients and patients overcome their mistrust of
the very professionals whose major role and responsibility it is to serve and
protect their interests. Many seniors complained that professionals were not
sufficiently concerned about receiving fragmented and frequently contradictory
information from the various professionals with whom they had dealings. Many
respondents with serious health problems were upset and frustrated by the professionals' lack of interest in discussing the complex choices related to initiating, withholding or terminating medical treatment.

One recommendation that has emerged from these studies is for practitioners
to engage more frequently in discussions concerning end-of-life health-related
issues directly with their elderly pa-
tients, as opposed to consulting se-
cretively with other family members,
and to provide the elderly patients
with reassurance that their wishes
and preferences in regard to medical
treatment or its detention will be
fully respected.

> *"One recommendation . . . is for practitioners to engage more frequently in discussions concerning end-of-life health-related issues directly with their elderly patients."*

Often, younger members of the pa-
tients' families lack the confidence or competence to handle end-of-life decisions for their elderly relatives. Thus, many seniors who have conflictual family
relationships prefer to rely on their physicians and other health care providers
to clarify complex medical or other social services choices open to them.

Given the recent interest of a growing number of elderly people to support
PAS legislation, it seems likely that physicians and other health care providers
may be called upon to engage in informal discussions concerning patients' access to PAS. One of the major concerns that emerged out of the findings of our
study and interviews is the naivete of many elderly PAS advocates regarding the
laws governing PAS procedures and the complexity of the issues involved. All
respondents, whether naive or well-informed, supported the notion that it
should be the primary responsibility of their primary health care providers to
initiate dialogue on the so-called "new discipline" of physician-assisted suicide
and the related privileges.

The laws pertaining to PAS are still quite unclear, and there have been few test cases in Canada. In the United States, however, numerous reports, books and articles that identify a few of the medical and ethical issues are beginning to appear. We encourage health care practitioners to talk with elderly adults about end-of-life issues and, to the degree to which the patients themselves are willing, provide accurate information on issues related to advance-care planning and other more remote medical choices such as PAS.

> *"We encourage health care practitioners to . . . provide accurate information on issues related to advance-care planning and . . . PAS."*

Physicians, social work personnel and other care providers should collaborate to refer their patients to seminars, workshops or other educational materials that are designed to inform older adults on current developments in legalized euthanasia practices, patient requests and physician responses to PAS requests. Additionally, health care providers need to be more familiar with the underlying attitudes, cultural values and religious preferences of their elderly patients so that in the event of decisional incapacity in patients, they are able to recommend and implement medical directives consistent with their individual patients' needs and preferences. Physicians, however, are urged to be quite open with their patients about their personal views in matters of PAS and advanced directives.

Quality of Life Is Critical

Although many elderly respondents were fearful about the impending threats to their health, they made it abundantly clear that the quality of their intellectual and emotional life was much more important to them than prolonging life. Contrary to stereotypes that portray the elderly as frail, confused, passive and vulnerable to public opinion, our observations about the older adults who participated in our study were that they had clear and consistent views about the quality of life they desire. Our study participants were not only vibrant and involved, but quite articulate about their rights to personal control in decision-making, autonomy and self-determination to pursue a chosen lifestyle. Few of our respondents viewed old age to be a downward trajectory, and very few were willing to accept that with increasing age they would be forced to compromise their quality of life. These observations about our respondents challenge traditional beliefs that most elderly people do not have any hopes or aspirations for their future. On the contrary, our findings show that many older adults desire to actively pursue challenging and stimulating activities and are reluctant to delegate decision-making powers with respect to their health and well-being.

Assisted Suicide Distorts the Meaning of Mercy

by Trudy Chun and Marian Wallace

About the authors: *Trudy Chun and Marian Wallace are writers for Concerned Women for America, a conservative, pro-family, pro-life organization.*

Over the past several decades, America has witnessed a strange and subtle shift in how society views life. In the 1960s, the shift began as some states began to remove the criminal penalties for abortion. In the 1970s, the U.S. Supreme Court *Roe v. Wade* decision put the federal government's stamp of approval on abortion nationwide. Today, the value of life is being obscured at the other end of the spectrum as courts grant the elderly and sick the so-called "right to die."

This "right to die" movement has entered society in two forms: assisted suicide and euthanasia, with the former beginning to give way to the latter. Assisted suicide occurs when the doctor provides the patient the means to kill himself—the doctor acts as an accomplice in the self-murder, so to speak. Euthanasia is the active killing of the patient by the doctor—the physician is the murderer in this case. More often today, physicians are initiating the desire for death.

The very laws once designed to protect a person's inalienable right to life now permit the elimination of those deemed unworthy to live. And in the name of compassion, doctors trained to heal and to prolong life are shortening and even snuffing it out altogether. Killing the patient as the cure is becoming an acceptable medical procedure in some circles. Nonetheless, changing public opinion and advances in modern pain relief and end-of-life care are shifting the debate in favor of pro-life advocates.

Many Americans view physician-assisted suicide as an acceptable practice. According to a March 1999 Gallup poll, 61 percent of all Americans believe physician-assisted suicide should be legal—down from 75 percent in a May 1996 *USA Today* poll. When the issue becomes personal, fewer Americans support it. Fifty-one percent of Americans said they would not consider physician-assisted suicide to end pain from a terminal illness, while 40 percent said they would. As may be expected, support for the idea of physician-assisted suicide diminished with age in the Gallup poll. While 62 percent of those between the ages of 18 and 29 supported physician-assisted suicide, 51 percent of those aged 65 said they do.

While acceptance of euthanasia and assisted suicide has diminished somewhat, euthanasia advocates continue their campaign. The manipulation of terms in the debate reveals their strategy of courting acceptance.

Euthanasia Is Murder

Christian writer C.S. Lewis coined the term "verbicide" to denote the murder of a word. That is what euthanasia advocates have done with the language of "compassion" and "mercy." In order to advance their agenda with the public, euthanasia advocates are cloaking doctors' deliberate homicide of patients in rosy phrases such as quality of life, death with dignity, voluntary euthanasia, and the right to die. Even "euthanasia"—which the dictionary defines as "killing an individual for reasons considered to be merciful"—comes from two Greek words meaning "good death." But no matter what they call it, euthanasia is still murder.

> *"In the name of compassion, doctors trained to heal and to prolong life are shortening and even snuffing it out altogether."*

Dr. Jack Kevorkian cast physician-assisted suicide and euthanasia into the national spotlight in the early 1990s. Kevorkian, a retired Michigan pathologist, claims to have helped approximately 130 people kill themselves. He calls his practice "medicide" and himself an "obitiarist." The man they call "Dr. Death" also proposes professionally staffed, well-equipped "obitoriums"—where the sick, elderly, or depressed could go to their demise voluntarily. In 1996, he opened his first suicide center north of Detroit. Fortunately, the building owner terminated Dr. Kevorkian's lease and his suicide center closed. Then, in 1999, after a nationally televised videotape showed Dr. Kevorkian ending the life of a terminally ill man, a Michigan jury convicted him and sentenced him to prison for murder.

The Civil Right to Die

Although Dr. Kevorkian is no longer in the national spotlight, death as the option of choice—abortion, infanticide, euthanasia and suicide—now has high-profile, big-money organizational support. Some of the most visible pro-death groups are Planned Parenthood, the National Abortion and Reproductive Rights Action League, the Hemlock Society, Choice in Dying, Americans Against Human Suffering and EXIT. Derek Humphry, cofounder of Hemlock, voices a common viewpoint: "Individual freedom requires that all persons be allowed to control their own destiny. . . . This is the ultimate civil liberty. . . . If we cannot die by our choice, then we are not free people." The decision to die is increasingly viewed as a civil "right."

In January 1997, lawyers representing some physicians and terminally ill patients urged the U.S. Supreme Court to rule that the Constitution allows individuals the right to terminate their lives with the assistance of a physician. This action came in response to appellate court rulings in Washington and New York, where state laws banned assisted suicide. Both rulings concluded that terminally ill patients had a right to a physician-assisted suicide. In its ruling, the U.S. Court of Appeals for the Ninth Circuit in Seattle said the constitutional "liberty"

> *"Euthanasia advocates are cloaking doctors' deliberate homicide of patients in rosy phrases such as quality of life, death with dignity . . . and the right to die."*

reasoning in *Planned Parenthood v. Casey*, which reaffirmed a woman's "right" to choose abortion, influenced their decision. That so-called "right," the judges concluded, also applied to the end of life.

In the New York state ruling, the Federal Court of Appeals for the Second Circuit based its similar finding on the 14th Amendment's "equal protection" clause. The judges argued that terminally ill patients had the right to hasten their own death by refusing treatment. Physicians therefore could lawfully order the removal of life-support systems. In addition, doctors should not be prosecuted for actively administering lethal drugs to patients when they request help in accelerating their deaths.

The New York Times editorialized that the two courts "have issued humane and sound rulings." In both cases, it noted the defendants "claimed a sovereign right over their own bodies." Ernest Van Den Haag, an advocate of suicide, observed in the June 12, 1995, issue of *National Review*, "Only in our time has it come to be believed that individuals . . . own themselves. . . . Owners can dispose of what they own as they see fit."

The U.S. Supreme Court reversed both decisions, however, stating that neither state law violated the 14th Amendment of the U.S. Constitution. The Court noted, "They neither infringe fundamental rights nor involve suspect classifications." Furthermore, the Court argued the Equal Protection Clause of the Fourteenth Amendment "creates no substantive rights," including a so-called right to die.

Francis Schaeffer, renowned Christian philosopher and theologian, credited the influx of humanistic thought in society for the increasing disrespect for human life. "If man is not made in the image of God, nothing then stands in the way of inhumanity. There is no good reason why mankind should be perceived as special," he wrote in *Whatever Happened to the Human Race?* "Human life is cheapened. We can see this in many of the major issues being debated in our society today: abortion, infanticide, euthanasia. . . ."

Euthanasia advocates are also redefining what it means to be a person. In their book, *In Defense of Life*, Keith Fournier and William Watkins dissect "ethicist" Joseph Fletcher's 15 "indicators of personhood." These include: an IQ greater than 40; self-awareness; self-control; a sense of time; capability of relating to and concern for others; communication; control of existence and [degree of brain] function. Alarmed, Fournier and Watkins wrote: "When judged by these criteria, the preborn, newborn, and seriously developmentally disabled would be disqualified as human persons." Sufferers of dementia or anyone brain-damaged would also be non-persons. "Ethicist" Peter Singer agrees that personhood should be defined according to what we can do, rather than who we are. He has even advocated allowing parents of severely disabled infants to put their children to death in some painless way. This kind of thinking about "defective humans" is disturbingly reminiscent of the euthanasia program that accompanied the rise of Nazism.

A Nazi Legacy

In *A Sign for Cain*, the eminent Dr. Fredric Wertham documented exhaustively the physician-sponsored mass murder of civilians in pre-World War II Germany. Well before they were dismantled and moved to the concentration camps, gas chambers were installed in six leading psychiatric hospitals. Under the guise of "help for the dying," "mercy killings," and "destruction of life devoid of value," university professors of psychiatry, hospital directors and their staff members systematically exterminated hundreds of thousands of "superfluous people"—mental patients, the elderly, and sick and handicapped children. Criteria for such "undesirables" included "useless eaters," the unfit, unproductive and misfit.

Wertham stressed the concept of "life not worth living" was not a Nazi invention. As early as the 1920s, respected physicians wrote about "absolutely worthless human beings" and the urgently necessary "killing of those who cannot be rescued." In fact, even in 1895, a widely used German medical textbook advocated the "right to death."

However, in 1939, a note from Adolf Hitler to his own private doctor and chancellery officials extended "the authority of physicians" so that

> "[In the Netherlands] 'one can do away with the comatose and children with severe malformations.'"

"a mercy death may be granted to patients who according to human judgment are incurably ill." Nearly the same language has been used in the various "right to die" decisions of America's high courts.

Holland's Contribution

In the Netherlands, the lower house of the Dutch parliament has passed a bill to permit euthanasia, paving the way for the open practice of giving doctors or relatives a "license to kill" unconscious patients. Dutch Dr. Karel Gunning, president of the World Federation of Pro-life Doctors, revealed that official figures estimate approximately 3,200 cases of euthanasia occur each year. This practice has caused a number of sick and poor Dutch to start carrying a printed card in their pockets that states they do not want doctors to put them to death.

> *"Physicians are healers. . . . The inability of physicians to prevent death does not imply that they are free to help cause death."*

According to Dr. Gunning, the euthanasia law simply legalizes what has been done secretly for years.

"In the beginning, the explicit request of the patient was necessary," he said. "Now, one can do away with the comatose and children with severe malformations. Initially, euthanasia was allowed only for terminal patients, but later it was extended to people with psychic depression." As happened in the United States, he also believes that this "path to death" began in 1971 when the Dutch Medical Association approved abortion. This act removed "the unconditional defense of human life."

America has been sliding down the same slippery slope as Holland, spurred by the same pro-euthanasia arguments and utilizing the same tactics.

Just as Dutch doctors had secretly performed euthanasia before a law was passed allowing it, American doctors have done the same. In a Washington state survey, 26 percent of responding doctors anonymously admitted they had been asked to help a patient die. Those same doctors actually gave 24 percent of their ailing patients prescriptions that induced death. Although chronic pain was a factor, researchers found that patients were most often motivated toward suicide by nonphysical concerns, such as "losing control, being a burden, being dependent, and losing dignity."

In February 1999, columnist Nat Hentoff wrote of Oregon's legalization of physician-assisted suicide and its decision to provide the service without cost to low-income residents. Noting the cruel hypocrisy of the decision, Hentoff quoted Ric Burger, spokesman for disabled citizens in Oregon, "The fact that the state of Oregon will not properly fund our personal-attendant services, yet will pay for us to die, amounts to nothing less than cultural genocide."

Ethical Quagmire

Secular medical ethicists also fear downright coercion in laws allowing doctors to help with suicide. They point out that not-so-subtle pressure—to save taxpayers' money—could be placed on those patients who are poorest, most isolated, and least attended. The idea is, "if you can afford it, you [can] get good care," said Zail Berry, former medical director of Hospice of Washington, D.C. "If you can't, you get a prescription for [a barbiturate] from a Medicaid doc."

Renowned medical ethicist Dr. Arthur Caplan agrees, worrying that with an aging population and an overburdened health care system, physician-assisted suicide will become not the "option of last resort . . . [but] the attractive solution of first resort." In an interview with PBS's "Frontline," Dr. Caplan stated, "I worry . . . that suddenly within the society, the notion will come that the older and disabled who are expensive should do the responsible thing and leave. I don't want to be in that place, and I'm not persuaded that this culture or this society isn't going to get us to that place."

In 1997, when the Supreme Court considered whether physician-assisted suicide was a constitutional right, Justice David Souter noted the slippery slope that followed. "A physician who would provide a drug for a patient to administer might well go the further step of administering the drug himself," he stated in a concurring opinion, "so the barrier between assisted suicide and euthanasia could become porous as well as the line between voluntary [and involuntary] euthanasia."

Evidence in other nations demonstrates this. The *Medical Journal of Australia* published a 1996 study of deaths in Australia. Thirty percent of all deaths are "intentionally accelerated by a doctor," by means such as withholding treatment. Moreover, only 4 percent of cases resulted from a direct response to a request from the patient—indicating the other patients were killed without consent. A patient's true desires are not usually clear.

"We must provide comforting care for the critically ill—food and water, pain medication, oxygen and a loving touch."

A study in the British medical journal *The Lancet* revealed terminal cancer patients often have second thoughts about dying. Dr. Harvey Max Chochinov, a professor of psychiatry and family medicine at the University of Manitoba (Canada), said, "Will to live is a construct that is highly changeable." Surveying 168 terminal cancer patients aged 31 to 89, Dr. Chochinov and his team found "a patient could have vast temporary changes in his outlook." The study revealed causes of unwillingness to live, such as depression, were treatable.

The Physician Is a Healer

At its heart, the Hippocratic Oath taken by physicians enjoins "Do no harm" and states: "I will give no deadly medicine, even if asked." Thomas Reardon, past president of the American Medical Association (AMA) said, "Physicians are healers. . . . The inability of physicians to prevent death does not imply that they are free to help cause death."

Under-treatment has been a problem for many terminally ill patients, noted Dr Richard Payne, chief of pain-control services at New York's Memorial Sloan-Kettering Cancer Center. The AMA has consistently opposed any attempts to legalize or promote physician-assisted suicide. In a policy paper on the issue, revised in 1999, the AMA even states, "Requests for physician-assisted suicide should be a signal to the physician that the patient's needs are unmet and further evaluation to identify the elements contributing to the patient's suffering is necessary." Physician-assisted suicide is "fundamentally incompatible with the physician's role as healer," states the AMA.

Even more encouraging are results of a 1998 survey of the 3,299 members of the American Society of Clinical Oncology (ASCO), published in the October 3, 2000, issue of the *Annals of Internal Medicine*, concerning euthanasia and physician-assisted suicide of terminally ill cancer patients. In 1994, 23 percent of ASCO members supported euthanasia for "dying cancer patients in excruciating pain." By 1998, that number dropped to *below 7 percent*. Likewise, 22 percent of the oncologists supported physician-assisted suicide in 1998, down from 45 percent in 1994. Lead researcher Ezekiel J. Emanuel, M.D., Ph.D., stated the survey's results "emphasize the need to educate physicians about ways to provide high-quality pain management and palliative care to dying patients."

"Modern medicine was so brilliant at saving lives that we . . . forgot our traditional role of providing comfort at the end of life," said Christine K. Cassel, M.D., chair of the Henry L. Schwartz Department of Geriatrics at Mount Sinai School of Medicine. "Now we need to take the advances in modern medicine and apply them to relieving suffering." The palliative care movement is growing.

The Joint Commission on Accreditation of Healthcare Organizations (JC-AHO) pushed physicians in this direction in 1999 by implementing required palliative care (pain relief) standards. It gave hospitals, nursing homes and outpatient clinics accredited by JCAHO until January 2001 to comply. The new standards require that every patient's pain be measured and relief be provided from the moment he checks into the facility. Otherwise, the health organization risks losing accreditation. Calling this a "watershed event," Dr. Russell Portenoy, pain medicine chairman of New York's Beth Israel Medical Center, commented, "No one has ever promised patients no pain." Yet euthanasia advocates have fought tooth and nail to make it easier to kill those same patients.

It is crucial the distinction be made between prolonging life artificially—with unwanted "heroic measures"—and terminating life prematurely through deliberate intervention. The first may be unacceptable to many. But the second is clearly murder. Rather, we must provide comforting care for the critically ill— food and water, pain medication, oxygen and a loving touch. Hospice programs nationwide offer medical, spiritual, legal and financial services for dying persons and their families.

The Ethical Challenge

In a 1994 state referendum, Oregon voters voted to allow assisted suicide. In 1997, they reaffirmed the decision by an even larger majority. At least forty-six terminally ill people have since ended their lives with the assistance of their physician. In response, Sen. Don Nickles (R-Oklahoma) inserted the Pain Relief Promotion Act into a year-end tax bill in late 2000. It passed the U.S. House but died in the Senate.

Instead of reviving the Act in the 107th Congress, pro-family groups worked to have Oregon's assisted-suicide law stopped by another means.

A directive from former Attorney General Janet Reno had effectively allowed Oregon to impose physician-assisted suicide by permitting doctors to prescribe lethal doses of narcotics, claiming this is a "legitimate medical use." As soon as Sen. John Ashcroft was confirmed as President George W. Bush's attorney general, representatives from Concerned Women for America met with Department of Justice officials to ask Mr. Ashcroft to rescind Janet Reno's order.

> *"To end the life of another— or our own—because of wrenching debilitation or 'lack of quality' is to deny the reality of death."*

On November 6, 2001, Attorney General Ashcroft sent a letter to Drug Enforcement officials to ensure that Oregon complies with federal law, which must be uniformly followed by all the states, on the proper use of controlled substances. He clarified that any person who violates the Controlled Substances Act will lose his or her license to prescribe.

"Oregon's assisted suicide rate is 42 percent higher than the nation's, and the suicide rate for those 75 or older is 63 percent higher," said Suzanne Brownlow, Director of Concerned Women for America of Oregon. "Oregon's vote for doctor-assisted suicide was a deadly mistake."

Still defiant, the pro-death movement in Oregon has, with the help of a sympathetic judge, temporarily stopped Mr. Ashcroft's order in the courts. CWA will continue to work to stop Oregon's physician-assisted suicide.

By definition, a terminally ill person's life will end—as will all our lives. The ethical challenge is how, when and at whose hand? Without question, watching a loved one waste away and suffer incurable pain is horrific. Along with them, we suffer intensely. But are we seeking to put others out of *our* misery? To end the life of another—or our own—because of wrenching debilitation or "lack of quality" is to deny the reality of death.

Fundamentally, assisted suicide and euthanasia are issues concerning morals and ethics. Indeed, the so-called "right to die" mantra has become the "duty to die." Professor David Currow, vice president of Palliative Care Australia, commented, "To make every person who's facing death think about euthanasia is an enormous impost on people who are already feeling isolated and frightened. The issue reaches to the very core of how a society views life. And it sets America sliding down a slippery slope toward destruction.

Assisted Suicide Distorts the Meaning of Personal Autonomy

by Jerome R. Wernow

About the author: *Jerome R. Wernow is executive director of the Northwest Center for Bioethics in Portland, Oregon. The Northwest Center for Bioethics is an alliance of physicians and other health care professionals, attorneys, accountants, clergy, theologians, philosophers, and medical ethicists dedicated to promoting the inherent value of human life through guidance in medico-ethical decision making.*

A contemplative of old, François Fenelon, once remarked, "Death only troubles the carnal." By voting for a policy that would allow an individual to commit suicide with the help of a physician, a majority of the Oregon public sought to secure personal control over this "troublesome enemy." Opponents of physician-assisted suicide (PAS) contend that its legalization only increases such trouble by, for example, paving the way for eventual social acceptance of legalized involuntary euthanasia of the weaker members of society. Following the November 1994 vote, opponents launched many challenges to the legalization of PAS, forestalling its actual legal practice. These challenges include the initial district court test in 1994, its eventual Supreme Court defeat as a state's rights issue in 1997, a second state initiative in 1997 (Measure 51), an initial challenge and loss by DEA [Drug Enforcement Administration] Administrator Thomas Constantine in 1999 (in the DEA's attempt to regulate the use of controlled substances), and the overturning of a challenge by U.S. Attorney General John Ashcroft [in 2002]. Euthanasia advocates have responded to such challenges by framing the debate as a matter of individual and state autonomy rights against an imposition of Christian pro-life morality. The short reflection that follows comes to you by way of observations from a local in the debate—a local who is more convinced than ever that the so-called dignified and autonomous decision of PAS remains a grand illusion and that those who promote and participate in this practice fail to escape the troubling reality that they so intend to control.

Physician-assisted suicide has been practiced legally in Oregon for four years [as of 2002]. Current law permits state residents to self-administer lethal doses of medications prescribed by their physicians for the purpose of terminating life. The law in no way permits any form of euthanasia or lethal injection in which someone else is directly involved in ending a patient's life. In order to receive a lethal prescription, a person must be capable of making health care decisions, capable of self-administering the lethal dose, and expected to die within 6 months.

The Barbarity of PAS

As a pharmacist, my first area of concern is with the safety and efficacy of PAS. In 1997, an entire anti-PAS campaign focused solely on whether lethal doses of oral barbiturates were truly a 100% "safe and effective means" of terminating a person's life. In September of 1997, Barbara Combs-Lee, leader of the pro-PAS movement, cleverly paraded statistics of "safety and efficacy" in the first major debate promoting legalization of the practice. Neither the press nor the moderators of the debate seemed to note, or were willing to entertain questions (including mine) regarding, the drug failure rates for which Combs-Lee failed to account. Unfortunately, the illusion of efficacy persists in spite of four years of statistics that demonstrate the inefficacy of oral barbiturates as life-ending agents.

The peak activity of short-acting barbiturates should kill a patient within 30 minutes to 3 hours. Patients who "linger" beyond six hours die from something other than the primary desired effect of lethal respiratory depression, and those who endure such a prolonged dying process often suffer great trauma. Although measures for 12 of the 91 cases from 1998–2001 were not even recorded, at least 7 failures of drug safety and efficacy occurred based on normal standards of PAS as practiced in the Netherlands. Also of concern is the fact that once the drug of choice (secobarbitol) is discontinued by the manufacturer, the second drug of choice (oral pentobarbitol) is typically also unavailable from the manufacturer. When these medications cannot be obtained, PAS practitioners will need to resort to medications unproven in their lethality—or

"The so-called dignified and autonomous decision of PAS remains a grand illusion."

perhaps to lethal injection under the guise of palliative sedation.

The illusion that PAS is a safe and effective practice arises from conceptualizing safety and efficacy apart from considerations of the peacefulness of death. Proponents of PAS assert that no adverse effects occurred to patients using the drugs of choice; however, they do not consider the barbarity and trauma of lingering death as constituting an adverse effect. The trauma experienced by now deceased ALS [amyotropic lateral sclerosis] patient Pat Matheny and his brother-in-law raises questions about the efficacy of PAS. Details of Matheny's death are not clear, but the flurry of reports in *The Oregonian* cast doubts that his demise was a peaceful one. Unfortunately, the portrayal of the nature of Matheny's death as unusual served to further the illusion that an individual has autonomy over the time and manner of death.

Informed Consent Questioned

Anecdotal evidence, such as the Kate Cheney case in which questions regarding mental competence and possible coercion by family members were raised, creates doubt that the criteria of informed consent is readily met in PAS cases. According to *The Oregonian*, one psychiatrist felt that Ms. Cheney suffered from dementia and that her daughter's agenda may have overshadowed the will of her mother. The pro-PAS bias of the journalist was evident as she went to great lengths to demonstrate the presence of mother-daughter love, as well as to portray the psychiatrist's opinion as an infringement upon Ms. Cheney's autonomous right to PAS.

What strikes me as most peculiar about the *Oregon Health Department Reports* is the infrequency with which patients requesting PAS undergo psychiatric evaluation. This lack of evaluation is odd, given the plethora of

> *"Those who promote and participate in [PAS] fail to escape the troubling reality that they so intend to control."*

studies suggesting that physicians not trained in psychiatry are often unable to diagnose depression accurately. The absence of routine psychiatric evaluation and the very real possibility of depression also renders the provision of informed consent uncertain.

A major rationale behind the defense of PAS is the radical individualism that is part of the Oregon culture. The "sacred cow" at issue is concern for loss of autonomy. Other top motivators such as "loss of bodily control" and being a "family burden" are easily subsumed under the autonomy category. The loss of a utilitarian valued "pleasurable state of consciousness" proved to be a popular concern as well. (Interestingly, "pain control," which was originally a major argument for permitting PAS, was only a minor category of concern over the last four years.)

The Appeal to Autonomy Is Dangerous

It is my contention that the many challenges to PAS have unfortunately resulted in increased support of the practice by those Oregonians who were originally unsure of their position. Such persons often have shifted their concern from the possible abuse and lack of safety of PAS to an issue of the state's rights and citizens' autonomy. Opponents who outspokenly equate PAS with murder tragically misread the cultural contours of an ethically relativistic and largely unchurched populace.

Calling for the radically individualistic citizens of Oregon to waive their autonomy or forfeit their voting choice in favor of a federal court decision resulted in a significant reduction in public opposition to PAS. Clearly, the landslide loss of Measure 51 (60%–40%) versus the 51%–49% vote of the original Measure 16 should be a

> *"A major rationale behind the defense of PAS is the radical individualism that is part of the Oregon culture."*

lesson of how not to overturn a law in Oregon. Will to power and the imposition of rules upon the fiercely individualistic Oregon residents shift the argument from the theater of reason to the stage of emotion, where myth or illusion will dominate any appeal to fact or rationality.

Take, for example, the nearly forgotten involuntary active euthanasia of an unconscious Corvallis woman brought into an Oregon ER in February of 1997. Following pleas from the woman's daughter, numerous procedures were used to end the woman's life, culminating in the lethal injection of succinylcholine. The attending physician did not deny the act, and a public emotional outcry in support of this practitioner led the prosecuting attorney to conclude that he would not be able to find a jury who would convict the physician of wrongdoing. He was probably correct, and that is my point. The discussion of PAS is so emotionally laden with pro-choice autonomy language that there is little, if any, resolve in the legal community to prosecute even the most blatant of violations—violations which, ironically, may rob patients of their autonomy.

After four years of the "Oregon Experience," I am more convinced than ever that Oregon's "sacred cow" of radical autonomy expressed in a suicidal "death with dignity" is nothing more than a grand illusion. It is, after all, a grand illusion to believe that one can really control the time and means of his or her death. This illusion has been borne out repeatedly, as problems with the safety and efficacy of PAS, as well as with obtaining truly informed consent for such a procedure and ensuring that it is performed only voluntarily, have been documented. Instead of embracing autonomy, we would all do well to recognize that the death we die is a result of the death lived throughout one's life—whether it is a death to self or a death for self.

Legalizing Assisted Suicide Would Harm Women

by Sidney Callahan

About the author: *Sidney Callahan, a Christian feminist, is a professor of psychology at Mercy College. She is also a columnist for* Commonweal *magazine and a contributor to many pro-life publications.*

Current movements to legalize physician-assisted suicide and euthanasia are using some familiar language. Choice. Autonomy. The moral right to control one's own body. In the United States, certain activists, physicians, and ethicists are making a moral argument for one's right to assisted suicide and euthanasia in order to control how and when one dies. Feminists and others must now confront the dilemma of whether this new liberty would contribute to human well-being. More specifically, would women benefit from these additional options at the end of life?

Women have for so long been denied full autonomy and respect in our society that it might be tempting for feminists to endorse a social measure that claims to increase women's freedom of choice. But feminists have learned to be cautious when new social or medical interventions are on offer. Proposals, which initially look positive, can result in unforeseen drawbacks and dangerous side effects—especially when medical technologies are involved. One only has to think of ongoing debates surrounding abortion, reproductive technologies, and hormonal therapies, to name but a few. Is there any consensus to be found among feminists, and if so, what would characterize a feminist critique of assisted suicide and euthanasia?

Women Will Be More Vulnerable

Women will be affected more directly by the euthanasia debate, simply by virtue of the fact that women live longer than men and in their old age command fewer financial and social resources. In a sexist society that also suffers from ageism or prejudiced and discrimination against the old, more women will

Sidney Callahan, "A Feminist Case Against Self-Determined Dying in Assisted Suicide and Euthanasia," *Studies in ProLife Feminism*, vol. 1, Fall 1995. Copyright © 1995 by the Feminism and Nonviolence Studies Association. Reproduced by permission.

end up living alone as fragile persons in need of care. As families become smaller and more dispersed, many women, particularly single, childless women, will not have nearby kin who can care for them or serve as their advocates within increasing complex health-care systems.

When the option or choice to end a life is morally permitted, the interpersonal situation changes. One must justify her or his choice to go on living, particularly when one is dependent upon others to some degree. Subtle pressures can all too easily emerge, pushing a person to stop being a burden on others by taking up resources and energy.

> *"Women will be affected more directly by the euthanasia debate, . . . women live longer than men and . . . command fewer financial and social resources."*

Women who have been socialized to be self-sacrificing may be the most vulnerable to such pressures. It is relevant to note that most of Dr. Jack Kevorkian's clients who have used his assisted-suicide machine have been women. People request assisted suicide when they are not yet in pain because they fear future debilitation and dependency. Fear of dependency is partly a fear of losing power and self-control, but it can also be a fear that others will not take care of you. To become ill is to enter the land of vulnerability where what you need above all is an unconditional entitlement to receive appropriate care.

The Slippery Slope

Feminists will be pessimistic if they look to the way women have been treated in health-care facilities devoted to birth and reproductive health care, or to the way women on welfare have fared. It is instructive also to look at the way abortion moved from being approved of as a tragic choice in exceptional cases to becoming a routinized necessity with only the most perfunctory of counseling or alternatives offered to women. Individual choices have a way of quickly becoming routine procedures in the larger institutions of society. A quick medicalized technological "solution" to problems can take over.

In our own disorganized, economically stressed, market-driven American health system, with so many of the poor having inadequate health insurance, many abuses could be expected. Little legal supervision or regulation could really be effective. Certain physicians would undoubtedly become known for their willingness to approve suicide and euthanasia requests, and perhaps, as with abortion, special for-profit clinics would be set up. Poor and uninsured old persons—particularly women, minorities and persons with disabilities—would be most at risk.

Do women stand to benefit from the right to assisted suicide and euthanasia? Hardly. In fact, women, once again, would pay the ultimate price.

Chapter 2

Should Assisted-Suicide Decisions Be Made by the States?

CURRENT CONTROVERSIES

Chapter Preface

Physician-assisted suicide (PAS) is not specifically prohibited by the Constitution of the United States or any federal law. Neither, according to two 1997 Supreme Court decisions, is a "right to die" constitutionally guaranteed. Chief Justice William Rehnquist observed, "Throughout the nation, Americans are engaged in an earnest and profound debate about the morality, legality, and practicality of physician-assisted suicide. Our holding permits this debate to continue, as it should in a democratic society." The debate about PAS occurs mainly at a state level because, according to contemporary interpretations of federalism—the division of authority between the federal government and the states—it falls to each state individually to determine whether PAS should be legal within its borders.

Thirty-seven states have banned assisted suicide—including PAS—by specific statute, and twelve more make it illegal under common law or homicide statutes. As of this writing, Oregon is the only state to legalize PAS. The Death with Dignity Act (DWD) was originally passed in 1994 through Oregon's initiative process. Although the innovative legislation contained strict safeguards and allowed PAS only under certain very specifically outlined circumstances, it was immediately challenged in federal court. In August 1995 U.S. district judge Michael Hogan declared Oregon's DWD unconstitutional because it violated the equal protection clause of the Fourteenth Amendment. His decision was overturned. The U.S. Supreme Court denied a final hearing to DWD opponents, and the law was allowed to go into effect on October 27, 1997. However, in reexamining the act, the Oregon legislature discovered many facts regarding assisted suicide that were either unknown or not brought to light during the original vote. The legislature decided to return the act to the November 1997 ballot, recommending that Oregon voters repeal it. However, by an overwhelming majority, voters chose not to repeal the act, affirming their desire for PAS a second time.

The passage and use of physician-assisted suicide laws by a single state has changed the debate about PAS by providing a real-life laboratory where the ramifications of the practice can be assessed. Authors in the following chapter debate the many issues surrounding assisted suicide and federalism. As time passes, the Oregon laboratory will provide much insight into how the legalization of physician-assisted suicide affects society.

Allowing the States to Make Assisted-Suicide Decisions Will Not Harm America

by Michael C. Dorf

About the author: *Michael C. Dorf is vice dean and professor of law at Columbia University.*

In early November [2001], Attorney General John Ashcroft directed the Drug Enforcement [Administration] to investigate and prosecute Oregon doctors who prescribe life-ending medication to terminally ill patients. The action is to take place pursuant to the federal Controlled Substances Act. Yet state law makes physician-assisted suicide legal in Oregon.

Almost immediately, federal judge Robert Jones issued an order enjoining enforcement of the new policy until November 20, so that he could take evidence and hear further arguments about the policy.

Ashcroft's decision, which reverses the policy of former Attorney General Janet Reno, raises difficult questions of statutory and constitutional interpretation. However the courts ultimately resolve those issues, the decision is vulnerable as a matter of public policy. There can be legitimate grounds for federal law displacing state law. But the Oregon experience does not justify federal intervention on this issue.

The Supreme Court has decided to leave the physician-assisted suicide issue to the states, and Ashcroft, who is a proponent of federalism, ought to follow the Court's lead on this issue.

Physician-Assisted Suicide: The Court Stays Agnostic

In 1997, the U.S. Supreme Court rejected constitutional challenges to laws barring physician-assisted suicide in the states of New York and Washington.

In *Washington v. Glucksberg*, the Court concluded that the states had legitimate interests justifying their bans. Those interests include the sanctity of all human life, ensuring the integrity of the medical profession, and preventing patients from succumbing to the pressure to end their lives that might result from a regime of legalized assisted suicide.

Although the Court in *Glucksberg* did not find the arguments for physician-assisted suicide sufficient to establish a constitutional right, neither did it say that states are *required* to prohibit physician-assisted suicide. And indeed, there are sound policy grounds for thinking the practice should be legal.

> *"The Supreme Court has decided to leave the physician-assisted suicide issue to the states, and Ashcroft . . . ought to follow the Court's lead."*

Most fundamentally, libertarians object to the government imposing a conception of life's sanctity on a person whose very own life is at stake. In addition, there is an efficacy question: anonymous surveys show that doctors in most states already act to speed the deaths of their terminally ill patients, but clandestinely and without regulation; legalizing the practice could prevent the problems associated with secrecy.

Finally, laws barring physician-assisted suicide can lead to inadequate pain medication by doctors who fear that their intent will be misinterpreted. Granted, most states formally permit doctors to prescribe sufficient doses of narcotics to treat a dying patient's pain even if that will have the "side effect" of hastening death. Yet despite this formal permission, doctors often undermedicate because they fear criminal penalties if they are deemed to have crossed the hazy line between treating pain and assisting suicide.

Because of the complexity of the issue, the justices concluded that the Constitution does not dictate one answer or another. Writing for the majority in *Glucksberg*, Chief Justice Rehnquist observed: "Throughout the Nation, Americans are engaged in an earnest and profound debate about the morality, legality, and practicality of physician-assisted suicide. Our holding permits this debate to continue, as it should in a democratic society."

Oregon's Death With Dignity Act

So far, the debate over physician-assisted suicide has been rather one-sided. Forty-nine states prohibit doctors (or anyone else) from dispensing controlled substances for the purpose of ending a patient's life.

Oregon is the exception. In 1994, 51 percent of Oregon voters approved a referendum establishing the state's Death With Dignity Act.

Lawsuits delayed the Act's implementation for several years. The state legislature also sought the Act's repeal. But in 1997, 60 percent of Oregon voters opted to retain it. The Act has been in effect since then.

The Death With Dignity Act legalizes physician-assisted suicide, but only under tightly restricted circumstances. For example, it does not permit doctors themselves to administer lethal medication in the manner practiced by Dr. Jack Kevorkian.

Instead, a physician can prescribe a lethal dose of medication to a terminally ill patient who then decides if and when to use it. Self-administration, the law's defenders say, helps ensure that the patient is acting voluntarily.

There are other restrictions, as well. For instance, a patient's request for lethal medication must be in writing and signed before two witnesses who confirm that the patient is acting voluntarily. Furthermore, the Act requires that before such a prescription can be given, two physicians must examine the patient and his or her medical records and confirm that the patient suffers from "an incurable and irreversible disease that has been medically confirmed and will, within reasonable medical judgment, produce death within six months."

Even then, the prescription may not be written until 48 hours after the written request and 15 days after the patient's first oral request—effectively creating waiting periods during which a patient can change his or her mind, and in which relatives or friends can intervene to argue against suicide if they choose.

Federal Law and the Oregon Act

Under the Supremacy Clause of the U.S. Constitution, when there is a conflict between federal law and state law, federal law prevails. Attorney General Ashcroft takes the position that Oregon's Death With Dignity Act must give way to the federal Controlled Substances Act or "CSA."

The CSA is the principal federal drug law. It classifies drugs into five "schedules." Some drugs, such as heroin and LSD, are placed in schedule I, meaning they have no legal uses.

As the CSA recognizes, however, many other drugs have "a useful and legitimate medical purpose and are necessary to maintain the health and general welfare of the American people." Therefore, physicians can lawfully dispense most controlled substances.

According to Attorney General Ashcroft, prescribing a controlled substance to facilitate a patient's suicide is not a "legitimate medical purpose" within the meaning of the CSA. Thus, his new policy would treat a doctor who fills a patient's request under Oregon's Death With Dignity Act as violating the terms of the federal license to prescribe controlled substances.

> *"Because of the complexity of the issue, the justices concluded that the Constitution does not dictate one answer or another."*

The immediate practical result for an Oregon physician would be the loss of the ability to prescribe medicine and the possibility of a prison sentence. In other words, the Attorney General's reading of the CSA would have the practical effect of voiding Oregon's Death With Dignity Act, because few if any

Oregon physicians would be willing to risk delicensing and prison.

By temporarily enjoining enforcement of the new policy, judge [Robert] Jones signaled that there is a substantial possibility that, after a full hearing, he will reject Ashcroft's interpretation of the CSA, which is somewhat strained.[1]

After all, former Attorney General Reno read the CSA differently. Even though the Clinton Administration generally opposed physician-assisted suicide, in 1998 Reno declared: "There is no evidence that Congress, in the CSA, intended to displace the states as the primary regulators of the medical profession, or to override a state's determination as to what constitutes legitimate medical practice in the absence of a federal law prohibiting that practice."

> *"The Death With Dignity Act legalizes physician-assisted suicide, but only under tightly restricted circumstances."*

Even if former Attorney General Reno had the better view of the CSA, there is still a chance that Attorney General Ashcroft will prevail before Judge Jones or on appeal to the Ninth Circuit Court of Appeals or the Supreme Court. In part, that is because executive officials charged with enforcing federal law are generally given some deference to interpret the law as they see fit, at least where the statutory language is ambiguous.

It would not be surprising, therefore, if further arguments over the CSA's effect on the Death With Dignity Act focus not so much on what the CSA means, as on whether that meaning is clear. If the courts hold that its meaning is not clear, then Ashcroft's interpretation could prevail because of the deference the law affords him (as would the possible contrary interpretation of a future attorney general, who would be entitled to the same deference in holding a different view).

We can also expect Oregon to argue that the CSA should be narrowly construed to protect state sovereignty. The state will likely invoke recent decisions of the Supreme Court that cut back on the scope of Congressional power to regulate interstate commerce.

Federal Law vs. State Law

Defenders of the Oregon law, including some people who personally oppose legalized physician-assisted suicide, have accused the Bush Administration of hypocrisy. Does the attorney general only favor states' rights when the states are exercising their rights in a manner that pleases him and the president?

In order to evaluate the hypocrisy charge, one needs some way of distinguishing appropriate from inappropriate federal action. Even someone who believes strongly in state sovereignty will allow that there are circumstances when fed-

---

1. Judge Robert E. Jones ruled against Attorney General John Ashcroft's interpretation of the CSA on April 17, 2002, placing a permanent injunction on the Ashcroft directive.

eral policy should prevail. The relevant question is whether those circumstances are present here.

One valid reason for federal regulation is that actions in one state can have substantial effects on other states. For example, if heroin sales were completely legal in Oregon, other states' efforts to combat heroin sales would be severely undermined. Heroin legally sold in Oregon would become illegal heroin elsewhere in the country.

Is there a similar risk with the lethal medication prescribed under Oregon's Death With Dignity Act? Not really.

The Act's restrictions mean that a very small quantity of drugs is being dispensed and the Act's reporting requirements make it relatively easy to trace those drugs that are dispensed.

Nor is there a worry that Oregon will become a magnet for people who want to evade their own states' prohibitions on physician-assisted suicide. The Act only permits prescription of lethal medication to patients who can prove that they are Oregon residents.

National Values

Federal legislation may also be desirable if a state policy contravenes some fundamental value. If Oregon were to legalize slavery, we would see nothing wrong with the federal government overriding that choice.

Of course, the Constitution itself prohibits slavery, and the federal government would be acting under its aegis. By contrast, as the Supreme Court recognized in *Glucksberg*, the Constitution is silent on the question of physician-assisted suicide.

Still, something can be a matter of fundamental national policy even if it is not in the Constitution. Federal statutes prohibiting private discrimination on the grounds of age, disability, national origin, race, religion, and sex all go further than the Constitution itself requires; yet no one now doubts their validity.

Here too, however, physician-assisted suicide is different. No federal statute clearly prohibits the practice. On the contrary, two years ago [1999] the House of Representatives passed a bill that would have directly superseded the Oregon law, but the bill died in the Senate.

> *"According to . . . Ashcroft, prescribing a controlled substance to facilitate a patient's suicide is not a 'legitimate medical purpose.'"*

That fact is significant. More than any other institution, the Senate is the federal body that represents the states. If federal law is to displace the choice of the Oregon voters, it should be through a federal law that has passed the Senate. In bypassing both the voters of Oregon and Congress, Attorney General Ashcroft is attempting to short-circuit the democratic process that the Supreme Court invited in *Glucksberg*.

55

States Have the Authority to Allow the Use of Federally Controlled Substances for Physician-Assisted Suicide

by Robert E. Jones

About the author: *Robert E. Jones is a U.S. district judge for the District of Oregon.*

Editor's Note: The following viewpoint was excerpted from the U.S. District Court for the District of Oregon decision in State of Oregon v. John Ashcroft *(2002).*

After surviving voter and legal challenges, the 1994 Oregon Death with Dignity Act ("Oregon Act"), finally went into effect in October 1997. On November 6, 2001, with no advance warning to Oregon representatives, Attorney General John Ashcroft (herein referred to as "Ashcroft") fired the first shot in the battle between the state of Oregon and the federal government over which government has the ultimate authority to decide what constitutes the legitimate practice of medicine, at least when schedule II substances regulated under the Controlled Substances Act ("CSA"), are involved. Ashcroft began the battle by issuing the so-called "Ashcroft directive,"—a few paragraphs published in the Federal Register on November 9, 2001, in which Ashcroft declares, in relevant part, that

• controlled substances may not be dispensed to assist suicide, thus reversing the position taken by his predecessor, Attorney General Janet Reno, in June 1998.

• assisting suicide is not a "legitimate medical purpose" and that prescribing, dispensing, or administering federally controlled substances to assist suicide violates the CSA.

Robert E. Jones, opinion and order, *State of Oregon v. John Ashcroft*, Civil No. 01-1647-JO, 2002.

• prescribing, dispensing, or administering federally controlled substances to assist suicide may "render [a physician's] registration . . . inconsistent with the public interest" and therefore subject to possible suspension or revocation. . . .

Stifling "Earnest and Profound Debate"

Through his directive, Ashcroft evidently sought to stifle an ongoing "earnest and profound debate" in the various states concerning physician-assisted suicide. In *Washington v. Glucksberg*, the Supreme Court was called upon to decide whether the state of Washington's statutory ban on assisted suicide violated the Due Process Clause. In a thoughtful opinion, the Court acknowledged that "[t]hroughout the Nation, Americans are engaged in an earnest and profound debate about the morality, legality and practicality

> *"Congress' overarching concern in enacting the [Controlled Substances Act] was the problem of drug abuse and illegal trafficking in drugs."*

of physician-assisted suicide." The Court recounted the various states' "serious, thoughtful examinations" of the issues in this difficult debate, including Oregon's 1994 enactment of the Oregon Act. The Court declined to "strike down the considered policy choice" of the State of Washington, deferring instead to that state's resolution of the debate.

In her concurring opinion in *Glucksberg*, Justice [Sandra Day] O'Connor further elaborated that

> There is no reason to think the democratic process will not strike the proper balance between the interests of terminally ill, mentally competent individuals who would seek to end their suffering and the State's interests in protecting those who might seek to end life mistakenly or under pressure. . . . States are presently undertaking extensive and serious evaluation of physician-assisted suicide and other related issues. . . . In such circumstances, "the . . . challenging task of crafting appropriate procedures for safeguarding . . . liberty interests is entrusted to the 'laboratory' of the States . . . in the first instance."

As the Court acknowledged in *Glucksberg*, the citizens of Oregon, through their democratic initiative process, have chosen to resolve the moral, legal, and ethical debate on physician-assisted suicide for themselves by voting—not once, but twice—in favor of the Oregon Act. The Oregon Act attempts to resolve this "earnest and profound debate" by "strik[ing] the proper balance between the interests of terminally ill, mentally competent individuals who would seek to end their suffering and the State's interests in protecting those who might seek to end life mistakenly or under pressure."

Ashcroft and the Oregon Act

With publication of the Ashcroft directive, Ashcroft essentially nullified the Oregon Act and four years of Oregon experience in implementing it. In response to what it perceived as an unwarranted and unauthorized intrusion into the sovereign interests of Oregon, the medical practices of Oregon physicians, and the end-of-life decisions made by terminally-ill Oregonians, plaintiff state of Oregon ("plaintiff") immediately commenced this lawsuit to, among other things, enjoin Ashcroft and the other defendants from giving the Ashcroft directive any legal effect. A temporary restraining order, issued on November 8, 2001, remains in effect.[1]

Despite the enormity of the debate over physician-assisted suicide, the issues in this case are legal ones and, as pertain to my disposition, are fairly narrowly drawn. My resolution of the legal issues does not require any delving into the complex religious, moral, ethical, medical, emotional or psychological controversies that surround physician-assisted suicide or "hastened death" (as the parties sometimes describe it), because in Oregon, those controversies have been—for now—put to rest.

The case presently is before me on several motions: (1) plaintiff's motion for summary judgment; (2) intervenors' motions for summary judgment or partial summary judgment; and (3) defendants' motion to dismiss and alternative motion for summary judgment. For the reasons stated below, I grant plaintiff's and intervenors' motions for summary judgment in part and today enter a permanent injunction enjoining defendants from enforcing, applying, or otherwise giving any legal effect to the Ashcroft directive at issue in this case. Those portions of plaintiff's and intervenors' motions not addressed in this opinion are denied as moot. Defendants' motion to dismiss and alternative motion for summary judgment are denied.

The Controlled Substances Act

Congress enacted the CSA, as Title II of the Comprehensive Drug Abuse Prevention and Control Act of 1970. The CSA provides a comprehensive federal scheme for regulation and control of certain drugs and other substances. The congressional findings supporting Title II reveal that Congress' overarching concern in enacting the CSA was the problem of drug abuse and illegal trafficking in drugs.

> *"The [Controlled Substances Act] does not prohibit practitioners from prescribing and dispensing controlled substances."*

The CSA establishes five schedules of controlled substances, ranging from schedule I substances, which have no accepted medical use and can be utilized only in very limited contexts, to schedules II, III, IV, and V substances, which have recognized uses and can be manufactured, distributed, possessed and used, subject to the restrictions of the CSA. The CSA sets forth initial schedules, and specifies procedures

---

1. A permanent injunction was entered on April 17, 2002.

by which the Attorney General may add, remove, or transfer substances to or between schedules.

The CSA makes it unlawful for any person to manufacture, distribute, or dispense any controlled substance "[e]xcept as authorized by [the CSA]." As pertinent in this case, physicians who prescribe controlled substances and pharmacists who fill the prescriptions are considered "practitioners" who "dispense" controlled substances. To obtain authorization to do so, practitioners must register with the Attorney General and obtain a Drug Enforcement Agency ("DEA") certificate of registration.

> *"The Ashcroft directive is not entitled to deference under any standard and is invalid."*

Under the CSA as originally enacted, state-licensed practitioners were entitled to be registered with the DEA as a matter of right. ("Practitioners shall be registered to dispense . . . controlled substances in schedule II, III, IV, or V if they are authorized to dispense . . . under the law of the State in which they practice"); (registration mandatory if applicant authorized under state law). The Attorney General could suspend or revoke a practitioner's registration only if the registrant (1) materially falsified an application; (2) was convicted of a felony relating to controlled substances; or (3) had his or her state license or registration suspended or revoked.

Congress has amended the CSA many times since 1970. With each amendment, Congress further attempted to address the problems of drug abuse and illegal trafficking in drugs. In 1984, apparently concerned with the domestic diversion of otherwise legitimate medical controlled substances into the illegal market by registered practitioners, Congress again amended the CSA. As pertinent here, the 1984 amendment empowered the Attorney General to deny, suspend, or revoke a practitioner's DEA registration if the Attorney General "determines that the issuance of such registration would be inconsistent with the public interest."

In 1971, under authority delegated by the Attorney General, the predecessor to the Administrator of the DEA adopted formal regulations implementing the CSA. One of the regulations . . . provides, in relevant part:

> A prescription for a controlled substance to be effective must be issued for a *legitimate medical purpose* by an individual practitioner acting in the usual course of his professional practice. . . . An order purporting to be a prescription issued not in the usual course of professional treatment or in legitimate and authorized research is not a prescription within the meaning and intent of section 309 of the Act . . . and the person knowingly filling such a purported prescription, as well as the person issuing it, shall be subject to the penalties provided for violations of the provisions of law relating to controlled substances. . . .

Legitimate Medical Purpose

The determination of what constitutes a legitimate medical practice or purpose traditionally has been left to the individual states. State statutes, state medical boards, and state regulations control the practice of medicine. The CSA was never intended, and the USDOJ [U.S. Department of Justice] and DEA were never authorized, to establish a national medical practice or act as a national medical board. To allow an attorney general—an appointed executive whose tenure depends entirely on whatever administration occupies the White House—to determine the legitimacy of a particular medical practice without a specific congressional grant of such authority would be unprecedented and extraordinary. As stated, the practice of medicine is based on state standards, recognizing, of course, national enactments that, within constitutional limits, specifically and clearly define what is lawful and what is not. Without doubt there is tremendous disagreement among highly respected medical practitioners as to whether assisted suicide or hastened death is a legitimate medical practice, but opponents have been heard and, absent a specific prohibitive federal statute, the Oregon voters have made the legal, albeit controversial, decision that such a practice is legitimate in this sovereign state.

The Ashcroft directive attempts to define the term "legitimate medical purpose" to exclude use of controlled substances for otherwise legal physician-assisted suicide where Congress failed to do so despite multiple opportunities. Obviously, Congress knows how to do so, as manifested in its abandoned attempts to restrict assisted suicide nationwide. Because former Attorney General Reno concluded that the CSA has no application to the Oregon Act, Representative [Henry J.] Hyde introduced two bills in the House of Representatives to specifically address the Oregon Act. The first bill, the Lethal Drug Use Prevention Act of 1998, would have amended the CSA to directly authorize the suspension or revocation of a practitioner's DEA registration if the registrant intentionally dispensed or distributed a controlled substance for the purpose of assisting the suicide or euthanasia of another individual. The second bill, the Pain Relief Promotion Act, attempted to clarify the CSA to provide that the alleviation of pain is a legitimate medical purpose, but that the CSA did not permit the use of controlled substances to cause death or assist in a suicide. While the second bill passed the House, neither bill passed the Senate, and neither was signed into law.

> *"The fact that opposition to assisted suicide may be fully justified . . . does not permit a federal statute to be manipulated . . . to satisfy even a worthy goal."*

Even though both acts failed in Congress, certain congressional leaders made a good faith effort to get through the administrative door that which they could not get through the congressional door, seeking refuge with the newly-appointed Attorney General whose ideology matched their views, and this is precisely what occurred. The Executive Branch immediately began its efforts to re-write the law to achieve its goal of abolishing assisted suicide anywhere. Although congressional action attempting to control matters traditionally left to the state may raise constitutional issues for any future legislation in this field, suffice it to say that at this juncture, neither the U.S. Constitution nor the Bill of Rights speaks to assisted suicide, neither providing for it as a personal right nor prohibiting it.

I again emphasize that I resolve this case as a matter of statutory interpretation, and my interpretation of the statutory text and meaning is that the CSA does not prohibit practitioners from prescribing and dispensing controlled substances in compliance with a carefully-worded state legislative act. Thus, the Ashcroft directive is not entitled to deference under any standard and is invalid. I also emphasize that my task is not to criticize those who oppose the concept of assisted suicide for any reason. Many of our citizens, including the highest respected leaders of this country, oppose assisted suicide. But the fact that opposition to assisted suicide may be fully justified, morally, ethically, religiously or otherwise, does not permit a federal statute to be manipulated from its true meaning to satisfy even a worthy goal. As the Supreme Court has warned, courts should be "out of the business of reviewing the wisdom of statutes" (*Usery v. Turner Elkhorn Mining Co.*), a proposition not to be taken "cum grano salis" (with a grain of salt).

The Federal Government's Attempt to Ban Assisted Suicide Threatens Federalism

by Nelson Lund

About the author: *Nelson Lund is a professor at George Mason University School of Law.*

Alone among the American states, Oregon has legalized physician-assisted suicide. This step was thoroughly debated and solemnly taken by the voters of Oregon not once but twice. In 1994, a narrow majority approved the policy in a formal referendum, and a much larger majority rejected a repeal initiative three years later.

But now, in a ruling issued November 9, [2001,] Attorney General John Ashcroft has reversed a decision of his predecessor, Janet Reno, and decided that Oregon doctors may no longer use federally regulated drugs to assist their patients in committing suicide. This decision raises important and troubling questions. Although I support the goal of discouraging physician-assisted suicide, I also believe that Ashcroft is pursuing that goal in a way that may undermine a fundamental constitutional principle.

To see why the Attorney General's approach to the problem is questionable, we need to begin with a closer look at the problem itself. In my view, the people of Oregon made a serious mistake in legalizing assisted suicide. Much of the current enthusiasm for this practice is driven by a perfectly understandable yearning for patient autonomy and by an equally understandable reluctance to let the frequently arrogant medical profession force us to endure degrading, technologically extended deaths. Unfortunately, the legalization of assisted suicide is also a big step down a road that will finally reduce patient autonomy rather than enhance it.

Nelson Lund, "Why Ashcroft Is Wrong on Assisted Suicide," *Commentary*, vol. 113, February 2002.

Doctors are uniquely empowered by their technical knowledge and by the nature of their work to kill their fellow citizens without getting caught. The principal check on that power has been the Hippocratic ethic, which forbids physicians from ever playing any part in deliberately hastening the death of any patient. In the movement for assisted suicide, that ethic is now under serious attack. It is under attack, moreover, at the very moment when strong new incentives have been created for doctors to step out of the narrow role of healers and to take on a political function for which they are eminently ill-suited.

Allocation of Scarce Health-Care Resources

This new function involves the allocation of scarce health-care resources, and it is one that has fallen to doctors as a direct result of our present crisis in health-care financing. The crisis itself has two main causes. First, scientific and technological advances have given doctors a huge new array of expensive tools for treating disease and prolonging life. Second, government policies have created a system of "third-party payers" in which patients and doctors alike have lost the incentive to conserve on expenditures, even when the cost of a treatment exceeds its expected benefits.

Inevitably, governments and insurance companies have been forced to seek new methods to prevent uncontrolled spending and waste. What we have gotten is "managed care," a form of increasingly politicized rationing that replaces the market discipline under which patients themselves once decided how much of their own money to spend on which medical services.

Oregon itself offers an instructive example. Several years ago, the state adopted a Medicaid rationing plan that assigned a priority to each of hundreds of different medical treatments. Under this plan, funds for lower-ranking treatments would be withheld in order to conserve money for those needing a higher-ranking treatment. When the plan was first proposed, treatments for the late stages of AIDS were assigned a low ranking because they were expensive and largely unsuccessful. But the AIDS lobby campaigned to raise the priority of these treatments, and it succeeded. Meanwhile, patients in analogous situations—like very low-birth-weight babies and patients with advanced cancer—continued to have funds withheld for the simple reason that they were politically less powerful.

Similar political forces will continue to push the health-care system to conserve resources by withholding care from the most expensive and politically least appealing patients.

> *"Ashcroft is [discouraging physician-assisted suicide] in a way that may undermine a fundamental constitutional principle."*

Whether it happens directly through law and regulation, or informally, very sick patients who are elderly or whose prospects for recovery are thought to be small are going to be prime targets for "hastened deaths." And the neatest justification for a hastened death is that the patient himself asked for help in committing suicide.

Family members and physicians have always faced special stresses in dealing with apparently doomed patients. Once physician-assisted suicide is legalized, there will be strong temptations to pressure such patients to accelerate the inevitable. This pressure will be especially effective with those who are clinically depressed. There will also be strong temptations for doctors and families to decide that some patients would want to die if only they could make a rational decision.

The Netherlands' Experience

The Netherlands' experience with assisted suicide shows that the slippery slope to euthanasia is no mere bugaboo. That nation has been running an experiment much like Oregon's for almost three decades. By extremely conservative estimates, almost 1 percent of all deaths in the Netherlands result from euthanasia performed without the patient's consent, including a large number of cases where the patient was totally competent. Nor are Dutch physicians who practice assisted suicide and euthanasia primarily concerned with their patients' pain and suffering. Reasons more commonly cited are no expectation of improvement; low quality of life; futility of medical therapy; and the difficulty that relatives have in coping with their sick kin.

> *"Congress has never said whether or not physicians may use regulated drugs to help their patients commit suicide."*

We need not go down this road. The fear that obsessive doctors will inflict a demeaning death by means of high-tech "heroic measures" is entirely legitimate, but no patient need consent to unwanted medical treatments, and directives given in advance can guard against their use on those who are unconscious. And if doctors are too often ignoring "do not resuscitate" orders, as they may be, the answer is hardly to give them a new power that can easily be used to substitute their judgment for their patients' as to whether a life is worth living. Yet this is exactly the power that the people of Oregon have decided to give their physicians.

Still, whether they were right or wrong to do so was not the question before Attorney General Ashcroft. He was charged with determining whether federal law requires or permits him to undermine the policy adopted, wisely or not, by Oregon's voters.

Prescription Drugs and Suicide

Physicians who decide to help their patients kill themselves typically employ a lethal combination of prescription drugs whose use is regulated by federal law under a framework that began to develop as long ago as 1914. The regulatory statutes have been repeatedly altered, and they have by now become quite detailed and complex. Nevertheless, and despite all the details, certain key provisions are surprisingly vague: in particular, Congress has never said whether or not physicians may use regulated drugs to help their patients commit suicide.

After the voters of Oregon emphatically reaffirmed their decision to allow assisted suicide in 1997, Attorney General Reno found nothing in the law to forbid the use of prescription drugs for this purpose.

In reversing the Reno position in November, Ashcroft relied on a lengthy legal opinion from the Justice Department. In order to understand its strengths and weaknesses, we need to begin with a brief summary of the law.

> *"It may be more useful to ask whether the Attorney General's decision . . . is consistent with the proper division of responsibilities between the state and federal governments."*

If a physician is licensed by a state to dispense prescription drugs, he must also be given a permit to do so under federal law—unless the Attorney General, which in practice usually means the Drug Enforcement Administration (DEA), determines that granting such a permit "would be inconsistent with the public interest." The statute Congress wrote, however, says nothing at all about what constitutes proper or improper use of these drugs by a physician who has a permit to dispense them.

In 1975, a doctor tried to use this statutory silence to defend himself when he was prosecuted for operating as a drug dealer. The Supreme Court rejected his defense on the ground that the statute implicitly requires doctors to act "within accepted limits." This meant, the Court concluded, that a doctor must act "as a physician," dispensing drugs only "in the course of professional practice or research."

We are left with the following question: given the Supreme Court's interpretation of the statute's intent, did Congress mean the "accepted limits" of professional practice to be defined separately by each state's law or by a national consensus? Because state laws seldom conflict in any relevant respect, it would usually make no difference. In the 1975 case, for example, the defendant gave inadequate physical examinations or none at all, ignored the results of the few tests he performed, prescribed whatever amount of drugs the "patient" asked for, and graduated his fee according to the number of tablets prescribed. No state authorizes doctors to behave in this manner.

In 1984, Congress amended the statute to allow the Attorney General to revoke a doctor's federal license for acts inconsistent with the "public interest." (This amendment was apparently triggered by a concern that some states were not being sufficiently vigorous in yanking licenses from physicians who dispensed drugs in an abusive manner.) The Justice Department opinion assumes that this "public-interest" standard must be uniform throughout the nation. It then goes on to show, quite convincingly, that the legitimacy of physician-assisted suicide has been rejected by almost all of the state governments that have considered the issue, by all of the major organizations of the medical profession, and in various ways by the federal government itself. If the "accepted limits" of medical practice must be established by finding a national consensus, Oregon clearly is a deviant jurisdiction that has departed from the consensus view.

Standards

Plausible as the Justice Department's conclusion may seem, its argument is not quite persuasive. Physician-assisted suicide may well be inconsistent with what the Attorney General and I believe is in the public interest, but it does not constitute the obvious abandonment of the physician's role that occurs when a doctor starts selling addictive drugs at a fixed price to anyone who asks. Moreover, the Supreme Court's sensible conclusion that Congress did not mean to authorize individual doctors to set their own professional standards does not imply that Congress forbade state governments from experimenting with nontraditional standards of medical practice. Finally, there is a real difference between lax enforcement of agreed-upon standards by some states (the apparent concern of Congress in 1984) and Oregon's deliberate adoption of a different standard altogether. Congress could decide to override such experiments with a uniform national standard, but it has never done so expressly or by clear implication.

Nor has this congressional inaction resulted from inattentiveness to the Oregon law. After that state's voters first approved assisted suicide, Congress took note of it in a new statute that prohibited any use of federal funds for this practice. The Justice Department's opinion cites that statute as evidence of congressional disagreement with Oregon's decision, which is fair enough, but the statute also stopped far short of forbidding Oregon physicians to use federally regulated drugs in a manner permitted by state law. The failure of Congress to go farther than it did actually reinforces the conclusion that Congress has not decided to use federal law to interfere with Oregon's new policy. On the contrary, when Congress decided to restrict the use of federal funds, it also decided not to impose additional restrictions.

The Justice Department's legal opinion also seeks support in a 2001 Supreme Court ruling that effectively nullified a California law authorizing the use of marijuana for medical purposes. This decision certainly does confirm that state law cannot immunize a physician from the requirements of federal drug laws. In the medical-marijuana case, however, an outright conflict between state and federal laws was undeniably present—the federal statute specifically listed marijuana as a substance that Congress had determined has no legitimate medical uses. Since no such explicit congressional decision exists in the context of physician-assisted suicide, the Court's 2001 decision cannot prop-

> *"Benefits arise from leaving the states to deal with local concerns."*

erly be invoked to support interfering with the operation of Oregon's new law.

The medical-marijuana decision highlights an additional problem with the Justice Department position. A standard rule requires courts to resolve statutory ambiguities in a way that avoids raising serious constitutional questions. That rule did not apply in the medical-marijuana case because the statute was completely unambiguous. With respect to assisted suicide, however, the federal statute is ambiguous at best.

And the Justice Department's position does raise constitutional questions. In the marijuana case, the Court pointedly noted that it was not deciding "the underlying constitutional issues," which included the question of whether the federal drug-control statute "exceeds Congress's power under the commerce clause." Until a few years ago, such a cautionary note would never have appeared in a Supreme Court opinion: for more than a half-century, the Court had effectively taken the position that virtually any federal regulation Congress saw fit to enact would be upheld as an exercise of its power to regulate interstate commerce. In a recent series of decisions, however, the Court has begun to define or restore some constitutional limits on Congress's regulatory authority.

Although there is little reason to think that the current Court would find the drug laws in general to be unconstitutional, the principles that have been revived in recent decisions might well support a narrower attack on the Attorney General's effort to frustrate Oregon's experiment with physician-assisted suicide. Indeed, a federal court has already suspended the enforcement of Ashcroft's policy, and an initial decision on the merits of this challenge is expected in the spring.[1] The case may eventually reach the Supreme Court, and a victory for Ashcroft's position is by no means certain.

> *"There is no obvious need for the federal government to interfere with Oregon's [physician-assisted suicide] experiment."*

Political Jurisdiction

Rather than guess just where the Supreme Court will go, however, it may be more useful to ask whether the Attorney General's decision—which at the very least was not compelled by anything in the statute itself—is consistent with the proper division of responsibilities between the state and federal governments.

Some of the deepest and most intractable questions in the design of representative government have to do with the appropriate size of a political jurisdiction. James Madison offered a quick summary of the American answer:

> It must be confessed that in this, as in most other cases, there is a mean, on both sides of which inconveniences will be found to lie. By enlarging too

---

1. Judge Robert E. Jones ruled against Attorney General John Ashcroft on April 17, 2002, placing a permanent injunction on the Ashcroft directive.

much the number of electors, you render the representative too little acquainted with all their local circumstances and lesser interests; as by reducing it too much, you render him unduly attached to these, and too little fit to comprehend and pursue great and national objects. The federal Constitution forms a happy combination in this respect; the great and aggregate interests being referred to the national, the local and particular to the State legislatures.

Madison might have added that this "happy combination" is easier to describe in words than to maintain in practice. Writing almost a half-century later, Alexis de Tocqueville was impressed with how stable the combination had remained. This he attributed in large measure (though by no means exclusively) to what he saw as a genuinely novel device in our Constitution. When the thirteen original states created the federal system, they gave to the new government the power not only to make laws but to administer them directly, without intermediation by the constitutive states. This idea, which seems obvious to us today, was so remarkable that Tocqueville was able to say there was still no word for the resulting form of government, even several decades after it had been put into place. He himself described what we had in the United States not as a federal government but as an "incomplete national government."

Three principal benefits arise from leaving the states to deal with local concerns. First, a multiplicity of jurisdictions creates choices that enable citizens to achieve the mix of policies that most closely satisfies their individual wants and needs. Second, and closely related, federalism promotes competition among jurisdictions: state governments that commit serious errors in satisfying their residents' preferences incur the costs of emigration (and immigration forgone) by the taxpayers who make government possible. Finally, the allocation of political power to the state level inhibits the ability of national government to shift costs and benefits from one place to another, and thus to create incentives for pork-barrel policies whose costs exceed their benefits. (Agricultural subsidies and Western water projects are familiar products of such perverse incentives.)

Competition among jurisdictions, however, is not an unmixed blessing. Although it is true, for example, that the national government is sometimes responsible for an inefficient redistribution of costs and benefits, it is also true that the national government can prevent inefficiencies that would otherwise occur. Standard examples include national defense and water pollution. If each state were left free to decide what contribution it would volunteer to the defense of the nation, it might become enormously difficult to achieve an adequate national defense in the first place; similarly, upstream jurisdictions have incentives to overpollute interstate rivers when they can thereby shift part of the costs of the pollution to their downstream neighbors.

> *"Every state in the union remains free to outlaw physician-assisted suicide and to enforce its laws as vigorously as it sees fit."*

Moreover, for every easy example of a function that is more appropriately performed at either the national or the local level, there are other examples where the appropriate allocation is fairly debatable. And even the easy examples have often been politically difficult to resolve correctly: when it comes to agricultural subsidies, for example, proponents can argue that the nation as a whole is better off when the food supply is less dependent on "unreliable foreign sources," or that market failures require the national government to prevent "ruinous competition" among farmers. More commonly, any time a problem is regarded as really serious, it will be said that the failure of the state governments to solve the problem demonstrates the need for national action.

The frustrating result is that everybody can genuflect to federalism as a matter of general principle without thereby committing himself to much of anything as a practical matter. Some sort of rationale is always available when federal jurisdiction would serve one's personal, political, or ideological interest, and the same goes for arguments in favor of protecting state autonomy. Still, having said all that, I believe that the question of physician-assisted suicide is a pretty easy case.

No Grounds for Federal Interference

People can and do have different preferences about this issue, which are presumably based on their differing assessments of the risks and benefits to themselves and those they care about. Convinced though I am that the risks of allowing physician-assisted suicide outweigh the benefits, it would be silly to pretend that no benefits exist, and presumptuous to suppose that I might not be wrong. Nor is it easy to see why Oregon and other state governments should be considered less capable than the federal government of settling on appropriate policies in the light of new experience and information, including new developments in medicine and the medical profession.

When the Supreme Court wisely declined to create a constitutional right to assisted suicide, Justice Sandra Day O'Connor pointed out that in this area there was no obvious need for judicial intrusion:

> Every one of us at some point may be affected by our own or a family member's terminal illness. There is no reason to think the democratic process will not strike the proper balance between the interests of terminally ill, mentally competent individuals who would seek to end their suffering and the state's interests in protecting those who might seek to end life mistakenly or under pressure.

For the very same reason, there is no obvious need for the federal government to interfere with Oregon's experiment.

That is hardly to say there will be no bad effects from Oregon's new policy. To the contrary, vulnerable people will likely be pressured to end their lives prematurely; others will become more distrustful of doctors, and perhaps less willing to submit to treatment. Some physicians will take another big step away from their proper role as healers and comforters, and will become increasingly corrupted by the very different role of deciding whose lives are worth living. Euthanasia of nonconsenting victims is also entirely possible.

As bad as these effects may be, however, they will be visited almost entirely on Oregonians, and will not threaten the citizens of other states. Nor will Oregon's policy necessarily spread to other states. Every state in the union remains free to outlaw physician-assisted suicide and to enforce its laws as vigorously as it sees fit. Oregon's practice can spread only if the people of other states conclude that the experiment has turned out to be a success.

> "The possibility of persuasion by example does not justify federal interference with Oregon's decision."

Besides, even a skeptic like me has to admit the very real possibility that Oregon's approach is not the worst imaginable. If, for example, the political and economic pressures for health-care rationing become significantly more intense, we may see a much more widespread denial of medical care to very feeble patients, including the withholding of food and water. If the alternative to a miserable death by dehydration turns out to be physician-assisted suicide or euthanasia, Oregon's approach may begin to look a lot less bad than it does today.

Federal Restraint Necessary

In any event, the possibility of persuasion by example does not justify federal interference with Oregon's decision. Rather, it provides a reason for federal restraint. As we have seen, Congress itself has exercised just such restraint, for it has not outlawed physician-assisted suicide or expressly forbidden the use of federally controlled drugs in carrying out this practice.

Perhaps the strongest argument for federal preemption of Oregon's policy is that it may lead to murder—and no state, certainly, should be free to ignore the most fundamental norms of civilized society. But this sounds more persuasive than it really is. For one thing, the Attorney General's decision forbids only the use of certain drugs, thus leaving doctors free to use other suicide techniques, as Jack Kevorkian did before he finally managed to get himself imprisoned. For another, every state (indeed, every government) does less than it could do to prevent murder, largely because preventative measures are subject to the law of diminishing returns. Oregon has not actually condoned murder, and its adoption of a new policy that may increase the number of murders is analytically similar to a decision to cut back on police services in order to free up funds for other pressing uses. One or the other may be a bad idea, but neither one amounts to a descent into barbarism.

In short, the Attorney General was not compelled to accept, and should have resisted, what is at best a strained interpretation of the law. Precisely because the courts are generally deferential to the executive's interpretation of regulatory statutes, and precisely because the courts have been highly reluctant to find that Congress has exceeded the limits of its authority to regulate interstate commerce, the Attorney General has a special responsibility to respect the principles of federalism in doubtful cases.

By making it more difficult for Oregon doctors to help their patients kill themselves, Attorney General Ashcroft's decision will probably have some salutary short-term effects. It will do so, unfortunately, only at the price of compromising a political principle with greater and historically demonstrated benefits to us all.

The Executive Branch's Attempt to Ban Assisted Suicide Threatens Democracy

by J. Paul Oetken

About the author: *J. Paul Oetken served as associate counsel to President Bill Clinton and as an attorney-advisor in the Department of Justice Office of Legal Counsel.*

Oregon Federal District Judge Robert E. Jones reaffirmed the validity of Oregon's assisted suicide law. He did so by formally overturning Attorney General John Ashcroft's prior decision that the Oregon law conflicted with federal drug laws.

Such a rejection of an executive branch decision by a judge is fairly unusual. Yet it is not nearly as remarkable as the overreaching exercise of power represented by Ashcroft's earlier decision.

While many have couched this dispute in terms of federalism, it is really about democracy—as Judge Jones correctly recognized.

Ashcroft's Ban

In November [2001], Ashcroft effectively adopted a federal ban on physician-assisted suicide, by ruling that the federal drug law prohibits that practice. Legally, the decision is an interpretation of the Controlled Substances Act, which is intended to prevent drug trafficking.

The Act says that regulated drugs may be prescribed by a physician only "in the course of professional practice." This phrase, in turn, has been interpreted by courts and agencies to mean that drugs may be prescribed only with a "legitimate medical purpose."

Dispensing drugs outside the course of professional practice—without a "legitimate medical purpose"—subjects a physician to revocation of her DEA [Drug Enforcement Administration] license and a possible felony conviction as well. The obvious target of the Act is a physician's knowing prescription of a regulated drug to a drug dealer or drug addict who lacks a medical reason for using the drug, and is motivated instead by profit or addiction.

Nevertheless, Ashcroft found in the Act's general language a prohibition of assisted suicide, even where a state has legalized and carefully regulated the practice. His interpretation is questionable in light of the Act's purposes, which have nothing to do with assisted suicide.

It is also particularly questionable in light of the fact that federal law has traditionally left the regulation of medical practice to the states. Indeed, the drug law specifies that it is not intended to override state law unless there is a direct conflict between the two.

The state of Oregon has legalized the practice of assisted suicide in narrow circumstances: where a terminally ill, mentally competent adult has been examined and interviewed by two independent physicians. Thus, the state has determined that assisting in a suicide, in strictly defined circumstances, is part of the "course of professional practice," and can be legitimate as a medical practice.

Disagreeing that the practice can ever be legitimate, Ashcroft read the federal drug law as overriding the law passed by Oregon's voters. Now, however, Judge Jones has overruled him, preventing enforcement of Ashcroft's interpretation (at least until Ashcroft's appeals, as is expected).

Democracy and Political Accountability

Judge Jones, who was appointed by the senior President [George] Bush, rejected Ashcroft's reading of the federal drug law as unfounded.

Specifically, he concluded that there is nothing in the federal law that "demonstrates or even suggests that Congress intended to delegate to the Attorney General or the DEA the authority to decide, as a matter of national policy, a question of such magnitude as whether physician-assisted suicide constitutes a legitimate medical purpose or practice." Instead, Judge Jones reasoned, that decision—as is traditional with medical practice issues—has been left to the individual states.

The dispute between the U.S. Attorney General and the Oregon Attorney General has been widely viewed as a dispute about federalism—about the power of a state versus the federal government. But in fact, it is not federalism that is at the heart of this debate.

> *"While many have couched this dispute [over physician-assisted suicide] in terms of federalism, it is really about democracy."*

It is true that Ashcroft's November decision reflects a robust view of federal power—which is ironic, given his usual solicitousness for states' rights, and no doubt explained by a commitment to pro-life political values. But as Judge Jones recognized, what the case is really about is democracy and political accountability—about the power of our elected Congress versus that of unelected executive branch officials.

It is Congress that has the power to make law, and Congress simply had not authorized the reading of the drug law that was adopted by Ashcroft. Rather, Ashcroft distorted beyond recognition a law designed to target illegal drug trafficking, attempting to transform it into an anti-physician-assisted suicide law.

> *"Debate over assisted suicide belongs in legislatures, state or federal. It should not be silenced by executive fiat."*

But as Judge Jones observed, "the fact that opposition to assisted suicide may be justified, morally, ethically, religiously or otherwise, does not permit a federal statute to be manipulated from its true meaning to satisfy even a worthy goal." Debate over assisted suicide belongs in legislatures, state or federal. It should not be silenced by executive fiat.

Indeed, opponents of assisted suicide, led by many members of the pro-life community, have been lobbying Congress for three years to enact a law that would prohibit assisted suicide. So far, they have been unable to rally the necessary political support for their bill.

Ashcroft attempted to hand them the win they have not been able to achieve. He tried to short-circuit the process of changing the law, along with the country's opportunity to debate and resolve the issue democratically, by interpreting an unrelated law purportedly to resolve the issue. But this fight should stay where it belongs, in the legislatures.

Patients in Pain Would Be Harmed

Another consequence of Ashcroft's misuse of the federal drug law would have been to create a more heavy-handed enforcement tool than the democratic process would have produced—and as a result, potentially to put many patients, both terminal and non-terminal, in jeopardy.

Recent bills introduced in Congress have included the caveat that physicians' efforts at pain management, even palliative care measures that hasten death, would not be subject to criminal prosecution or license revocation. Ashcroft's novel reading of the law had no such safe harbor.

As a result, the law as interpreted by Ashcroft would not only have prevented physicians in Oregon from assisting in suicides, but could potentially have had a chilling effect on physicians nationwide who seek to relieve their patients' pain. Since untreated pain itself has been shown, in some instances, to impede recovery, Ashcroft's decision would not only have caused patients needless suffering, but actually could have harmed their ability to get well.

Laws passed by Congress are always subject to interpretation. But Ashcroft's decision regarding assisted suicide, albeit phrased in terms of legality, lacked support in the law written by Congress and amounted to lawmaking by the Justice Department.

The federal district court has correctly resolved this dispute by assigning the thorny problem of whether to allow, and how to limit, physician-assisted suicide to its proper forum: the "laboratories" of the states. Their varied approaches to the issue may, over time, aid in forming a national consensus, making it possible for Congress to resolve it through national legislation.

States Do Not Have the Authority to Allow the Use of Federally Controlled Substances for Physician-Assisted Suicide

by the International Task Force on Euthanasia and Assisted Suicide

About the author: *The International Task Force on Euthanasia and Assisted Suicide (ITF) is an anti-assisted-suicide organization that addresses issues of euthanasia, assisted suicide, advance directives, assisted-suicide proposals, "right-to-die" cases, euthanasia practices in the Netherlands, disability rights, and pain control.*

Editor's Note: The following viewpoint was excerpted from the International Task Force on Euthanasia and Assisted Suicide's amicus curiae brief in State of Oregon v. John Ashcroft *(2002).*

Although this case [*State of Oregon v. John Ashcroft*] will be decided within the context of the debate over assisted suicide, it is not a case about whether the State of Oregon may permit the practice of assisted suicide within its borders. It is about whether a state can prevent the federal government from interpreting its own regulations. . . .

The District Court erred in concluding that the Controlled Substances Act, ("CSA"), does not "grant defendants the authority under the CSA to determine that prescribing controlled substances for purposes of physician-assisted suicide in compliance with Oregon law is not a 'legitimate medical purpose.'. . .

Congress granted authority to the Attorney General to carry out the CSA and the Drug Enforcement Administration (DEA) regulations that implement the CSA. . . .

International Task Force on Euthanasia and Assisted Suicide, brief of *Amicus Curiae, Oregon v. John Ashcroft*, Civil No. 01-1647-JO, 2002.

Attorney General [John] Ashcroft's Directive ("Ashcroft Directive") does not address the matter of whether assisted suicide may be considered a "legitimate medical *practice*" under Oregon law. Instead, it deals solely with whether using a federal registration to prescribe federally controlled substances to cause drug-induced death serves a "legitimate medical *purpose*" under the DEA regulations.

> *"Nothing in the Ashcroft Directive prevents Oregon physicians from engaging in assisted suicide under the Oregon Death with Dignity Act."*

The Court incorrectly assumes that the Ashcroft Directive usurps the rights of the State of Oregon to enact and carry out its own laws. Further, the Court mistakenly concluded that the Ashcroft Directive interferes with the practice of medicine.

Plaintiff-Intervenors also advanced this mistaken notion when they claimed that it was only because of the District Court's temporary injunction that Intervenors, a physician and a pharmacist, "can practice lawful medicine in Oregon." That claim lacks any shred of truth.

First, the Ashcroft Directive was prospective and, therefore, any prior use of federally controlled substances for assisted suicide would not subject a physician to investigation and possible revocation of a federal registration to prescribe or dispense federally controlled substances.

Second, if the Ashcroft Directive is implemented, and if a physician chooses to prescribe federally controlled substances for assisted suicide and if, after administrative proceedings, the physician's registration were revoked or suspended, that physician would still be able to lawfully practice medicine in Oregon.

Nothing in the Ashcroft Directive prevents the State of Oregon from enforcing its own statutes. Nothing in the Ashcroft Directive prevents the State of Oregon from controlling the process of licensing physicians to practice medicine. Nothing in the Ashcroft Directive prevents Oregon physicians from engaging in assisted suicide under the Oregon Death with Dignity Act, . . . ("ODWDA"). The Ashcroft Directive only precludes the use of a federal registration to prescribe controlled substances for the purpose of causing drug-induced deaths.

The Ashcroft Directive Does Not Control the Practice of Medicine

States regulate the practice of medicine. States issue medical licenses. Only states may revoke physicians' licenses to practice medicine.

The Attorney General, under the authority granted to him under the CSA, controls the dispensing of federally controlled substances. It is the Attorney General who registers physicians to prescribe federally controlled substances and it is the Attorney General who may suspend or revoke such registrations, in accordance with administrative procedures.

Physicians in Oregon are not required to have a federal registration to practice medicine. Without a federal registration, physicians may diagnose and treat patients. They may perform surgery. They may prescribe any of thousands of medications that are not federally controlled substances.

If the Ashcroft Directive is implemented, the conduct of a physician who prescribes federally controlled substances to assist suicide "*may* render his registration . . . inconsistent with the public interest and therefore subject to *possible* suspension or revocation. . . . Prescribing or providing medications for assisted suicide that are not controlled substances would not subject a practitioner's registration to any risk of suspension or revocation.

The Federal Government Has Authority over All Federally Controlled Substances

Since 1914, the federal government has had the authority to regulate controlled substances. The Controlled Substances Act (CSA) as enacted in 1970 and amended in 1984, provides a uniform national standard for the control of potentially dangerous drugs. The CSA makes it unlawful for any person, including physicians and pharmacists, to dispense or distribute any federally controlled substance "except as authorized.". . . One such exception permits physicians and pharmacists to distribute controlled substances if they obtain a registration from the Attorney General.

The right to distribute controlled substances upon registration is an *exception* to the total ban on distributing controlled substances. Under the CSA, Congress delegated authority to the Attorney General to register applicants "unless he determines that the issuance of such registration is inconsistent with the public interest." Among the factors that the Attorney General is to consider in determining the public interest are "such facts as may be relevant to and consistent with the public health and safety." Furthermore, the Attorney General is authorized to suspend or revoke a registration if he finds that the registrant "has committed such acts as would render his registration . . . inconsistent with the public interest. . . ."

Drug Safety and Public Health

When it passed the CSA, Congress found, "Many of the drugs included within this title have a useful and legitimate medical purpose and are necessary to maintain the health and general welfare of the American people." Thus, the CSA grants exemptions to the overall prohibition on dispensing controlled substances so that those substances may be dispensed for the useful and legitimate medical purposes that are necessary to maintain the health and general welfare of the American people.

Suicide, including suicide by intentional overdose of federally controlled substances, has never been considered an act that maintains the "health and general welfare" of the American people.

Plaintiffs would have this Court believe that there is an implied exception to the

CSA so that, for terminally ill patients, suicide—assisted by a physician—must be permitted. They provide no basis for claiming this exception.

Nowhere is there any evidence that "Congress intended protection only for persons suffering from curable diseases." In [*United States v.*] *Rutherford*, the U.S. Supreme Court noted that "the concept of safety . . . is not without meaning for terminal patients." In its discussion of the Food and Drug Administration's ("FDA") approval of drugs for use by the public, the Court declared, "For the terminally ill, *as for anyone else*, a drug is unsafe if its potential for inflicting death or physical injury is not offset by the possibility of therapeutic benefit."

> *"The Ashcroft Directive only precludes the use of a federal registration to prescribe controlled substances for the purpose of causing drug-induced deaths."*

If the FDA will not approve a drug for use if its *potential* for inducing death is not offset by the possibility of therapeutic benefit, it is preposterous to think the Attorney General should be compelled to authorize prescribing controlled substances for the specific *purpose* of inducing death.

Just as legislative history and consistent administrative interpretation of the Federal Food, Drug, and Cosmetic Act . . . ("FDCA") gave no implicit exception to the terms "safe" and "effective" for drugs used by the terminally ill, the CSA does not imply any exception to the meaning of "public health and safety" for those who are terminally ill.

The concept of "safety" applies equally to all patients under the FDCA, including terminally ill patients. So, also, the meaning of "public health and safety" is equally applicable to all patients—young and old, rich and poor, temporarily ill and terminally ill—under the CSA.

Moreover, if prescribing federally controlled substances for the purpose of causing drug-induced death for terminally ill patients were to be considered a legitimate medical purpose, the Attorney General would be compelled to consider such prescribing a legitimate medical purpose for any and all other patients if a state so decides.

Drug-Induced Death as a Threat to Public Health

Plaintiffs have asserted that, since the CSA does not explicitly state that assisted suicide is not a legitimate medical practice, Congress did not intend to prevent a practitioner from enabling a patient to take his or her life using federally controlled substances.

On the contrary, while, in 1984, no one envisioned that any medical professional would seriously claim that enabling drug-induced death was a "legitimate medical practice," there was great concern about the serious threat that drug-induced deaths posed to public health and safety.

When Congress amended the CSA in 1984, it did so to strengthen the ability of the Attorney General to deny, suspend or revoke the registration of practitioners who dispense federally controlled substances in a way that threatens public health and safety and to give him the authority to act in cases where a state was either unable or unwilling to intervene.

At that time, supporters of amending the Act based the need to expand the Attorney General's authority on the fact that "the most serious threat to public health and safety prompting the legal change was the frequency with which prescription drugs were involved in 'drug-induced deaths.'"

Indeed, common sense dictates that the basis for control of certain drugs is the prevention of threats to health and life. Throughout this nation's history, intentionally participating in causing or enabling drug-induced death has never been considered a "legitimate medical practice." Furthermore, suicide has never been viewed as a "treatment or therapy" for any medical condition. . . .

The State of Oregon Is Attempting to Exempt Itself from Provisions of the CSA

Maintaining a uniform national standard pertaining to federally controlled substances is vital to public health and safety. However, the State of Oregon has boldly tried to carve out a new and unprecedented exception for itself. In effect, Oregon is brazenly attempting to amend the CSA so that states have the authority that has traditionally belonged to the federal government.

This creates an untenable situation since it *bestows a right on Oregon* to declare practitioners immune from actions taken in violation of *federal regulations*. Under the Oregon scheme, the state, not the federal government, decides how a federal registration may be used and whether prescribing federally controlled substances is done for a legitimate federal purpose under federal law.

Although the State of Oregon has determined that practitioners may enable patients to end their lives with medications, they may not dictate that federally controlled substances be used to do so.

Oregon's Death with Dignity Act

The District Court declared that the Ashcroft directive "essentially nullified the Oregon Act." Likewise, the State of Oregon claimed, "If the DEA interpretation of the CSA were correct, it would effectively result in the preemption of portions of the Act." And Plaintiff-Intervenors argued, "The practices that are authorized by Oregon law *require* the use of controlled substances."

The Ashcroft Directive does not nullify the ODWDA. It does not result in preempting portions of the Act. And there is nothing in the Oregon law that requires the use of controlled substances.

The ODWDA permits physicians to "prescribe, but not administer, medication to enable a qualified patient to end his or her own life." Passage of the ODWDA approved the *act* of physician assisted suicide. However, the ODWDA does not specify the *means* by which the act is to be accomplished. Nothing in the

ODWDA limits "medication" to a federally controlled substance.

The Ashcroft Directive does not prevent physicians from engaging in the *act* of physician assisted suicide under the ODWDA. They may still write prescriptions for medication for the purpose of enabling patients to commit suicide. The Ashcroft Directive only addresses the *means*, by stating that practitioners may not use their federal registrations to prescribe federally controlled substances for the purpose of causing drug-induced deaths.

The Ashcroft Directive Does Not Apply to All Prescription Drugs

Although all federally controlled substances are prescription drugs, not all prescription medications are federally controlled substances. A federal registration is only required to dispense prescription medications that are federally controlled substances. The Ashcroft Directive applies only to those prescription drugs for which a federally issued license is necessary and only to those drugs when they are prescribed for the purpose of enabling a patient to commit suicide.

Self-Administration Under the ODWDA Is Broadly Interpreted

As previously noted, the ODWDA gives physicians the power to prescribe medication for the purpose of enabling a patient *to end his or her life*. It does not permit a physician or any other person to end a patient's life by lethal injection, mercy killing or active euthanasia.

It does require self-administration. However, self-administration does not necessitate great involvement on the part of the patient. Although physicians and others may not "administer" the lethal medication, they are precluded only from taking the final act. It is only the last act—the act that results in death—that must be taken by the patient under the ODWDA.

> *"Intentionally . . . causing or enabling drug-induced death has never been considered as a 'legitimate medical practice.'"*

There is a common misperception that all patients who have died under the ODWDA have done so after independently taking several pills after which they "slip peacefully away." In fact, the reality is far different. For example, the *Washington Post* described a woman's death in which Plaintiff Peter Rasmussen, M.D. participated. The story illustrates the quantity of pills, the degree of assistance that may be given to a patient, and the length of time it can take for a person to die after taking federally controlled substances by mouth. . . .

ODWDA Medication Options

The ODWDA refers to a prescription for "medication" but does not define the term. However, accepted definitions of "medication" include: "medicinal substance, a drug, and treatment with remedies." "Remedy," which falls within the meaning of "medication" is defined as "anything that relieves or cures a disease."

Shortly after passage of the ODWDA in 1994, Peter A. Goodwin, M.D. of the Oregon Health Sciences University who was one of the authors of the ODWDA appeared on ABC's *Nightline* to discuss the ODWDA. He explained that no route of administration of lethal medication would be excluded under the ODWDA "as long as the patient had full responsibility."

Thus, a prescription of "medication" as permitted under the ODWDA could encompass routes other than oral and [federally regulated] substances other than barbiturates. . . .

The Ashcroft Directive Does Not Contravene a Patient's Right to Palliative Care

Plaintiffs would have this Court believe that, unless a doctor has the right to prescribe federally controlled substances to end a patient's life, he or she cannot prescribe those substances to end a patient's pain.

The Ashcroft Directive Enhances the Right to Palliative Care

Plaintiffs claim that the Ashcroft Directive "contravenes the right to palliative care" and that it would cause a "chilling effect on doctors who prescribe medicine for palliative care." Recently, Kathryn Tucker, counsel for Plaintiff-Intervenors, compounded and exaggerated this misrepresentation when she stated that "the Ashcroft Directive would impair all patients *nationwide* from getting adequate pain medication."

This tired and unsuccessful assertion was also made by assisted suicide proponents in the *Vacco v. Quill* and [*State of Washington v.*] *Glucksberg* cases when they contended that there was no significant difference between prescribing drugs for pain control which *might* result in death and prescribing drugs *intended* to result in death.

The U.S. Supreme Court decisively rejected that contention. In some cases "painkilling drugs may hasten a patient's death, but the physician's purpose and intent is, or may be, only to ease his patient's pain. . . . The law has long used actors' intent or purpose to distinguish between two acts that may have the same result. . . . [T]he law distinguishes actions taken 'because of a given end [to induce death] from actions taken 'in spite of' their unintended but foreseen consequences [the possibility that pain control may increase the risk of death]."

"It is preposterous to think the Attorney General should be compelled to authorize prescribing controlled substances for the specific purpose of inducing death."

Far from creating legal barriers to the administration of federally controlled substances for pain relief, the Ashcroft Directive provides the strongest assurances ever given to doctors who prescribe controlled substances for the purpose of ending their patients' pain. It explicitly states that the "use of controlled substances to manage pain [is] promoted" and sets out a procedure whereby there will not be any increased monitoring or investigation of physicians' prescribing patterns of controlled substances used for pain relief.

In addition, on the same day he issued his directive, Attorney General Ashcroft sent a letter to physicians' groups stating that doctors "will have no reason to fear that prescription of controlled substances to control pain will lead to increased scrutiny by the DEA, even when high doses of painkilling drugs are necessary and even when dosages needed to control pain may increase the risk of death." He explained that, under the directive, physicians "should feel confident that they may prescribe federally controlled drugs to the full extent desirable to relieve pain without any fear that their prescriptions will be subject to greater questioning, investigation or any form of monitoring as a result of today's action."

> *"Oregon is ... attempting to amend the [Controlled Substances Act] so that states have the authority that has traditionally belonged to the federal government."*

Strikingly, when states pass laws that ban assisted suicide and those laws contain explicit assurances—such as that in the Ashcroft letter—that physicians may prescribe pain control that might unintentionally increase the risk of death, the per capita use of opioids for pain control rises dramatically. For example, in Louisiana, morphine consumption rose by 80 percent in the year its assisted suicide ban passed and had nearly tripled two years later. Likewise, according to official DEA figures, in the year before Rhode Island's ban on assisted suicide passed, it was 46th among the states in per capita use of morphine. However, use doubled in the year following the law's enactment, placing the state 19th in use of morphine.

The ODWDA Does Not Ensure That Patients Will Receive Adequate Pain Relief

After the ODWDA went into effect, a survey found that the number of Oregon patients who were reported as dying in moderate to severe pain increased. The ODWDA Act went into effect in late 1997. Prior to its implementation, 33 percent of family members reported that their loved ones died in moderate to severe pain. However, in 1998 which was the first full year that the ODWDA was in effect, that rate was 54 percent.

Barriers to Adequate Pain Control Are Unrelated to the Right to Prescribe Federally Controlled Substances

"Untreated and undertreated pain is nothing short of a national scandal" [according to Eric M. Chevlan and Wesley J. Smith]. However, barriers to pain control stem from factors unrelated to whether a physician has the right to prescribe for the purpose of enabling a patient to commit suicide. . . .

The Ashcroft Directive Deserves Deference

Nothing in federal law gives a state the authority to adopt standards that prevent the federal government from interpreting its own regulations.

The Ashcroft Directive is an agency interpretation, a textual regulation implementing the CSA, which the Attorney General is charged by Congress to administer.

When an agency interprets its own regulation, notice and comment is not required. "The APA [Administrative Procedures Act] requires that rules promulgated by administrative agencies undergo certain procedures *unless those rules are 'interpretive rules*, general statements of policy, or rules of agency organization, procedure, or practice.'" This is so even if there is a prior interpretation to the contrary. An agency is "not estopped from changing legal interpretation that she believes to be erroneous."

In this instance, Attorney General Janet Reno's Directive ("Reno Directive"), issued on June 5, 1998, was a prior interpretation of a regulation. Like Ashcroft's interpretation, Reno's interpretation did not undergo notice and comment. It is of interest that, unlike Ashcroft's interpretation, the interpretation expressed in the Reno Directive was not published in the Federal Register. Furthermore, the Reno Directive did not contain any history of the CSA or a textual analysis as the basis for the interpretation by which Reno exempted an entire state from long held national standards regarding controlled substances.

> *"The State of Oregon . . . may not dictate that federally controlled substances be used [by doctors to end a patient's life]."*

As an interpretation of a regulation, Ashcroft's Directive deserves deference if he is construing the provisions in a reasonable way. An "agency's interpretation [of its own regulations] must be given controlling weight unless it is plainly erroneous or inconsistent with the regulation. . . . But the ultimate criterion is the administrative interpretation, which becomes of controlling weight unless it is plainly erroneous or inconsistent with the regulation."

Certainly, the interpretation expressed in the Ashcroft Directive—that prescribing federally controlled substances to cause drug-induced death is inconsistent with public health and welfare—is not erroneous or inconsistent with the regulation.

Attorney General Ashcroft, in his directive, did not create a new regulation. As discussed above, he merely construed the textual phrases contained in the regulation. The fact that Attorney General Reno construed the phrase differently did not prevent Attorney General Ashcroft from making a different interpretation of that regulation, nor did it require Attorney General Ashcroft to do so only after notice and comment. Deference should be given to the Ashcroft Directive.

The Ashcroft Directive Is Appropriate

As this brief has demonstrated, the Ashcroft Directive is an appropriate interpretation of a regulation. By barring the use of a federal registration for the purpose of causing drug-induced death, it maintains a necessary national standard for dispensing federally controlled drugs. At the same time, it does not nullify a law enacted by the State of Oregon.

The District Court radically and erroneously bestowed the right on the State of Oregon to prevent the federal government from interpreting its own regulations. The District Court's judgment should be reversed and the Permanent Injunction should be lifted.

Allowing States to Violate Federal Laws by Legalizing Assisted Suicide Subverts Medical Ethics

by Wesley J. Smith

About the author: *Wesley J. Smith is an attorney, writer, and pro-life advocate. He is a consultant for the International Task Force on Euthanasia and Assisted Suicide and the author of* Culture of Death: The Assault on Medical Ethics in America.

Last month [April 2002], to the cheers of editorial writers throughout the country, a federal judge enjoined Attorney General John Ashcroft from revoking the federal licenses to prescribe controlled substances of Oregon doctors who legally assist in a patient's suicide. The Oregon lawsuit was filed last year [2001] when Ashcroft issued a directive in the Federal Register, proclaiming that assisted suicide was not a "legitimate medical purpose" under the Controlled Substances Act (CSA). But United States District Court Judge Robert E. Jones ruled that once Oregon determined that assisted suicide was a legitimate medical act, the federal government was bound to accede to the state's determination even when enforcing federal law.

The Pretty Case

[In May 2002], the European Court of Human Rights issued a ruling in another assisted-suicide case, the facts of which seem to have great bearing on whether assisted suicide is or is not a medical act. The case involved a terminally ill woman disabled by Lou Gehrig's disease (known as motor-neuron disease in Europe) named Diane Pretty. Mrs. Pretty wants to commit suicide. But her disease has progressed to the point where she cannot do the deed on her own. So last year, she filed suit in Britain seeking a court order guaranteeing that her husband would suffer no legal penalty for helping her kill herself, even though Britain's law prohibits assisted suicide.

Pretty's case is acutely relevant to Ashcroft's attempt to declare assisted suicide non-medical under the CSA. Consider the relief Mrs. Pretty requested from the British and EU [European Union] courts: She wanted her husband Brian to help kill her legally. Not her doctor; her husband who, relevantly, is not a physician and has no medical training other than that he may have picked up as a caregiver for his wife.

"Killing isn't medicine."

Pretty's lawsuit has been treated with great respect in the British and European courts. The trial court first gave its permission to bring the case and then spent a great deal of time hearing evidence and pondering the law before ultimately rejecting the claim. The House of Lords, the British equivalent of the Supreme Court, took the appeal and held a hearing that treated her arguments with utmost solemnity and seriousness. Then, when the Lords ruled against Mrs. Pretty, the EU Court agreed quickly to take up the matter to see if Britain's anti-assisted-suicide law violated the European Rights Convention.

Now imagine what would have happened if this case had not been about assisted suicide but about Mrs. Pretty wanting her husband to be allowed to perform surgery on her, such as the minor procedure required to insert her feeding tube into her abdomen. Or, what if she had brought the case requesting that her husband be allowed to decide the proper medication for her to take to alleviate the symptoms of her disease. She would have been laughed out of court! Why? Because those are actions that are clearly medical: Only licensed medical professionals can perform surgery or prescribe medications. Thus, the case would be deemed utterly frivolous and a waste of the court's time.

Notice also that Mrs. Pretty did not sue to prevent her husband from being prosecuted for practicing medicine without a license if he assisted her suicide. The very idea of such a suit is so ludicrous that it would have never occurred to her attorneys. Assisting a suicide, after all, isn't medicine.

Further proof of this is found in the advocacy of the euthanasia movement, which has established a cottage industry in suicide devices. For example, Derek Humphry, cofounder of the Hemlock Society, has established NuTech, which is devoted to promoting suicide-facilitation devices. As reported breathlessly in the *Economist* December 6, 2001, among these contraptions is the "DeBreather," a face-mask apparatus that recycles a suicidal person's own carbon dioxide toward the end of cutting off all oxygen.

How-to-commit-suicide videos Humphry promotes (and stars in), also extol the use helium and a plastic bag to bring life to an end.

Now ask yourself this question: Should Medicare pay for the expense of obtaining and using a DeBreather if the patient is over 65? Or should your local

HMO provide the device to patients as if it were durable medical equipment akin to an oxygen tank or a kidney-dialysis machine? Indeed, should helium be considered a palliative medical agent? The entire concept is preposterous, ridiculous. Why? Simply stated, killing isn't medicine.

A few years ago, Berkeley Assemblywoman Dion Aroner authored legislation to legalize physician-assisted suicide in California. At a public forum I confronted her and made the points I have just written above. Aroner nodded her head and acknowledged candidly that she would have preferred to keep doctors out of it. But, she said, she believed it necessary to bring assisted suicide under a medical umbrella for political reasons. Otherwise, her bill would have no chance of passage.

Assisted-suicide activists intentionally redefine, distort, and subvert medicine, medical ethics, and the morality of health-care public policy in pursuit of their dream of obtaining the right to "choose the time and manner" of their own deaths. But at least they have an excuse: They are death fundamentalists driven by a cancerous ideology that is as deeply felt as the most sincere expression of religious faith. But when a federal judge thwarts the United States attorney general from recognizing the obvious truth that intentional killing is not medical by forcing him to accept Oregon's twisted redefinition, not only has medicine been subverted but also has language and the law.

Assisted-Suicide Decisions Made by the States Threaten Human Life Protections

by the National Right to Life Committee and Oregon Right to Life

About the authors: *The National Right to Life Committee (NRLC) is an anti-assisted-suicide organization that seeks to protect all human life from conception to natural death. Oregon Right to Life (ORTL) is the Oregon affiliate of NRLC.*

Editors's Note: The following viewpoint was excerpted from an amicus curiae brief in State of Oregon v. John Ashcroft.

At the hearing on the motion for a Temporary Restraining Order, the Court asked in essence what governmental interest there is in the lives of persons who are terminally ill. This brief responds to that query with two interests: (1) government has an unqualified interest in protecting life and (2) government has an interest in equally protecting persons from self harm.

As to the first interest, precedents establish that government has an interest in protecting life that does not depend in any way on the quality of the life. For example, it is no defense to a homicide charge that the person killed had a low quality of life or short life expectancy.

As to the second interest, Oregon extends several protections against self harm to persons who are not terminally ill that are withdrawn from terminally ill persons by [Oregon's] "Death With Dignity Act [which permits physician-assisted suicide]." Chief Judge Michael R. Hogan for this Court found that the Act consequently violated the Equal Protection Clause. Both federal and state governments have an interest, indeed a duty, to protect persons equally. . . .

National Right to Life Committee and Oregon Right to Life, brief of *Amicus Curiae, State of Oregon v. John Ashcroft*, Civil No. 01-1647-JO, 2002.

Government Has an Unqualified Interest in Protecting Life

The United States has effectively asserted an unqualified federal governmental interest in protecting human life by construing the federal Controlled Substances Act ("CSA"), and its implementing regulations to forbid prescribing or dispensing controlled substances for the purpose of assisting suicide whether or not state law sanctions this practice for some persons. In contrast, Oregon has chosen not to serve this interest when the person seeking assisted suicide has a "terminal condition" and has followed certain procedures in accord with the Oregon Death With Dignity Act, (the "Oregon Act").

At the heart of the Plaintiffs' plea for relief is the assumption that a state's determination that physician-assisted suicide is a "legitimate medical practice" trumps any federal determination that it is not. Implicit in their claim is the notion that any federal governmental interest in protecting human life must yield to an individual's choice to commit suicide, at least when coupled with a state's determination to permit others to assist in implementing such a decision under certain circumstances.

To the contrary, the United States maintains an unqualified and compelling governmental interest in protecting human life that fully supports its construction of the CSA to preclude the use of federally controlled substances for assisting in suicide. In serving this most compelling interest through federal law, as it has through its interpretation of the CSA, the federal government is under no obligation whatever to acquiesce to any state's decision to refuse to do so through its own law. . . .

No Right to Assisted Suicide

The U.S. Supreme Court has firmly established that government is nowhere required to carve out any exception based on any "quality of life" to the uniform application of its laws intended to protect human lives. There is no such thing as a right to hasten one's own death. There is no right to suicide or to assisted suicide under any circumstance. Assuming the existence of a right to refuse medical treatment, any exercise of such a right is subject to searching governmental scrutiny and procedural safeguards. There is no special claim that any person might legitimately make based on a quality of life, such as the existence of a disability or terminal condition, that the law of homicide should not uniformly apply.

Assisted Suicide

In holding that there is no right to a hastened death by suicide or assisted suicide, the U.S. Supreme Court observed that an absolute prohibition on assisted suicide is also supported by a number of compelling interests. . . .

The same interest applies here to the federal government's interpretation of the CSA to uniformly apply to any use of a controlled substance for a killing purpose. Rather than legalizing physician-assisted suicide for the "terminally ill," Oregon might have legalized homicide by active euthanasia through lethal injection under some circumstances. It might have legalized assisted suicide for persons over a certain age or with certain disabilities. In service to an unqualified interest in protecting human life, the federal government is under no more obligation to bend its policy with regard to use of controlled substances to accommodate the Oregon Act than it would be to any other exception that Oregon might choose to carve out of its homicide code.

> *"The United States maintains an unqualified and compelling governmental interest in protecting human life."*

The Supreme Court rejected the claim that the government only has a "real interest in preserving the lives of those who can still contribute to society and have the potential to enjoy life." As did the State of Washington in *Glucksberg*, the federal government here has legitimately "rejected this sliding-scale approach and, [through its construction of the CSA], insists that all persons' lives, from beginning to end, regardless of physical or mental condition, are under the full protection of the law."

More specifically, the federal government is under no obligation to provide any exception to the CSA to permit assisted suicide for the "terminally ill," as Oregon has done. The U.S. Supreme Court has held that a claim of "terminal illness" creates no exception to otherwise uniformly applicable federal drug legislation. . . . Furthermore, although the concept of a "terminal condition" might be useful for some purposes, it may properly be regarded as far too vague, ambiguous, and open to abuse to form an exception to the use of direct means, such as use of controlled substances, for a killing purpose.

The government's construction of the CSA to apply uniformly to the use of controlled substances for a killing purpose is further supported by its interest "in protecting the vulnerable—including the poor, the elderly, and disabled persons—from abuse, neglect, and mistakes." As the Supreme Court declared (substituting federal for state government):

> [The government's] interest here goes beyond protecting the vulnerable from coercion; it extends to protecting disabled and terminally ill people from prejudice, negative and inaccurate stereotypes, and "societal indifference." The [federal government's] assisted suicide ban reflects and reinforces its policy that the lives of terminally ill, disabled, and elderly people must be no less valued than the lives of the young and healthy, and that a seriously disabled person's suicidal impulses should be interpreted and treated the same way as anyone else's.

Likewise, the government "may fear that permitting assisted suicide [through use of controlled substances] will start it down the path to voluntary and perhaps even involuntary euthanasia." If federal policy on controlled substances must bend to Oregon's will with regard to physician-assisted suicide, then it must likewise bend with regard [to] the decision of Oregon or some other state to legalize use of controlled substances for practices even more offensive to the federal government's manifest interest in protecting human life.

Clearly, therefore, the federal government may legitimately assert an unqualified interest in protecting human life in enforcement of the CSA by refusing to permit any exception in its application, whatever the Oregon Act might otherwise permit. Plaintiffs have no grounds on the merits to object to the government's construction of the CSA on such a basis, and they can assert no constitutionally cognizable hardship as a result of the government's construction. . . .

The Tail Must Not Wag the Dog

Both the federal government and an overwhelming majority of states have penalized assisted suicide without exception and have acted in various other ways in pursuit of an unqualified interest in protecting human life. . . .

Obviously, both state and federal governments might properly assert and enforce an unqualified interest in human life within their respective, sometimes concurrent jurisdictions. It is thus simply untrue that the U.S. Supreme Court ruled in *Glucksberg* that *only* the several states may regulate assisted suicide or experiment with its practice, as the Intervenor-Plaintiffs suggest. The federal government might choose to assert an unqualified interest in protecting human life within its sphere as much as the strong majority of states have chosen to do. *Glucksberg* emphasized that a ruling holding that there was indeed a right to assisted suicide would have ham-strung the majority of states that preferred to recognize an unqualified interest in protection of life through absolute bans on assisted suicide. Neither the *Glucksberg* majority nor the concurring opinion of Justice [Sandra Day] O'Connor in *Glucksberg* stated or implied that assisted suicide was a matter to be left solely to the states to the exclusion of the federal government.

In sum, the United States is entirely justified in serving an unqualified interest in protecting human life in its construction of the CSA to exclude prescribing or dispensing federally controlled substances for the purpose of assisting in suicide within its own jurisdictional realm. Oregon remains free to refuse to endorse or enforce its own law regarding the use of controlled substances and assisted suicide as it sees fit. Indeed, Oregon and the several states remain perfectly free to implement an even stricter policy regarding assisted suicide than that represented by the federal construction of the CSA. But Oregon is not a tail wagging the federal dog. That Oregon has legalized physician-assisted suicide and that some Oregonians may be denied use of federally controlled substances to commit suicide as the result of the federal interpretation of the CSA does not effectively nullify uniform application of federal drug laws that prohibit the use of controlled substances for any killing purpose. . . .

> *"The federal government is under no obligation to provide any exception to the [Controlled Substances Act] to permit assisted suicide for the 'terminally ill.'"*

Chapter 2

Government Has an Interest in Equally Protecting Life

Government also has an interest in protecting life equally, in keeping with the constitutional mandate of equal protection of the laws. As described in this [viewpoint], Oregon fails to provide such equal protection with its "Death With Dignity Act." By contrast, the United States accomplishes equal protection with its uniform national interpretation of the Controlled Substances Act. . . .

Oregon provides protections to its vulnerable citizens, as other states do, with several statutes against self-harm. It establishes a crime of manslaughter for aiding another to commit suicide; authorizes use of reasonable physical force to prevent suicide, defines a "mentally ill person" as, inter alia, "a person who, because of a mental disorder is . . . [d]angerous to self"; provides commitment proceedings for one who is a "mentally ill person," including emergency commitment proceedings where there is risk of "serious harm or danger to the person," and provides for disciplinary action of physicians for "unprofessional or dishonorable conduct," including conduct contrary to recognized professional standards or harmful to the patient. . . .

> *"The federal government may legitimately assert an unqualified interest in protecting human life."*

While the foregoing statutes protect most Oregon residents from self-harm and assisted suicide, Oregon has by its Act determined that the lives of persons who have the disability of a terminal disease are not entitled to the same protection from self-harm and assisted suicide as those not deemed terminally ill. It removes the presumptions from a request for assistance in suicide by a terminally ill person that exist for non-terminally ill persons.

The following are the key provisions of the Act: (1) a written request by an adult who has been determined by two physicians to be suffering from a terminal disease; (2) two witnesses who attest that the patient is capable, acting voluntarily, and not under coercion; (3) the attending physician shall inform the patient of his diagnosis, prognosis, potential risks in taking a lethal medication, the probable result, and the feasible alternatives; (4) the consulting physician shall examine the patient and his records, confirm in writing the diagnosis, verify that the patient is capable and acting voluntarily; (5) if either physician thinks the patient "may be suffering from a psychiatric or psychological disorder or depression causing impaired judgment," he is to refer the patient for counseling by a psychiatrist or psychologist; (6) the attending physician shall ask the patient to notify the next of kin of his request for medication; (7) a fifteen day waiting period; and (8) civil and criminal immunities for the physician acting in "good faith compliance" with the Act.

This Court reviewed these purported safeguards and their underlying presumptions, as compared to the general safeguards against self harm, and declared that the Act "singles out terminally ill persons who want to commit suicide and excludes them from protection of Oregon laws that apply to others."

This Court Held Unequal Protection Unconstitutional

The Fourteenth Amendment Equal Protection analysis this Court employed . . . was based on the constitutional doctrine that "prohibits the states from treating persons differently who are, in all relevant respects, alike." "Legislation is presumed valid if a classification drawn by a statute is rationally related to a legitimate state interest." "A classification rationally furthers a state interest when there is some fit between the disparate treatment and the legislative purpose.". . .

Because of these equal protection violations, this Court declared the Act unconstitutional: "[The Act] provides a means to commit suicide to a severely overinclusive class who may be competent, incompetent, unduly influenced, or abused by others. The state interest and the disparate treatment are not rationally related and [the Act], therefore, violates the Constitution of the United States" [as cited in *Lee v. Oregon*].

The United States' CSA Interpretation Treats All Equally

By contrast, the interpretation of the Controlled Substances Act presently before this Court, treats all Americans equally, whether they live in Oregon or elsewhere. It would bring the use of controlled substances in Oregon into line with their use in the rest of the Nation and with the standards of medical care across the Republic. The federal government has a powerful interest in treating its citizens all equally in such vital matters.

In sum, the United States has strong interests in protecting vulnerable persons, especially those who are terminally ill. It asserts those interests with its interpretation of the Controlled Substances Act. Oregon has a constitutional duty to similarly provide its citizens the equal protection of the law, which it ought to do.

The interpretation of the CSA by the United States is wholly reasonable and supported by powerful governmental interests and ought to be upheld against the present assault.

States Do Not Have the Authority to Exempt Physicians from Federal Laws

by Christopher Hook

About the author: *Christopher Hook is a consultant in hematology and medical oncology at the Mayo Clinic in Rochester, Minnesota. He is the founder of the Mayo Medical Center Ethics Consultation Service, a senior fellow of the Center for Bioethics and Human Dignity, and a member of the Christian Medical Association.*

The Pain Relief Promotion Act (PRPA) is an invaluable piece of legislation for the promotion of patients' right to freedom from unnecessary pain.[1] It also serves to add protection to their lives and dignity. While opponents have tried to label the legislation as nothing more than a means to restrict physician-assisted suicide (PAS), it is a liberating document, helping to ensure that physicians can aggressively treat pain without fear of possibly losing their licenses to practice medicine.

Presently, the Drug Enforcement [Administration] (DEA) may intervene in any physician-patient relationship if restricted substances, such as narcotics, are used in "large" quantities or might result in an earlier demise of the patient. The DEA may do so regardless of whether or not the quantities of medications were appropriately used to alleviate a patient's pain, and in which there was no primary goal of ending the patient's life. Physicians throughout the country have undergone the nightmare of "trials" before state authorities with the support of the DEA, sometimes losing their licenses for simply providing appropriate aggressive pain management.

---

1. The U.S. Senate adjourned in 2000 without passing the PRPA, rendering the bill dead for the 106th Congress. While some attempt was made to resurrect the bill in subsequent years, it was never passed.

Christopher Hook, testimony before the U.S. Senate, Washington, DC, September 7, 2000.

Physicians Fear the DEA

Though medical ethics has long understood that negative consequences may occur from beneficent means, and are consequently to be accepted to pursue the good, the DEA is not bound by medical tradition or reasoning. Consequently, many physicians are afraid to prescribe necessary and appropriate doses of narcotic analgesics lest they be investigated, brought before some state board or pursued by the DEA. As a hematologist/oncologist I have had to struggle many times to get referring physicians to provide sufficient analgesics in order to give our shared patients some reasonable quality of life, and freedom from needless suffering.

Just last week [in September 2000] I had another long discussion with a physician in another state about the medication requirements of one of my patients. This patient of five years suffers from a severe chronic pain syndrome resulting from a major motor vehicle accident and subsequent acute respiratory distress syndrome (ARDS). He spent many weeks on a ventilator in an intensive care unit and it is a miracle that he is alive today. But he, like many ARDS survivors, is left with a severe diffuse pain syndrome and requires fairly hefty doses of narcotic medications. His doses have been stable for the last two years. I have had him seen by pain specialists in our institution to explore other options of pain management, and they have repeatedly supported his current program. Most of last year I struggled to find him a physician at home who would continue to write renewal prescriptions for his medications. His primary physician abandoned him, refusing to write the prescriptions, for fear of investigation by state and/or federal officials. Other physicians have refused to take him as a patient claiming the same reason. Finally, we found a physician many miles from his home who would assume his care. Even then, I received a call from the physician expressing concern that he might be investigated by his state's Board, or the DEA, if he provided the prescriptions for my patient. Finally, after I reassured him that 1) the patient's narcotic doses had been stable over several months (documented), 2) that pain management specialists had independently evaluated the patient and recommended the current course of therapy (documented), 3) that I would come to his defense if such an investigation were initiated, and 4) that our professional obligations required us to provide the necessary treatment to control the patient's suffering, he agreed to write the prescriptions. This is all the result of the status quo. Those

> *"What we have in this situation is the claim that one state can override the authority and power of the DEA . . . or any other federal agency."*

who claim that the PRPA will cause a "chilling effect" on pain control in this country have the burden of proof to demonstrate that it would create a worse situation than currently exists, and they simply cannot do it.

American Patients Have a Right to Pain Control

Rather, the PRPA specifically declares "alleviating pain or discomfort in the usual course of professional practice is a legitimate medical purpose for the dispensing, distributing, or administering of a controlled substance that is consistent with public health and safety, even if the use of such a substance may increase the risk of death." When individual states have changed their own internal standards to adopt similar positions and language, the use of narcotics for pain control and efforts in palliative care have increased dramatically. However, patients elsewhere should not have to suffer based upon whether they happen to be in one of the more enlightened states or not. It is the right of every American patient to receive appropriate, aggressive pain control. This statement is the first clear articulation in national legislation of what has been the ethical and appropriate standard of care for patients in pain. It is a statement and protection long overdue.

Further, the PRPA recognizes the need for education of members of the medical profession and regulators to improve and support appropriate palliative care. This process will bring together members of the different disciplines to ensure that patients may receive the care they need and that physicians may treat without fear and unnecessary encumbrances.

"The PRPA takes nothing from Oregon. It simply reminds the state what it means to be a member of a union . . . under a central government."

The PRPA declares that the use of controlled substances for the deliberate killing of patients is forbidden, a statement that is simply consistent with the nature and purpose of the FDA [Food and Drug Administration] and the DEA. The FDA and DEA have been created by the Federal Government to ensure that pharmaceuticals are safe and effective and that powerful agents are not misused. Further, the use of any pharmaceutical to deliberately kill is incompatible with the ethical practice of medicine. This is a 2400 year old pillar of medical ethics and has served our patients well. To allow the use of controlled substances to explicitly kill is to make a mockery of the FDA, the DEA and the profession of medicine.

We should learn from history that whenever a society has allowed its physicians to kill, even for ostensibly beneficent purposes, serious abuses have occurred and physicians have become unworthy of trust. The experience of the German medical profession from the 1920's through the end of World War II is a glaring example, but many choose not to remember this. It was, however, physicians, empowered by the state to kill, who designed and implemented the means of the Holocaust.

For the past twenty years the Netherlands has continued to teach us this point. Though the requirements for euthanasia and physician-assisted suicide initially required that the patient initiate the request, nearly 1% of all deaths in Holland now occur with the deliberate killing of a patient without the patient's explicit request. Consequently, some patients now refuse to enter a hospital or a nursing home, or in some cases even to take medication, because they fear for their lives.

It is claimed that this will not happen in the "experiment" in Oregon [where physician-assisted suicide is legal], but it already is happening. The supposed safeguards to prevent abuse clearly do not work. The very

> *"Oregon is trying to coerce the Federal Government to support physician-assisted suicide by exempting its physicians from the rules that apply . . . in the remaining 49 states."*

first person killed under the Oregon plan demonstrates this. The woman had metastatic breast cancer, but was asymptomatic. She was discouraged because of this and wanted a lethal prescription. Her regular physician and oncologist believed she was clinically depressed and appropriately refused to give her the prescription. Data clearly has demonstrated that the majority of patients who are considering ending their lives are clinically depressed, and that with appropriate antidepressant therapy, or even the passage of time, the patient's desire for death will pass. Patients who are clinically depressed lack the decision-making capacity for such critical, life-affecting decisions. The patient, however, then called Compassion in Dying [a pro–assisted suicide group] and was referred to a physician who was guaranteed to write a prescription for a lethal overdose. Because the physicians who had a long-standing relationship with the patient had declared that she was depressed, this individual felt obligated to dispute this claim and arranged a 20 minute phone conversation with a psychologist who declared that she was not depressed. This is in spite of the fact that in a recent survey 94% of Oregon psychiatrists stated that they were not confident (51% stating they were not at all confident) that they could spot a judgment-impairing psychiatric problem in just one visit. The lethal prescription was written and the patient committed suicide. So much for safeguards.

A more recent case illustrates that, though required by law, the patient need not make the request. The patient was an elderly women suffering from dementia, and was declared incompetent by several physicians to request assisted-suicide. The patient's daughter went doctor shopping until she found someone who would write the prescription, despite the fact that the physician admitted, "the choices of the patient may be influenced by the family's wishes and the daughter was somewhat coercive".

Margaret Mead wrote in 1937,

> Throughout the primitive world the doctor and the sorcerer tended to be the same person. . . . He who had the power to cure would necessarily be able to kill. Depending on who was paying the bill, the doctor/witchdoctor could try to relieve pain or send the patient to another world. Then came a profound

change in the consciousness of the medical profession—made both literal and symbolic in the Hippocratic Oath. . . . One profession . . . was to be dedicated completely to life under all circumstances, regardless of rank, age or intellect—the life of the slave, the Emperor, . . . or the defective child. This is a priceless possession which we cannot afford to tarnish . . . but society is always attempting to make the physician into a killer—to kill the defective child at birth, to leave sleeping pills beside the bed of the cancer patient. . . . It is the duty of society to protect the physician from such requests.

Indeed. The PRPA reflects this wisdom. Assisted suicide is not a legitimate form of medical practice and should not be permitted.

And speaking of "who is paying the bill", the *Oregonian* reported in October of 1998 that the Oregon Medical Assistance Program would now pay for physician-assisted suicide but no longer would pay for adequate palliative care. Pain medications were capped at low levels. The program had also suspended funding for antidepressants, but later reversed that position under significant protest. So much for a system that is supposed to be committed to the dignity of the patient. All this tells a poor patient is that we are happy to kill you, but that you are not even worth the cost of appropriate comfort care.

Assisted Suicide Does Not Promote Dignity or Autonomy

It is often stated that assisted-suicide is a necessary means to preserve patients' dignity. The Oregon program is even called the Death With Dignity Act. Once and for all we should put an end to this false rhetoric. If one looks in the dictionary, there are two common usages of the term dignity: one meaning intrinsic worth, and the other referring to imputed dignity—the subjective perception of worth or decorum. Intrinsic worth or dignity is something that all of us possess by the mere fact that we are human beings and each of inestimable worth. It is something that cannot be lost or eroded by the presence of disability or illness. If we imply that illness can diminish our dignity we diminish the worth of every human being, a rather dangerous course. If we believe rather that we should focus on imputed dignity in the question of assisted suicide then we encounter another problem. The patient is forced to come to another person to receive the means of death and states, "I think my life no longer has value, I have lost my dignity". The physician in order to write the prescription must implicitly, if not explicitly, state, "I agree, your life no longer has meaning or value. Here take these. . .". At this point the physician has shredded any sense of imputed dignity the patient may have held onto. To agree to overtly kill another human being is the antithesis of respecting dignity by any definition.

> *"[The PRPA] recognizes the proper authority of federal agencies, specifically the DEA."*

This in essence leads to another commonly heard justification for assisted-suicide, that it promotes autonomy. As I have shown earlier, the majority of patients who request assisted suicide are depressed and lack decision-making capacity. Autonomy requires liberty and agency, the latter meaning decision-making capacity. Thus most requests for assisted-suicide are by definition not autonomous. Further, the Oregon program requires the permission and participation of others, so again it is not truly a promoter of autonomy. Any thoughts that the Oregon Death With Dignity Act promotes autonomy are illusory. Thus criticism that the PRPA will restrict the autonomy of Oregonians is false.

Is not the PRPA a usurpation of state's rights, a common complaint against the bill? The claim is that the Oregonians approved physician-assisted suicide and therefore the Federal Government has no jurisdiction in any realm that might interfere with that choice. To answer this question, I pose another question. Would we allow a state to authorize the sale of laetril, or other disproven, toxic drugs? What we have in this situation is the claim that one state can override the authority and power of the DEA, or ostensibly the FDA, or any other federal agency, which has regulatory authority throughout the United States. All physicians must have a DEA license to prescribe controlled substances, and yet somehow a state has now decided that the licensing agency for every other physician in the United States no longer has jurisdiction over its physicians. This would not be accepted for any other similar Federal authority and should not be accepted here. The PRPA takes nothing from Oregon. It simply reminds that state what it means to be a member of a union of states under a central government. Oregon is trying to coerce the Federal Government to support physician-assisted suicide by exempting its physicians from the rules that apply to any other physician in the remaining 49 states, an act of injustice and impropriety. We either have national regulatory agencies with uniform authority throughout the 50 states or we revert to a system of inconsistent and arbitrary behavior regarding critical issues of safety and justice. The choice should be clear.

The DEA Exercises Proper Authority

In summary, the PRPA is a valuable, long overdue piece of legislation promoting the freedom of patients to achieve relief from their pain, and of physicians to appropriately perform their duties. It recognizes the proper authority of federal agencies, specifically the DEA. It appropriately recognizes that the purpose of the medical profession and medication is to help, not to kill. In so doing it protects the safety of patients, the integrity of the medical profession and the dignity of us all.

Chapter 3

Would Legalizing Assisted Suicide Harm America's Healthcare?

Chapter Preface

"I will neither give a deadly drug to anybody who asked for it, nor will I make a suggestion to this effect." For many physicians and laypeople, this sentence from the classical Hippocratic Oath—recited for centuries by graduating medical students—is at the center of the debate surrounding the legalization of physician-assisted suicide (PAS). Opponents of PAS argue that allowing physicians to assist terminally ill patients in committing suicide would violate the Hippocratic Oath, perverting the medical profession by changing doctors from healers into technical dispensers of death. According to Leon R. Kass, physician and professor at the University of Chicago, "The venerable Hippocratic Oath clearly rules out physician-assisted suicide. Without this taboo, medicine ceases to be a trustworthy and ethical profession; without it, all of us will suffer—yes, more than we suffer now because some of us die too slowly."

Many ethicists argue that if physicians are allowed to violate the Hippocratic Oath by assisting in suicide, the doctor-patient relationship will be irreparably damaged. They maintain that it will be difficult if not impossible for patients to trust in their doctor's concern for their best interests when doctors can legally help them die. Further, critics insist that even the most conscientious doctors might have difficulty in being completely devoted to their patient's recovery if death becomes a treatment option.

Proponents of assisted suicide, however, argue that the procedure is a compassionate act in keeping with the highest traditions of the Hippocratic Oath. They maintain that allowing doctors to assist in the suicides of terminally ill patients offers suffering individuals a chance for a peaceful, easy death. A modern version of the oath written in 1964 and in wide use today does not specifically prohibit PAS. Instead it cautions, "If it is given me to save a life, all thanks. But it may also be within my power to take a life; this awesome responsibility must be faced with great humbleness and awareness of my own frailty. Above all, I must not play at God." This modern version of the Hippocratic Oath recognizes facets of modern medicine, such as technology and drugs that can keep ill people alive much longer, and a more equal doctor-patient relationship. As physician Agata Bednarz explains, "The more modern ethical issues at stake . . . could be the principle of patient autonomy and the idea of the quality of life as chosen and perceived by the patient—both key components in the patient-physician relationship."

Physicians, laypeople, and ethicists continue to debate whether PAS violates the Hippocratic Oath and damages the doctor-patient relationship. Authors in the following chapter explore the effects, both harmful and beneficial, of other aspects of PAS on American health care.

Legalizing Physician-Assisted Suicide Would Harm the Care of Terminally Ill Patients

by Ezekiel J. Emanuel

About the author: *Ezekiel J. Emanuel is the chair of the Department of Clinical Bioethics at the Warren G. Magnuson Clinical Center at the National Institutes of Health. He is also a breast oncologist.*

Euthanasia and physician-assisted suicide (PAS) are not ends in themselves with intrinsic value. At best, they are means to realize the end of a good death or, more accurately, a quality dying experience. The current debate has tended to focus on whether euthanasia or PAS is appropriate for this or that individual, or whether passive is the same as active euthanasia, or whether providing morphine for pain relief with the risk of respiratory depression and premature death is the same as euthanasia. But the issue that has exercised this country for the past five to ten years is legalization—or otherwise publicly sanctioning a social practice—of euthanasia or PAS. This issue is not about the morality of a specific decision regarding the care of an individual patient, but the ethics of having a particular social policy and practice. Ultimately, the ethical question we should consider is: Will legalizing—or permitting—euthanasia and PAS promote—or thwart—a good death for the 2.3 million Americans who die each year in the United States? Will people who die be helped or harmed by having euthanasia or PAS available to them?

In confronting this question, we must first acknowledge that figuring out the benefits and harms of permitting euthanasia or PAS is speculative, at best. As will become clear, we inherently lack some of the essential information we need for this assessment. But judgment under uncertainty and with incomplete

Ezekiel J. Emanuel, "What Is the Great Benefit of Legalizing Euthanasia or Physician-Assisted Suicide?" *Ethics*, vol. 109, April 1999. Copyright © 1999 by The University of Chicago. Reproduced by permission.

data is precisely the type of ethical judgment that we—laymen and legislators—must make in deciding whether on balance it is better to legalize euthanasia or PAS or not. And, far from being neutral, this uncertainty needs to be considered in this ethical evaluation. Nevertheless, articulating and estimating the benefits and harms of legalization can be quite helpful in clarifying the stakes of the choice.

Furthermore, any reasonable commentator on this issue must acknowledge that no matter which social policy regarding euthanasia or PAS is adopted—legalization or maintaining the current policy of permitting them in individual cases—there will be both benefits and harms. Legalization would inevitably generate abuses, cases in which people's lives were intentionally ended when they should not have been because they were coerced, or because appropriate palliative measures were not provided, or because they did not consent. As [Dan W.] Brock, a staunch proponent of legalizing euthanasia and PAS, has acknowledged, stringent safeguards can "not eliminate . . . the potential for abuse." Similarly, opponents must acknowledge that if neither euthanasia nor PAS is permitted, some patients experiencing unremitting pain will be prevented from ending their lives and will suffer needlessly. And other patients who might not use euthanasia or PAS but would receive some reassurance by knowing these are possible options would not have this psychological benefit if they remain illegal. The ethical question is how do the benefits and harms of legalization compare.

Likely Benefits of Legalizing Euthanasia and PAS

Proponents of euthanasia and PAS identify three main benefits to legalization: (1) realizing individual autonomy, (2) reducing needless pain and suffering, and (3) providing psychological reassurance to dying patients.

Benefit 1: Realizing Autonomy

Autonomy is an essential American value and should not be dismissed. Yet, . . . it is controversial whether permitting euthanasia or PAS is essential to realizing individual autonomy. I cannot enter this debate. But it is worth noting that polls suggest that most people do not find securing individual autonomy sufficient justification for legalizing euthanasia or PAS. Intentionally ending a person's life is an act that requires another person's participation, and requires giving that other person a good reason to participate. Without a good reason beyond preference or personal life plans, people would not permit it. Indeed, the notion that individual autonomy is not a sufficient

"Polls suggest that most people do not find securing individual autonomy sufficient justification for legalizing euthanasia or PAS."

justification is embodied in the safeguards incorporated into most proposals for legalization. The key safeguards require that the patient initiate and freely and repeatedly request euthanasia or PAS; that there be unremitting pain or uncontrolled physical suffering that cannot be relieved except by euthanasia or PAS; and that a second physician consult on the case to be sure of the patient's prognosis and that the patient is acting voluntarily and understands his or her decision. Having more than the first safeguard acknowledges that autonomy is an insufficient justification for euthanasia or PAS, that these interventions must also realize a good besides autonomy, such as relief of unremitting and excruciating pain.

Benefit 2: Relief of Pain and Suffering

If we legalize euthanasia or PAS, how many people will have their needless pain and suffering relieved? To determine this number we need to know five factors: (1) how many dying people there are each year; (2) what proportion of these patients have a recognizable and distinct dying process during which they can request euthanasia or PAS; (3) what proportion of these patients would be competent to request euthanasia or PAS; (4) what proportion of these patients would have unremitting pain that would justify euthanasia or PAS; and (5) what proportion of these patients would actually want euthanasia or PAS. . . .

Combining all five factors, I estimate that each year, of the 2.3 million Americans who die, approximately 5,000 to 25,000 patients might have a distinct dying process with significant and unremitting pain, desire euthanasia or PAS, and be competent to repeatedly request and consent to euthanasia or PAS. (This is 0.5 percent to 2.5 percent of the 1 million people who have a dying process and are competent to request euthanasia or PAS. These proportions are based on the 5 percent who have unremitting pain with optimal pain control therapy combined with only 10 percent to 50 percent of patients with pain who desire euthanasia or PAS.)

> *"To put this into proper perspective, 1 percent or fewer deaths would be improved by legalizing euthanasia and PAS."*

An alternative method to calculate the proportion of dying patients who might benefit from euthanasia or PAS is to use available Dutch data to estimate those who might benefit from euthanasia and PAS. This method is based on two factors: the proportion of all decedents that would use euthanasia or PAS and the proportion that would do so for reasons of unremitting pain. Factor 1: According to the latest data, approximately 2.4 percent of all Dutch decedents had a distinct dying process, were competent to request euthanasia or PAS, and died from euthanasia or PAS. Factor 2: According to these same data, in only a third of cases did pain play any role in the patient's decision to seek euthanasia or PAS. These and other Dutch data have suggested that pain was the sole or dominant reason for euthanasia or PAS in 11 percent or fewer cases. Recent studies in the United States have suggested that among euthanasia and PAS cases in the United States pain also plays a relatively minor role in requests for euthanasia and PAS. Interviews with physicians suggest that in about one-third of cases pain is the motivating factor for the request for euthanasia or PAS. A recent survey of physicians indicated that 24 percent of patients who received euthanasia and 54 percent of patients who received PAS were experiencing pain. Combining these data suggests that if euthanasia or PAS were legalized fewer than 20,000 dying Americans might use these interventions to end their lives for reasons of unremitting pain. (This is based on noting that 2.4 percent of all dying patients in the United States is 55,000 people and that one-third of this is less than 20,000 people.)

> *"Overall, the benefit of legalizing euthanasia or PAS is improvement in the dying experience for a maximum of 25,000 terminally ill patients."*

Thus . . . I believe we can say that, at best, legalizing euthanasia or PAS would benefit by relieving unremitting and excruciating pain 25,000 or fewer of the 2.3 million Americans who die each year.

Benefit 3: Psychological Reassurance

No one has directly asked sick, let alone terminally ill, patients whether having euthanasia or PAS available as an option would be reassuring. The closest available data revealed that 41.6 percent of cancer patients—not all of whom were terminally ill—and 44.4 percent of the public thought discussions with their physicians about end-of-life care that included discussion of euthanasia and PAS would increase their trust in their physicians.

Overall, the firmest benefit of legalizing euthanasia and PAS would be to relieve the excruciating and unremitting pain of 25,000 or fewer dying Americans each year. To put this into proper perspective, 1 percent or fewer deaths would be improved by legalizing euthanasia and PAS. In addition, approximately 40 percent of Americans might get some psychological reassurance knowing that euthanasia or PAS were possible alternatives if their dying was too painful.

Likely Harms of Legalizing Euthanasia or PAS

What are the potential harms of legalizing euthanasia or PAS? Opponents identify six potential harms: (1) undermining the integrity of the medical profession; (2) creation of psychological anxiety and distress in patients from the possibility of euthanasia or PAS; (3) coercion of patients to use euthanasia or PAS against their wishes; (4) provision of euthanasia or PAS to patients prior to implementing optimal palliative care interventions; (5) provision of euthanasia or PAS to patients without their full informed consent because of either mental illness or mental incompetence; and (6) psychological distress and harm to surviving family members of the patient.

For almost all these harms there are few firm data. These harms are much harder to empirically evaluate; they require studying many deaths for the smaller proportion that occur by euthanasia or PAS and then assessing them for coercion, less than optimal palliative interventions, mental competence of the patient, and so forth. No research group has been able to assemble a representative and reasonably large enough number of cases to study and to do so would require enormous resources. (Small numbers of cases are likely to be unrepresentative and very deceptive.) Furthermore, determining how many of these harms might occur depends upon knowing how many dying patients might use euthanasia and PAS if they became legal or socially sanctioned. And for this we only have the Dutch data, and must guess about how well they translate to the United States.

Harm 1: Undermining the Medical Profession

Whether euthanasia or PAS harms the medical profession is an interpretive issue and probably depends upon other factors, such as the social role of the profession, that vary over time. While the data indicate that in the majority of cases physicians do not regret having performed euthanasia and PAS and would do so again in similar circumstances, a significant minority have regret and more. In a study my colleagues and I did, we found that about 25 percent of physicians regret having performed euthanasia or PAS in some cases because it did not lead to a good death for the patient or family. (This regret was not associated with fear of prosecution, which was also asked about.) Other physicians reported significant emotional burden from having performed euthanasia and PAS that, in some cases, even led to changes in practice patterns. [Diane] Meier and colleagues reported that 18 percent of physicians who performed PAS and 12 percent who performed euthanasia were uncomfortable with having assisted in ending a patient's life. In addition, at least 7 percent of physicians would not repeat the acts in similar cases in the future. One of the leading advocates of euthanasia and PAS in Australia said of his actions that he felt like an "executioner." "Regret" by a minority of physicians who perform euthanasia or PAS does not constitute a fundamental change in the profession. But such findings do suggest problems and adverse effects that should not be ignored.

Harm 2: Psychological Anxiety

There are some data about whether euthanasia or PAS would disrupt the trust necessary for the physician-patient relationship and generate psychological distress, not reassurance. In the same survey where patients and the public indicated that discussions with physicians about end-of-life care that included discussion of euthanasia and PAS would increase their trust in their doctor, an almost equal proportion of cancer patients thought such discussion would decrease trust in their physician. More importantly, my colleagues and I found that 19.0 percent of cancer patients and 26.5 percent of the public would change from physicians who discussed euthanasia or PAS with them. Indeed, patients with significant

> *"Supporters of legalization of euthanasia and PAS tend to be financially well-off, well-educated, white, nonreligious, and under sixty-five years of age."*

pain were more likely to want to change physicians. While far from definitive, these data indicate that whatever psychological reassurance some patients might experience from legalizing euthanasia or PAS is likely to be offset by increases in psychological anxiety and distress induced in other patients, and the most adverse impact will be on the very patients most in need of help, those with significant pain.

Harm 3: Coercion to Use Euthanasia or PAS

Coercion of the patient is most likely to come from his or her family either because of financial or caregiving burdens. Unfortunately, there really are no substantive data that permit quantification of the number of dying patients that might be coerced to receive euthanasia or PAS. There are some anecdotes about such coercive pressures, such as the DeLury case in New York in which a husband was convicted of pressuring his wife, who suffered from severe multiple sclerosis, to intentionally end her life. According to his own diaries his motive was to eliminate the burdens he was experiencing in caring for her. Similarly, there are data that suggest financial pressures could lead to coercion. The SUPPORT study found that in 24 percent of cases, families of terminally ill patients lost most or all of their savings because of medical care costs. In addition, in as yet unpublished data, my colleagues and I found that 8.6 percent of caregivers of patients who had just died reported that the patients' medical care imposed a "great economic burden" on the family. While there are no data on whether economic pressures from illness lead to coercion of patients to seek euthanasia or PAS, data do indicate that these pressures alone—independent of other factors of ill health such as severity of illness and poor physical functioning—incline family members not to want life-sustaining treatments for their dying relatives. And while there are no data on how many requests for euthanasia and PAS are motivated by family pressures due to financial burdens, we have reported that in 7.9 percent of actual cases of euthanasia and PAS in the United States financial burden was a core motive. More needs to be done to understand the impact of these financial pressures on desires for euthanasia or PAS and whether they lead to coercive family pressure to seek euthanasia or PAS. Existing data are suggestive that such pressures might exist and do influence preferences at the end of life.

> *"The harms of legalization are likely to fall on vulnerable members of our population."*

Independent of financial burdens, terminally ill patients also impose significant caregiving responsibilities on families that could lead to coercive pressures to request euthanasia or PAS. For instance, the SUPPORT study reported that in 34 percent of families dying patients required a large amount of caregiving assistance. We found that more than one-third of terminally ill patients reported significant or moderate caregiving needs for transportation, nursing care, homemaking, and personal care with 16.3 percent having significant caregiving needs. Such caregiving needs adversely affect the patients' families—family members of patients with significant needs are more likely to be depressed and to report that the patient is interfering with their lives. More importantly, we found that, second only to depression, having high caregiving needs was a significant predictor for terminally ill patients having seriously thought about euthanasia or PAS. Whether this interest in euthanasia or PAS was the result of family coercion or pressure, as it was in the DeLury case, could not be determined from these data.

> *"Focusing ... on debating, campaigning, litigating, and studying euthanasia and PAS is beginning to detract from ... improving end-of-life care."*

We cannot accurately estimate the numbers of dying patients who might be coerced to request euthanasia or PAS because of financial or caregiving burdens. However, these data indicate that this is likely to exist and to be a real factor, and they influence a large proportion of the 2.3 million Americans who die, more than just the 2–3 percent of dying patients who might desire euthanasia or PAS. Among the 1 million competent patients with a dying process who might be eligible to request euthanasia or PAS, these data suggest that 86,000 to 240,000 (8.6 percent to 24 percent of 1 million dying patients) impose significant financial burdens, while 160,000 to 340,000 (16 percent to 34 percent of 1 million dying patients) impose significant caregiving burdens on their families. If just a few percent of these patients are coerced to request euthanasia or PAS, then the number of patients who might be harmed by legalization of these interventions begins to equal and exceed the number of dying patients who might benefit from legalization. And such patients can be harmed even if the coercive pressures are resisted simply because they have had to confront these pressures at a time of vulnerability and because such pressure is likely to disrupt the already intricate task of negotiating a good death.

Harm 4: Premature Euthanasia or PAS

Properly utilized euthanasia and PAS are "last ditch" interventions, interventions that can be justified only after appropriate palliative options are attempted. In the Netherlands, physicians report that in 9 percent of euthanasia cases in nursing homes not all palliative measures were utilized prior to ending the patient's life. My colleagues and I . . . reported that all patients whose lives were ended by euthanasia or PAS and who had pain were on opioid narcotics. But some of these patients were not given all optimal care: 60 percent were not receiving hospice care; in addition, less than 10 percent received psychiatric evaluations for depression, and at least one depressed patient who was given euthanasia refused psychiatric care. How many depressed patients were not diagnosed or not given proper treatment but were given euthanasia or PAS we could not determine. Others have reported that in 39 percent of cases patients who were given euthanasia were depressed, and in 19 percent of cases patients given PAS were depressed. These data suggest a lack of adequate palliative care for psychological symptoms prior to use of euthanasia and PAS. Another recent survey of all oncologists in the United States revealed the surprising finding that those oncologists who reported that administrative, financial, and other barriers prevented them from providing all the care they wanted for their terminally ill patients were much more likely to have performed euthanasia or PAS in the last year (1997–98). All these data indicate that in both the Netherlands and the United States, many patients who received euthanasia and PAS received these interventions before all appropriate palliative interventions had been implemented. Again, it is impossible to estimate how many dying patients would have ended their lives to relieve pain and suffering before appropriate palliative measures were instituted if euthanasia and PAS were legalized. But these data suggest that such actions occur in the Netherlands despite safeguards; it is hard to imagine that with legalization the frequency of euthanasia or PAS without adequate palliative care would decline in the United States. And the total numbers of patients would increase if the number of patients receiving euthanasia and PAS increased.

Harm 5: Euthanasia for Incompetent Patients

In the Netherlands, it has been documented that slightly more than 20 percent of patients who received euthanasia were not mentally competent to consent to euthanasia when their lives were ended. In only 53 percent of these cases did the patient ever express interest in receiving euthanasia. Recent data from two studies in the United States suggest that a high proportion of euthanasia cases occur in mentally incompetent patients. A national survey of physicians revealed that in 5–7 percent of cases of euthanasia and PAS, patients were mentally confused more than 50 percent of the time when given these interventions. In another 5.3 percent of cases patients were also unconscious when given euthanasia. More importantly, my colleagues and I found that in 15 percent of euthanasia cases, patients were not involved in the decision to end their lives, sometimes even when they were competent. Thus, it appears that in 15–20 percent of the cases there will be provision of euthanasia without patient's consent. This occurs when the action is illegal and the penalties high and in the Netherlands with explicit and established safeguards barring such practices.

> *"Attention and resources focused on euthanasia and PAS are likely to impair, not improve, the care of the 2.3 million decedents by diverting valuable resources."*

Harm 6: Family Suffering

. . . Euthanasia and PAS are decisions that go beyond the individual patients and affect the family who live long after the event. There are no data on the positive or negative long-term effects on families of patients whose lives are ended by euthanasia and PAS.

Overall, the benefit of legalizing euthanasia or PAS is improvement in the dying experience for a maximum of 25,000 terminally ill patients with unremitting pain. The benefit from psychological reassurance for patients is likely to be offset by increases in anxiety and psychological distress of other patients. The existing data do not permit us to estimate how many terminally ill patients might experience coercion to request euthanasia or PAS and to receive euthanasia or PAS without having received optimal palliative care or without having given their informed consent. However, each year hundreds of thousands of terminally ill patients would be at risk for these harms. Even if a small percentage of terminally ill patients suffer these harms, the benefits from legalizing euthanasia or PAS would be overwhelmed. Under such circumstances are the benefits of legalization of euthanasia and PAS worth the risk of harms? The case for rushing forward does not seem very strong.

The Inequitable Distribution of the Benefits and Harms

Finally, there is a point of equity that hardly gets mentioned in the debate about the legalization of euthanasia and PAS. Part of the reason there is such a rush to legalize euthanasia and PAS is that the benefits and the harms are not likely to be fairly distributed; the advocates are likely to reap the benefits while avoiding most of the harms.

The pressure to legalize euthanasia and PAS comes from relatively educated, well-off, politically vocal people. Polls consistently demonstrate that supporters of legalization of euthanasia and PAS tend to be financially well-off, well-educated, white, nonreligious, and under sixty-five years of age. (How ironic that this sociodemographic description fits most federal judges, as well as philosophers and other academics.) These are people who have positions of authority in society, who control their work and home environments, and who are used to realizing their life plans. If euthanasia or PAS were legalized they would receive the benefits, especially the reassurance of knowing these options are available. Furthermore, they are likely to be protected from the harms of legalization. They tend to have good health insurance, intact, supportive families, and the social skills and know-how to get what they want from an increasingly bureaucratized health care system.

Conversely, the harms of legalization are likely to fall on vulnerable members of our population. Coercion to opt for euthanasia or PAS and inadequate uses of palliative care are likely to fall on financially less well-off and comparatively powerless patients who may not be insured or may be underinsured, who cannot get all the medical services they need, for whom the costs of care are likely to constitute a large financial burden, and who may not have the social skills to navigate the health care system. Again, the polling data suggest that the poor, African-Americans, and older people tend to oppose legalization of euthanasia and PAS. They know their interests and know that they are most vulnerable to abuse. Further, the data on actual practices both from the Netherlands and the United States, including all of Dr. Kevorkian's cases, suggest that women are much more likely to be the recipients of euthanasia or PAS than are men. Our data from oncologists showed that in 60 percent of euthanasia and PAS cases females were the patients.

The benefits and harms of legalizing euthanasia and PAS are likely to reinforce inequities in the delivery of health care services and the disparities of wealth and power in our society. And there is very little that the proposed safeguards will do to prevent this, since these sociodemographic disparities are common in the health care system and have been quite resistant to strenuous efforts to eliminate them.

Legalization Will Impair End-of-Life Care

Will legalization of euthanasia and PAS significantly improve the care of the 2.3 million patients in the United States who die each year? There is no compelling evidence that the answer is in the affirmative. And the focusing of so much attention and energy on debating, campaigning, litigating, and studying euthanasia and PAS is beginning to detract from the primary goal of improving end-of-life care. There are important challenges to providing better end-of-life care. These include providing better and more mental health care, home care, and spiritual care. The health care system has scarce resources, especially scarce time, money, attention span, managerial talent, and so forth. The euthanasia and PAS debate has been useful in focusing some of these scarce resources on the dying and in galvanizing improvements in care of the dying. Much of the nation, including the medical establishment, national foundations, and the National Institutes of Health, is focused on improving end-of-life care. Continued attention and resources focused on euthanasia and PAS are likely to impair, not improve, the care of the 2.3 million decedents by diverting valuable resources.

Legalizing Physician-Assisted Suicide Would Lead to Abuses

by Marilyn Golden

About the author: *Marilyn Golden is a policy analyst for the Disability Rights Education and Defense Fund (DREDF) and a member of the executive committee of the California Disability Alliance (CDA).*

In 1999, faced with a bill in the California legislature to legalize assisted suicide, the Disability Rights Education and Defense Fund (DREDF) joined ten other nationally prominent disability organizations in adopting a position against the legalization of assisted suicide and euthanasia.

The 1999 California bill went down to defeat, due in part to an opposition coalition spanning the political spectrum from left to right. That coalition represented disability rights organizations, workers, poor people, physicians and other health-care workers, hospice organizations, Catholics, and right-to-life organizations. The opposition to legalization of assisted suicide is often mischaracterized as composed of religious conservatives, but most current opposition coalitions include many persons and organizations whose opposition is based on their progressive politics.

A similar coalition defeated a referendum on the same proposal in Maine in 2000. What happened in Maine is a perfect example of the general public's typical reaction to assisted suicide proposals. Early polls showed strong support, before the general public was educated about the dangers of legalization. As this education occurred, the polls slowly but steadily shifted, with the opposition gaining in each. At the time of the election, polls showed the opposition exceeding the support, and the referendum failed.

In 2002 and 2003, DREDF worked with a similar coalition in Hawaii to defeat the same bill.

DREDF Opposes Legalization of Assisted Suicide

Assisted suicide seems, at first blush, like a good thing to have available. But on closer inspection, there are many reasons legalization is a very serious mistake. Supporters often focus solely on superficial issues of choice and self-determination. It is crucial to look deeper.

We must separate our private wishes for what we each may hope to have available for ourselves some day and, rather, focus on the significant dangers of legalizing assisted suicide as public policy in this society as it operates today. Assisted suicide would have many unintended consequences.

A Very Few Helped—a Great Many Harmed

The movement for legalization of assisted suicide is driven by anecdotes of people who suffer greatly in the period before death. But the overwhelming majority of these anecdotes describes either situations for which legal alternatives exist today, or situations in which the individual would not be legally eligible for assisted suicide. It is legal in every U.S. state for an individual to create an advance directive that requires the withdrawal of treatment under any conditions the person wishes. It is legal for a patient to refuse any treatment or to require any treatment to be withdrawn. It is legal to receive sufficient pain-killers to be comfortable, even if they might hasten death. And if someone who is imminently dying is in significant discomfort, it is legal for the individual to be sedated to the point that the discomfort is relieved. Moreover, if someone has a chronic illness that is not terminal, that individual is not eligible for assisted suicide under any proposal in the U.S., nor under the Oregon Death with Dignity Act (Oregon is the only state where assisted suicide is legal). Furthermore, any individual whose illness has brought about depression that affects the individual's judgment is also ineligible, according to every U.S. proposal as well as Oregon's law. Consequently, the number of people whose situations would actually be eligible for assisted suicide is extremely low.

> *"Assisted suicide would have many unintended consequences."*

The very small number of people who may benefit from legalizing assisted suicide will tend to be affluent, white, and in possession of good health insurance coverage. At the same time, large numbers of people, particularly among those less privileged in society, would be at significant risk of harm.

Managed Care and Assisted Suicide Are a Deadly Mix

Perhaps the most significant problem is the deadly mix between assisted suicide and profit-driven managed health care. Again and again, health maintenance organizations (HMOs) and managed care bureaucracies have overruled physicians' treatment decisions. These actions have sometimes hastened patients' deaths. The cost of the lethal medication generally used for assisted suicide is about $35 to $50, far cheaper than the cost of treatment for most long-term medical conditions. The incentive to save money by denying treatment already poses a significant danger. This danger would be far greater if assisted suicide is legal.

Assisted suicide is likely to accelerate the decline in quality of our health care system. A 1998 study from Georgetown University's Center for Clinical Bioethics underscores the link between profit-driven managed health care and assisted suicide. The research found a strong links between cost-cutting pressure on physicians and their willingness to prescribe lethal drugs to patients, were it legal to do so. The study warns that there must be

> *"The cost of lethal medication . . . for assisted suicide is about $35 to $50, far cheaper than the cost of treatment for most long-term medical conditions."*

"a sobering degree of caution in legalizing [assisted suicide] in a medical care environment that is characterized by increasing pressure on physicians to control the cost of care".

The deadly impact of legalizing assisted suicide would fall hardest on socially and economically disadvantaged people who have less access to medical resources and who already find themselves discriminated against by the health care system. As Paul Longmore, Professor of History at San Francisco State University and a foremost disability advocate on this subject, has stated, "Poor people, people of color, elderly people, people with chronic or progressive conditions or disabilities, and anyone who is, in fact, terminally ill will find themselves at serious risk".

Rex Greene, M.D., Medical Director of the Dorothy E. Schneider Cancer Center at Mills Health Center in San Mateo, California and a leader in bioethics, health policy and oncology, underscored the heightened danger to the poor. He said, "The most powerful predictor of ill health is [people's] income. [Legalization of assisted suicide] plays right into the hands of managed care."

Supporters of assisted suicide frequently say that HMOs will not use this procedure as a way to deal with costly patients. They cite a 1998 study in the *New England Journal of Medicine* that estimated the savings of allowing people to die before their last month of life at $627 million. Supporters argue that this is a mere .07% of the nation's total annual health care costs. But significant problems in this study make it an unsuitable basis for claims about assisted suicide's potential impact. The researchers based their findings on the average cost to Medicare of patients with only four weeks or less to live. Yet assisted suicide proposals (as well as the law in Oregon) define terminal illness as having *six months* to live. The researchers also assumed that about 2.7% of the total number of people who die in the U.S. would opt for assisted suicide, based on reported assisted suicide and euthanasia deaths in the Netherlands. But the failure of large numbers of Dutch physicians to report such deaths casts considerable doubt on this estimate. And how can one compare the U.S. to a country that has universal health care? Taken together, these factors would skew the costs much higher.

Fear, Bias, and Prejudice Against Disability

Fear, bias, and prejudice against disability play a significant role in assisted suicide. Who ends up using assisted suicide? Supporters advocate its legalization by arguing that it would relieve untreated pain and discomfort at the end of life. But *all but one* of the people in Oregon who were reported to have used that state's assisted suicide law during its first year wanted suicide *not* because of pain, but for fear of losing functional ability, autonomy, or control of bodily functions. Oregon's subsequent reports have documented similar results. Furthermore, in the Netherlands, more than half the physicians surveyed say the main reason given by patients for seeking death is "loss of dignity".

This fear of disability typically underlies assisted suicide. Said one assisted suicide advocate, "Pain is not the main reason we want to die. It's the indignity. It's the inability to get out of bed or get onto the toilet . . . [People] . . . say, 'I can't stand my mother—my husband—wiping my behind.' It's about dignity". But as many thousands of people with disabilities who rely on personal assistance have learned, needing help is not undignified, and death is not better than reliance on assistance. Have we gotten to the point that we will abet suicides because people need help using the toilet?

Diane Coleman, President and Founder of Not Dead Yet, a grassroots disability organization opposed to legalizing assisted suicide, has written that the "public image of severe disability as a fate worse than death . . . become(s) grounds for carving out a deadly exception to longstanding laws and public policies about suicide intervention services. . . . Legalizing assisted suicide means that some people who say they want to die will receive suicide intervention, while others will receive suicide assistance. The difference between these two groups of people will be their health or disability status, leading to a two-tiered system that results in death to the socially devalued group".

Depression Underlies Some Requests for Assisted Suicide

Suicide requests from people with terminal illness are usually based on fear and depression. As Herbert Hendin, M.D., Medical Director of the American Foundation for Suicide Prevention and a leading U.S. expert on suicide, stated in Congressional testimony in 1996, "a request for assisted suicide is . . . usually made with as much ambivalence as are most suicide attempts. If the doctor does not recognize that ambivalence as well as the anxiety and depression that underlie the patient's request for death, the patient may become trapped by that request and die in a state of unrecognized terror".

Most cases of depression among terminally ill people can be successfully treated. Yet primary care physicians are generally not exports in diagnosing depression. Where assisted suicide is legalized, the depression remains undiagnosed, and the only treatment consists of a lethal prescription.

Assisted suicide proposals and Oregon's law are based on the faulty assumption that it is possible to make a clear distinction between those who are terminally ill with six months to live, and everyone else. Everyone else is supposedly protected and not eligible for assisted suicide. But it is extremely common for medical prognoses of a short life expectancy to be wrong. Studies show that only cancer patients show a predictable decline and even then, it's only in the last few weeks of life. With every disease other than cancer, there is no predictability at all. Prognoses are based on statistical averages, which are nearly useless in predicting what will happen to an individual patient. Thus, the potential effect of assisted suicide is extremely broad, far beyond the supposedly narrow group its proponents claim. The affected group could include many people who may be mistakenly diagnosed as terminal but who have many meaningful years of life ahead of them.

> *"Have we gotten to the point that we will abet suicide because people need help using the toilet?"*

This also poses considerable danger to people with new or progressive disabilities or diseases. Research overwhelmingly shows that people with new disabilities frequently go through initial despondency and suicidal feelings, but later adapt well and find great satisfaction in their lives. However, the adaptation usually takes considerably longer than the mere two week waiting period required by assisted suicide proposals and Oregon's law. People with new diagnoses of terminal illness appear to go through similar stages. In that early period before one learns the truth about how good one's quality of life can be, it would be all too easy, if assisted suicide is legal, to make the final choice, one that is irrevocable.

Other Alleged Safeguards

Neither do other alleged safeguards offer any real protections. In Oregon's law and similar proposals, physicians are not permitted to write lethal prescription under inappropriate conditions that are defined in the law. This is seen as a "safeguard." But in several Oregon cases, suicidal patients engaged in "doctor shopping." When the first physician each of these patients approached refused to comply with the request for assisted suicide because the patient didn't meet the conditions of the law, the patient sought out another physician who agreed. The compliant physicians were often assisted suicide advocates. Such was the case of Kate Cheney, age 85, as described in *The Oregonian* in October 1999. Her physician refused to prescribe lethal medication, because he thought the request, rather than being Ms. Cheney's free choice, actually resulted from pressure by her assertive daughter who felt burdened with care giving. So the family found another doctor, and Ms. Cheney soon used the prescribed drugs and died.

Another purported safeguard is that physicians are required to discuss alternatives to assisted suicide. However, there is no requirement that these alternatives be made available. Kate Cheney's case exemplifies this. Further, the Kate Cheney case demonstrates the shocking laxness with which safeguards in Oregon are being followed. Ms. Cheney decided to take the lethal medication after spending just a week in a nursing home, to give her family a break from caretaking. The chronology shows that Cheney felt she had only three choices: burdening her family, the hell of a nursing home, or death.

> *"Once society authorizes assisted suicide for . . . terminally ill patients . . . it will be difficult if not impossible to contain the option to such a limited group."*

After reading about the case of Kate Cheney, Diane Coleman of Not Dead Yet sent a letter via the Internet to Dr. Robert Richardson, a physician involved in Cheney's care. It stated, in part:

> In my role as a long term care advocate, I have heard for years of Oregon's claim to operate the most progressive long-term care programs in the country, model programs that emphasize in-home and community based services, even for the most frail elderly. What in-home services was Ms. Cheney receiving? How is it that Ms. Cheney had to spend a week in a nursing home to give her family respite from caregiving? Did Ms. Cheney and her family know of other respite options? If not, who failed to tell them? How can their actions have been based on the informed consent promised in Oregon's law? Or did the family choose the nursing home respite option with the knowledge of other alternatives (an even more disturbing possibility)? What ongoing support options were explored to reduce the daily need for family caregiving? There are many ways to resolve the feeling of being a burden on family, and the family's feelings of being burdened. In what way were these issues explored? In this context, family relationships are complex, and the emotional dynamics could not realistically be uncovered in a brief consultation.

> It appears from the newspaper account, as well as your response to Dr. Hamilton, that these issues were not meaningfully addressed Ms. Cheney appears to have been given the message that she had three choices—to be a burden on family, to go to a nursing home, or to die. After a week in a nursing home, an experience I wouldn't wish on my opponents except perhaps to educate them, it appears that Ms. Cheney felt she had only one option. How is this a voluntary and uncoerced decision based on informed consent?

Coleman never received an answer from Dr. Richardson.

There *is* one foolproof safeguard in current assisted suicide proposals and Oregon's law—but it is for HMOs and physicians: the "good faith" standard.

This "safeguard" provides that no person will be subject to any form of legal liability if they acted in "good faith." The claim of a "good faith" effort to meet the requirements of the law is virtually impossible to disprove. Moreover, this particular provision renders all other "safeguards" effectively unenforceable. Even more alarming, for all other medical procedures, practitioners are liable under a much stronger legal standard, that of negligence. Yet, even if negligent, practitioners of assisted suicide will not be found violating the law, as long as they practice in good faith.

Diane Coleman continues, ". . . is society really ready to ignore the risks, tolerate the abuse, marginalize or cover up the mistakes, and implicitly agree that some lives—many lives—are expendable, in order to enact a law that immunizes health care providers and other participants assisted suicide?"

"Narrow" Proposals Will Inevitably Expand

Proponents claim that assisted suicide will be narrowly limited to those who are terminally ill, but these so-called "narrow" proposals will inevitably be expanded. The New York State Task Force on Life and the Law wrote in 1997: "Once society authorizes assisted suicide for . . . terminally ill patients experiencing unrelievable suffering, it will be difficult if not impossible to contain the option to much a limited group. Individuals who are not (able to make the choice for themselves), who are not terminally ill, or who cannot self-administer lethal drugs will also seek the option of assisted suicide, and no principled basis will exist to deny (it)".

The longest experience we have with assisted suicide is in the Netherlands, where active euthanasia as well as assisted suicide are practiced. The Netherlands has become a frightening laboratory experiment because assisted suicide and euthanasia have meant that "pressure for improved palliative care appears to have evaporated," according to Herbert Hendin, M.D., in his Congressional testimony in 1996. Hendin was one of only three foreign observers given the opportunity to study these medical practices in the Netherlands in depth, to discuss specific cases with leading practitioners, and to interview Dutch government-sponsored euthanasia researchers. He documented how assisted suicide and euthanasia have become not the rare exception, but the rule for people with terminal illness in the Netherlands.

"Given the absence of any real choice, death by assisted suicide becomes not an act of personal autonomy, but an act of desperation."

"Over the past two decades," Hendin continued, "the Netherlands has moved from assisted suicide to euthanasia, from euthanasia for the terminally ill to euthanasia for the chronically ill, from euthanasia for physical illness to euthanasia for psychological distress and from voluntary euthanasia to nonvoluntary and involuntary euthanasia. Once the Dutch accepted assisted suicide it was not possible legally or morally to deny more active medical (assistance to die), i.e. euthanasia, to those who could not effect their own deaths. Nor could they deny assisted suicide or euthanasia to the chronically ill who have longer to suffer than the terminally ill or to those who have psychological pain not associated with physical disease. To do so would be a form of discrimination. Involuntary euthanasia has been justified as necessitated by the need to make decisions for patients not [medically] competent to choose for themselves". Hendin describes how, for a substantial number of people in the Netherlands physicians have ended their patients' lives without consultation with the patients.

U.S. advocates of legalization, attempting to distinguish the Oregon experience from that in the Netherlands, argue that the numbers of reported users of assisted suicide in Oregon are low. But in fact the number of people requesting lethal drugs has grown. In the beginning, the numbers were low in the Netherlands as well, but usage grew along with social acceptance of the practice. There is no reason to believe that legalization in the U.S. would not be followed, in twenty years or more, with the kind of extraordinary growth that has taken place in the Netherlands.

Furthermore, assisted suicide proponents and medical personnel alike have established that taking lethal drugs by mouth is often ineffective in fulfilling its intended purpose. The body expels the drugs through vomiting, or the person falls into a lengthy state of unconsciousness rather than dying promptly, as assisted suicide advocates wish. Such ineffective suicide attempts happen in a substantial percentage of cases. Estimates range from 15% to 25%. The way to prevent these "problems," in the view of euthanasia advocates, is by legalizing injections by physicians—that is, legalizing active euthanasia. This is an inevitable next step if society first accepts assisted suicide as a legitimate option.

Assisted suicide proponents tell us that none of these things will happen here. But why not? How can the proponents, or anyone, stop it? If the next step is wrong, then taking this step is tantamount to taking the next step.

Claims of Free Choice Are Illusory

Assisted suicide purports to be about free choice and self-determination. But there is significant danger that many people would take this "escape" due to external pressure. For example, elderly individuals who don't want to be a financial or caretaking burden on their families might choose assisted death. In Oregon's third year Report, "a startling 63% of [reported cases] cited fear of being a 'burden on family, friends or caregivers' as a reason for their suicide".

Also very troubling, research has documented widespread elder abuse in this country. The perpetrators are often family members. Such abuse could easily lead to pressures on elders to "choose" assisted suicide.

In addition, leaders and researchers in the African-American and Latino communities have expressed their fears that pressures to choose death would be applied disproportionately to their communities.

Still others would undergo assisted suicide because they lack good health care, or in-home support, and are terrified about going to a nursing home. As Diane Coleman noted regarding Oregon's law, "Nor is there any requirement that sufficient home and community-based long-term care services be provided to relieve the demands on family members and ease the individual's feelings of being a 'burden' . . . The inadequacy of the in-home long-term care system is central to the assisted suicide and euthanasia debate".

While the proponents of legalization argue that it would guarantee choice, assisted suicide would actually result in deaths due to a *lack* of choice. Real choice would require adequate home and community-based long-term care; universal health insurance; housing that is available, accessible, and affordable; and other social supports. In a perverse twist, widespread acceptance of assisted suicide is likely to *reduce* pressure on society to provide these very kinds of support services, thus reducing genuine options even further, just as Herbert Hendin observed that widespread use of euthanasia in the Netherlands has substantially decreased pressure there for improved palliative care, by decreasing demand for it.

As [San Francisco State University professor of history] Paul Longmore has stated, "Given the absence of any real choice, death by assisted suicide becomes not an act of personal autonomy, but an act of desperation. It is fictional freedom; it is phony autonomy".

Legalizing Assisted Suicide Would Lead to Involuntary Killing

by Oregon Right to Life

About the author: Oregon Right to Life (ORTL) is the state's oldest and largest politically active pro-life organization.

On November 8, 1994, Oregon became the first government in the world to legalize physician-assisted suicide. The law was ruled unconstitutional due to unequal protection under the law. "What are the boundary lines, if any, to state-sanctioned suicide?" the federal judge asked (*Lee v. Oregon*). "Where in the Constitution do we find distinctions between the terminally ill with six months to live, the terminally ill with one year to live, paraplegics, the disabled, or any category of people who have their own reasons for not wanting to continue living?" In 1997 the Ninth Circuit Court overturned the decision on the grounds that the plaintiffs did not have legal standing to bring the case to court. In November of 1997 a measure which would have repealed the law was rejected by Oregon voters. Oregon became the first jurisdiction in the world to begin experimenting with legalized assisted suicide.

It is important to distinguish between physician-assisted suicide and refusing medical treatment. Physician-assisted suicide involves a physician prescribing lethal drugs for a patient with the knowledge that the patient intends to use the drugs to commit suicide. Refusing medical treatment is turning down treatment expected to prolong life. What does this mean? Refusing a ventilator, or some other life sustaining machine or treatment is not assisted suicide and is already legal in all states. The intent of refusing medical treatment is not to end life, but to allow nature to take its course. With physician-assisted suicide the intent is to kill the patient. Euthanasia is the lethal injection of the patient by the doctor.

In the 1997 Supreme Court case, *Washington v. Glucksberg*, physician-assisted suicide was rejected as a constitutional right because "the right to autonomy clashes with the right to life in our constitutional system. . . . Death is the extinguishment of rights, not the triumph of one right over another." The U.S. Supreme Court upheld both the New York and Washington statutes prohibiting assisted suicide in all cases by a 9-0 vote. Physician-assisted suicide is not a right protected by our Constitution.

Opponents of assisted suicide are concerned about the many abuses that could occur if it is legalized. In addition to the many dangerous effects that opponents and judges feel it would have on society's attitudes towards suicide, they are concerned about:

"The main concern about physician-assisted suicide is the inability to create safeguards or contain assisted suicide to any boundaries."

• The power and pressures placed on physicians and how it will affect their role as healer.

• Protecting vulnerable groups including the poor, the elderly, and disabled persons from abuse, neglect and mistakes; "No matter how carefully any guidelines are framed, assisted suicide and euthanasia will be practiced through the prism of social inequality and bias that characterizes the delivery of services in all segments of all society, including health care".

• Health care cost containment; "The growing concern about health care cost increases the risks presented by legalizing assisted suicide and euthanasia".

The main concern about physician-assisted suicide is the inability to create safeguards or contain assisted suicide to any boundaries. In ruling Oregon's law unconstitutional the federal judge stated that if assisted suicide is legalized, it must be legal for everyone, "The attempt to restrict such rights to the terminally ill is illusory" *(Lee v. Oregon).*

Advocates of physician-assisted suicide claim that it is meant for patients in uncontrollable pain with only six months or less left to live. They claim the Oregon law is successful. However, in the years of Oregon's law, there has not been one documented case of assisted suicide being used for untreatable pain. Instead, patients are using assisted suicide for psychological and social concerns. Since legalizing assisted suicide, Oregonians have seen first-hand what really happens. *When physician-assisted suicide is legalized, safeguards don't work.*

Oregon's Safeguards Are Not Effective

In April 2001, the Netherlands legalized physician-assisted suicide and euthanasia. Legalized euthanasia operates under the pre-existing guidelines by which "unofficial" euthanasia and physician-assisted suicide had operated for many years. In the Netherlands:

• Euthanasia has expanded to infants, the depressed, and the chronically ill.

• Children as young as 12 with parental consent and those as young as 16 with parental notification can access euthanasia.

• The percentage of deaths from euthanasia has continued to increase.

• 80% of euthanasia deaths are not requested by the patient.

• Virtually every guideline set up by the Dutch . . ."has failed to protect patients or has been modified or violated" [according to Suzanne Daley].

The first known case of physician-assisted suicide was a woman in her mid-80's who had been battling breast cancer for twenty years. Her long-time physician refused to prescribe a lethal dosage; a second physician diagnosed her as depressed and also refused the assisted suicide request. The woman then sought the help of assisted suicide advocates who found a physician willing to prescribe a lethal overdose. The doctor who wrote the lethal prescription knew her 2½ weeks. In a taped conversation with the woman before her suicide, she lamented she could no longer pick her flowers. She added, "I am looking forward to [suicide] because, being I was always active, I cannot possibly see myself living out two more months like this. . . . I will be relieved of all the stress I have". A depressed patient was Oregon's first known assisted suicide victim.

Matheny Case

Patrick Matheny was 43 years old and diagnosed with ALS (Lou Gehrig's disease). After obtaining the pills by Federal Express, he struggled with the decision of when to use them. By the time he decided to take the lethal drugs he was unable to adequately swallow and his brother-in-law admitted to "helping" him. It is illegal under Oregon's law for a patient to receive help in suicide. A legal opinion from the Oregon Department of Justice was requested. The Deputy Attorney General answered that it would "seem logical to conclude that persons who are unable to selfmedicate" are discriminated against. If the law is judged to be discriminatory, it will open the door to legalized euthanasia. A patient hardly able to swallow has pushed the boundary lines of assisted suicide to lethal injection by doctors.

> *"Assisted suicide is paid for by tax dollars; adequate pain management, adequate living assistance for the disabled and some life-sustaining treatments are not covered."*

Cheney Case

Kate Cheney was an elderly woman diagnosed with an inoperable tumor. When she requested assisted suicide, her daughter felt her first doctor was "dismissive" of the request and sought another doctor. Kate's second doctor ordered a psychiatric evaluation. The psychiatrist found that the patient did "not seem to be explicitly pushing for [assisted suicide]," had difficulty with short-term memory and lacked the "very high level of capacity required to weigh options about assisted suicide". He refused the suicide request, saying Kate's apparent dementia, combined with pressure from her daughter, made him wonder whose agenda the lethal drug request really was. Kate seemed to accept the refusal, but her daughter became angry. A second opinion from a psychologist resulted in an approval, although she also noted Kate's memory problems and that Kate's "choices may be influenced by her family's wishes, and her daughter . . . may be somewhat coercive." Cheney did not take the prescription right away. It was not until she spent a week at a nursing home that she finally took the lethal prescription. A patient suffering beginning stages of dementia and under pressure from her family was a known assisted suicide victim.

In February 1998, the Oregon State Health Commission added assisted suicide to its list of services to be provided under the Oregon Health Plan. Assisted suicide, listed under "comfort care," was now to be paid for by tax dollars for those of low income. The state has created financial pressures favoring suicide over good care. Assisted suicide is paid for by tax dollars; adequate pain management, adequate living assistance for the disabled and some life-sustaining treatments are not covered.

Depression Predicts a Request for Death

The Oregon Health Division issues a yearly summary of assisted suicide using information derived from prescribing doctors. No supporting documentation or independent evaluation is provided to determine the assisted suicide was performed in accordance with the law. All information is forbidden to inspection.

The Health Division acknowledged that it had no way to "detect doctors who fail to report assisted deaths or commit other violations of the law".

National studies show that among patients requesting assisted suicide, depression is the only factor that significantly predicts the request for death. Sixty-seven percent of suicides are because of psychiatric depression. By Oregon's fifth year, only 13% of suicide victims received psychiatric counseling.

Social isolation and concerns about loss of autonomy and control over bodily function were the causes of assisted suicide. Did patients receive adequate information on alternative palliative care? Were concerns about loss of autonomy and other fears adequately addressed? Was the assisted suicide truly the patient's "last resort"?

Oregon's safeguards are illusory. Assisted suicide has spread beyond the type of people it supposedly was reserved for. A shroud of secrecy encompasses the reporting process of assisted suicide. However, publicized assisted suicide cases have proven:
• "Doctor shopping" interferes with long-time physician/patient relationships
• Familial pressure may promote suicide
• Assisted suicide will expand to euthanasia
• Patients suffering from depression and dementia are receiving physician-assisted suicide.

Once assisted suicide is legalized, it becomes impossible to contain. Once assisted suicide is legalized, it becomes impossible to protect the vulnerable and mentally ill. Once assisted suicide is legalized, it becomes, essentially, death on demand.

Assisted Suicide Would Be Mandated for Economic Reasons

by Wesley J. Smith

About the author: *Wesley J. Smith is an attorney, writer, and pro-life advocate. He is a consultant for the International Task Force on Euthanasia and Assisted Suicide and the author of* Culture of Death: The Assault on Medical Ethics in America.

When liberals ask me why they should oppose physician-assisted suicide (PAS), I always reply, "I can summarize a big reason in just three letters: HMO [Health Maintenance Organization]."

That always raises an eyebrow. Liberals hate HMOs.

Then I ask, "Do you know how much it costs for the drugs used in an assisted suicide?" They usually shake their heads, no. Answering my own question, I say, "About forty bucks," adding, "Since HMOs make money by cutting costs, and it could cost $40,000 (or more) to provide suicidal patients with proper care so that they don't want assisted suicide, the economic force of gravity is obvious." More often than not, my liberal interlocutor will say, "Gee, I never thought about that before," and agree that the HMO factor is a very serious problem confronting the assisted-suicide movement.

Most people haven't yet made the money connection between assisted suicide and the increasing strains on health-care budgets. That may be because reporters, who are usually eager to expose potential financial conflicts of interest in other public-policy issues, tend to be blind to the economic stakes involved in the assisted-suicide controversy. They prefer to see it as a matter of "choice," • or of "compassion," or of modernism-versus-religion. Yet, the realization that assisted suicide will, in the end, be largely about money, is becoming increasingly difficult to ignore.

Take Oregon, where assisted suicide is legal. While the assisted-suicide law does not compel any doctor or HMO to participate in the self-destruction of patients, only Catholic HMOs have said no. Indeed, Kaiser/Permanente Northwest's doctors are known to have written lethal prescriptions under the Oregon law.

But now, Kaiser isn't merely permitting doctors to assist in patient suicides, it is actively soliciting its doctors to participate in the deadly practice. As revealed by the anti-assisted-suicide medical group Physicians for Compassionate Care, a Kaiser executive recently e-mailed a memo to more than 800 Kaiser doctors soliciting PAS-doctor volunteers.

Doctors Are Recruited for PAS

The memo reveals that to the apparent chagrin of Kaiser, to their credit, few plan doctors are willing to participate in the killing of their own patients. Hence, the executive urges any Kaiser doctor willing to "act as Attending Physician under the [assisted suicide] law for YOUR patients" and doctors "willing to act as "Attending Physician under the law for members who ARE NOT your patients" to contact "Marcia L. Liberson or Robert H. Richardson, MD, KPNW Ethics Services." (Emphasis in the memo.)

> *"The realization that assisted suicide will, in the end, be largely about money, is becoming increasingly difficult to ignore."*

Since "attending physicians" write the lethal prescriptions under the Oregon law, Kaiser is apparently willing to permit its doctors to write lethal prescriptions for patients they have not treated.

For opponents of assisted suicide who are closely following events in Oregon, Robert Richardson is already notorious as the HMO administrator who greenlighted the assisted suicide of Kate Cheney. Cheney, as reported by the *Oregonian*, was a terminal cancer patient who was probably suffering from dementia when she asked for a lethal prescription, raising serious and significant questions about her mental competence. Rather than prescribe lethal drugs, her doctor referred her to a psychiatrist who reported that "she does not seem to be explicitly pushing for this." He also determined that she did not have the "very high capacity required to weigh options about assisted suicide." Accordingly, the psychiatrist nixed the lethal prescription.

Advocates of legalized assisted suicide might, at this point, smile happily and say that this is the way the law is supposed to operate: a vulnerable and perhaps incompetent woman's life had been protected.

But proving that "protective guidelines" don't really protect, that wasn't the end of Cheney's story. Her daughter insisted that Kaiser permit another psychiatric opinion. Kaiser agreed to the request.

This time, the consultation was a clinical psychologist rather than an M.D.

psychiatrist. Like the first report, the psychologist found that Cheney had significant memory problems. For example, she could not recall when she had been diagnosed with terminal cancer. The psychologist also worried that Cheney's decision to die "may be influenced by her family's wishes." Still, despite these reservations, the psychologist determined that Cheney was competent to commit suicide.

The Suicide Was Approved

The final decision to approve the assisted suicide was made by Richardson. Despite two mental-health professionals' significant concerns about Cheney's mental state and the potential that familial pressure was involved in her decision, after he interviewed Cheney, Richardson approved the writing of a lethal prescription.

It is worth noting that Cheney did not take the poison pills right away. Her assisted suicide took place only after she was sent to a nursing home for a week. Tellingly, she took the pills on the very day of her return home. No doctor was present. Nor was her mental status assessed at that time. That is because under the Oregon law, once the prescription is written, death doctors need have no more to do with the suicidal patient.

When the Cheney case became public, Richardson angrily claimed that his decision had nothing to do with money. And, to be fair, there is no doubt that if the relatively few people reported as committing assisted suicide so far in Oregon is correct, Kaiser and other participating HMOs have not yet saved a great deal of money by agreeing to facilitate the assisted suicides of their terminally ill members. But if the reluctance of good doctors such as those currently refusing to participate in patient self-killing at Kaiser is ever overcome, the financial facts could change. Indeed, if assisted suicide ever became nationalized and a routine "medical treatment," significant money could be saved—and hence made—by the HMO industry from the hastened deaths of their patients.

This is the view of none other than assisted-suicide guru, Derek Humphry, cofounder of the Hemlock Society and a heavy lifter in support of the Oregon law. Humphry now claims that money is the "unspoken argument" in favor of legalizing assisted suicide. Specifically, in his most recent book *Freedom to Die*, co-authored with Mary Clement, the authors write that "the hastened demise of people with only a short time left would free resources for others," an amount they predict could run into the "hundreds of billions of dollars." Moreover, the authors claim that "economic necessity" is the ultimate force driving the assisted-suicide movement, to the point that it "is the main answer to the question [about legalizing PAS], 'Why Now?'"

> *"If assisted suicide ever became nationalized and a routine 'medical treatment,' significant money could be saved . . . by the HMO industry."*

Logic is certainly on their side. With the advent of managed care, profits in health care increasingly come from cutting costs. With assisted suicides costing such little money, what "treatment" could be more cost effective than assisted suicide? And since it is a well-known human failing that our values often follow our pocketbooks, ignoring the significant financial stakes involved in the assisted-suicide debate is to overlook a crucial part of the story.

Legalized Assisted Suicide Would Damage the Physician-Patient Relationship

by Physicians for Compassionate Care

About the author: *Physicians for Compassionate Care is an anti-assisted-suicide association of physicians and other health professionals.*

Experience with physician-assisted suicide in the state of Oregon has revealed that it occurs in a complex medical, social, and economic system, making the individual patient vulnerable to adverse influence. There is evidence that family members and others sometimes pressure the patient to commit assisted suicide. It has unfairly discriminated against vulnerable individuals and has put seriously ill individuals contemplating suicide at dangerous and unequal risk of death by failing to provide equal protection of their lives. One vulnerable class of individuals, those labeled "terminally ill," have been devalued and are no longer afforded the same protection against assisted suicide which other Oregonians enjoy. This failure to assure equal protection has resulted in some of the depressed and mentally infirm who have been labeled terminally ill receiving assisted suicide instead of medical care. . . .

Damage to the Doctor-Patient Relationship

The U.S. Supreme Court in [*Washington v.*] *Glucksberg* recognized the legitimate public interest in protecting the doctor-patient relationship. It concluded that, "The State also has an interest in protecting the integrity and ethics of the medical profession."

The American Medical Association (AMA) along with other medical and physicians' groups have concluded, "Physician-assisted suicide is fundamen-

Physicians for Compassionate Care, "Physicians for Compassionate Care Friend of the Court Brief on *Oregon v. Ashcroft* et al.," www.pccef.org, November 8, 2001. Copyright © 2001 by the Physicians for Compassionate Care Educational Foundation. Reproduced by permission.

tally incompatible with the physician's role as healer, would be difficult or impossible to control, and would pose serious societal risks." The New York Task Force on Life and the Law agreed that lifting protections against doctor-assisted suicide would undermine trust essential to the doctor-patient relationship. Since that relationship is based on the assumption that the doctor values the life of each patient equally, the erosion of that relationship becomes inevitable, once some patients' lives are no longer considered equally valuable and equally deserving of protection as other people's lives.

This mistrust caused by allowing doctor-assisted suicide expands to the entire medical system, which doctors represent. In the Netherlands, for example, loss of trust has resulted in the finding "that 60 percent of older people were afraid that their lives could be ended against their will."

This erosion of trust has already become apparent in Oregon [where physician-assisted suicide (PAS) is legal]. For example, one Oregon Health Plan patient had to leave hospice care because of shifts he noticed in the attitudes of hospice personnel. He went to the hospital to have a procedure to relieve painful pressure from a closed space in his abdomen. He reported that he was shocked and hurt when his hospice nurse saw him and criticized him, "What are you doing here? You are a hospice patient." Regardless of the motivation for the nurse's queries, the feeling of trust between this patient and his nurse and the hospice system in general had been undermined by the legalization of doctor-assisted suicide. He no longer trusted the doctor-patient relationship or the nurse-patient relationship.

> *"This mistrust caused by allowing doctor-assisted suicide expands to the entire medical system, which doctors represent."*

Unfortunately, this feeling of mistrust may have been warranted. Five seriously ill patients in a Sheridan, Oregon, hospice were given excessive doses of morphine by a nurse, between November, 1997, and January, 1998, just after the Oregon assisted-suicide law was implemented, according to criminal investigators. The overdoses resulted in the deaths of four of the five patients. Some patients were determined by investigators to have refused pain medication and were given it nonetheless. Another was given repeated narcotic doses when he was unconscious or unresponsive. The one woman who survived had been placed on hospice, which meant that she had been determined to be "terminally ill" and to have less than six months to live by the nurse who eventually gave her a life threatening overdose. In fact, she failed to meet the criteria for "terminal illness" because two years later she was still alive.

Her experience with the attempts to kill her with a lethal overdose of federally controlled substances, however, undermined her trust in the medical care system to the extent that she insists on always sleeping with her door locked.

The erosion of trust in the doctor-patient relationship, and more broadly in the complex medical system in which people are actually treated, has already begun in the state of Oregon as it has in the Netherlands [where PAS is also legal], thereby harming public interest in protecting the integrity and ethics of the medical profession and of the medical system in which doctors practice. . . .

Doctor-Assisted Suicide Is Complex

Doctor-assisted suicide is not a private action, but takes place in a complex medical, social and economic setting. The social and institutional nature of doctor-assisted suicide subjects the discouraged or anxious patient to influence and coercion. It discriminates against a vulnerable class of individuals, those labeled "terminally ill," as well as the mentally ill and/or alcoholic who are put especially at increased risk.

Because assisted suicide is not a "private" and "autonomous" act, it endangers not only the individual contemplating assisted suicide, but also the general welfare of society and the public interests of the state. It is destructive to the doctor-patient relationship and leads to the creation of economic circumstances favoring assisted suicide over more expensive responses to serious illness. Because it cannot be adequately monitored, it is impossible to control and inevitably leads to the introduction of lethal injection for difficult cases.

Legalizing Assisted Suicide Would Help Physicians Reduce the Suffering of Terminally Ill Patients

by Peter Rogatz

About the author: *Peter Rogatz is a physician and founding member of Compassion in Dying of New York, a member of the Ethics Committee of Hospice Care Network, and a member of the Committee on Bioethical Issues of the Medical Society of the State of New York.*

Physician-assisted suicide is among the most hotly debated bioethical issues of our time. Every reasonable person prefers that no patient ever contemplate suicide (with or without assistance) and recent improvements in pain management have begun to reduce the number of patients seeking such assistance. However, there are some patients who experience terrible suffering that can't be relieved by any of the therapeutic or palliative techniques medicine and nursing have to offer, and some of those patients desperately seek deliverance.

Physician-assisted suicide isn't about physicians becoming killers. It's about patients whose suffering we can't relieve, and about not turning away from them when they ask for help. Will there be physicians who feel they can't do this? Of course, and they shouldn't be obliged to. But if other physicians consider it merciful to help such patients by merely writing a prescription, it is unreasonable to place them in jeopardy of criminal prosecution, loss of license, or other penalty for doing so.

Many arguments are put forward for maintaining the prohibition against physician-assisted suicide, but I believe they are outweighed by two fundamental principles that support ending the prohibition: patient autonomy (the right to control one's own body) and the physician's duty to relieve suffering.

Society recognizes the competent patient's right to autonomy (to decide what will or won't be done to his or her body). There is almost universal agreement that a competent adult has the right to self-determination, including the right to have life-sustaining treatment withheld or withdrawn. Suicide, once illegal throughout the United States, is no longer illegal in any part of the country. Yet assisting a person to take her or his own life is prohibited in every state but Oregon. If patients seek such help, it is cruel to leave them to fend for themselves, weighing options that are both traumatic and uncertain, when humane assistance could be made available.

Physician's Obligation Is to Relieve Suffering

The physician's obligations are many but, when cure is impossible and palliation has failed to achieve its objectives, there is always a residual obligation to relieve suffering. Ultimately, if the physician has exhausted all reasonable palliative measures, it is the patient—and only the patient—who can judge whether death is harmful or a good to be sought. Marcia Angell, former executive editor of the *New England Journal of Medicine*, has put it this way:

> The highest ethical imperative of doctors should be to provide care in whatever way best serves patients' interests, in accord with each patient's wishes, not with a theoretical commitment to preserve life no matter what the cost in suffering. . . . The greatest harm we can do is to consign a desperate patient to unbearable Suffering—or force the patient to seek out a stranger like Dr. [Jack] Kevorkian [a Michigan physician who assisted in suicides].

Let's examine the key arguments made against physician-assisted suicide. First, much weight is placed on the Hippocratic injunction to do no harm. It has been asserted that sanctioning physician-assisted suicide "would give doctors a license to kill," and physicians who accede to such requests have been branded by some as murderers. This is both illogical and inflammatory. Withdrawal of life-sustaining treatment—for example, disconnecting a ventilator at a patient's request—is accepted by society, yet this requires a more definitive act by a physician than prescribing a medication that a patient has requested and is free to take or not, as he or she sees fit. Why should the latter be perceived as doing harm when the former is not? Rather than characterizing this as "killing," we should see it as bringing the dying process to a merciful end. The physician who complies with a plea for final release from a patient facing death under unbearable conditions is doing good, not harm, and her or his

> *"The physician who complies with a plea for final release from a patient facing death under unbearable conditions is doing good, not harm."*

actions are entirely consonant with the Hippocratic tradition.

Second, it is argued that requests for assisted suicide come largely from patients who haven't received adequate pain control or who are clinically depressed and haven't been properly diagnosed or treated. There is no question that proper management of such conditions would significantly reduce the number of patients who consider suicide; any sanctioning of assistance should be contingent upon prior management of pain and depression.

Loss of Dignity

However, treatable pain is not the only reason, or even the most common reason, why patients seek to end their lives. Severe body wasting, intractable vomiting, urinary and bowel incontinence, immobility, and total dependence are recognized as more important than pain in the desire for hastened death. There is a growing awareness that loss of dignity and of those attributes that we associate particularly with being human are the factors that most commonly reduce patients to a state of unrelieved misery and desperation.

Third, it is argued that permitting physician-assisted suicide would undermine the sense of trust that patients have in their doctors. This is curious reasoning; patients are not lying in bed wondering if their physicians are going to kill them, and permitting assisted suicide shouldn't create such fears, since the act of administering a fatal dose would be solely within the control of the patient. Rather than undermining a patient's trust, I would expect the legalization of physician-assisted suicide to enhance that trust. I have spoken with a great many people who feel that they would like to be able to trust their physicians to provide such help in the event of unrelieved suffering, and making that possible

"The slippery slope argument discounts the real harm of failing to respond to the pleas of real people and considers ... the ... harm that might be done ... at some future time."

would give such patients a greater sense of security. Furthermore, some patients have taken their own lives at a relatively early stage of terminal illness precisely because they feared that progressively increasing disability, without anyone to assist them, would rob them of this option at a later time when they were truly desperate. A patient contemplating suicide would be much less likely to take such a step if he or she were confident of receiving assistance in the future if so desired.

Fourth, it is argued that patients don't need assistance to commit suicide; they can manage it all by themselves. This seems both callous and unrealistic. Are patients to shoot themselves, jump from a window, starve themselves to death, or rig a pipe to the car exhaust? All of these methods have been used by patients in the final stages of desperation, but it is a hideous experience for both patient and survivors. Even patients who can't contemplate such traumatic acts and instead manage to hoard a supply of lethal drugs may be too weak to complete the process without help and therefore face a high risk of failure, with dreadful consequences for themselves and their families.

Suicide Requests Are Not Rare

Fifth, it is argued that requests for assisted suicide are not frequent enough to warrant changing the law. Interestingly, some physicians say they have rarely, if ever, received such requests, while others say they have often received requests. This is a curious discrepancy, but I think it can be explained: the patient who seeks help with suicide will cautiously test a physician's receptivity to the idea and simply won't approach a physician who is unreceptive. Thus, there are two subsets of physicians in this situation: those who are open to the idea of assisted suicide and those who aren't. Patients are likely to seek help from the former but not from the latter.

A study carried out . . . by the University of Washington School of Medicine queried 828 physicians (a 25 percent sample of primary care physicians and all physicians in selected medical subspecialties) with a response rate of 57 percent. Of these respondents, 12 percent reported receiving one or more explicit requests for assisted suicide, and one-fourth of the patients requesting such assistance received prescriptions.

> *"I believe that removing the prohibition against physician assistance . . . is likely to reduce the incentive for suicide."*

A survey of physicians in San Francisco treating AIDS patients brought responses from half, and 53 percent of those respondents reported helping patients take their own lives by prescribing lethal doses of narcotics. Clearly, requests for assisted suicide can't be dismissed as rare occurrences.

Sixth, it is argued that sanctioning assisted suicide would fail to address the needs of patients who are incompetent. This is obviously true, since proposals for legalization specify that assistance be given only to a patient who is competent and who requests it. However, in essence, this argument says that, because we can't establish a procedure that will deal with every patient, we won't make assisted suicide available to any patient. What logic! Imagine the outcry if that logic were applied to a procedure such as organ transplantation, which has benefited so many people in this country.

Seventh, it is argued that once we open the door to physician-assisted suicide we will find ourselves on a slippery slope leading to coercion and involuntary euthanasia of vulnerable patients. Why so? We have learned to grapple with many slippery slopes in medicine (such as Do Not Resuscitate (DNR) orders) and the withdrawal of life support. We don't deal with those slippery slopes by prohibition but, rather, by adopting reasonable ground rules and setting appropriate limits.

The slippery slope argument discounts the real harm of failing to respond to the pleas of real people and considers only the potential harm that might be done to others at some future time and place. As in the case of other slippery slopes, theoretical future harm can be mitigated by establishing appropriate criteria that would have to be met before a patient could receive assistance. Such criteria have been outlined frequently. Stated briefly, they include:

1. The patient must have an incurable condition causing severe, unrelenting suffering.

2. The patient must understand his or her condition and prognosis, which must be verified by an independent second opinion.

3. All reasonable palliative measures must have been presented to and considered by the patient.

4. The patient must clearly and repeatedly request assistance in dying.

5. A psychiatric consultation must be held to establish if the patient is suffering from a treatable depression.

6. The prescribing physician, absent a close preexisting relationship (which would be ideal), must get to know the patient well enough to understand the reasons for her or his request.

7. No physician should be expected to violate his or her own basic values. A physician who is unwilling to assist the patient should facilitate transfer to another physician who would be prepared to do so.

8. All of the foregoing must be clearly documented.

Application of the above criteria would substantially reduce the risk of abuse but couldn't guarantee that abuse would never occur. We must recognize, however, that abuses occur today (in part because we tolerate covert action that is subject to no safeguards at all). A more open process would, in the words of philosopher and ethicist Margaret Battin, "prod us to develop much stronger protections for the kinds of choices about death we already make in what are often quite casual, cavalier ways."

Protecting the Vulnerable

It seems improbable that assisted suicide would pose a special danger to the elderly, infirm, and disabled. To paraphrase John Maynard Keynes, in the long run we are all elderly, infirm, or disabled and, since society well knows this, serious attention would surely be given to adequate protections against abuse.

> *"Those physicians who wish to fulfill what they perceive to be their humane responsibilities to their patients shouldn't be forced by . . . prohibition into covert action."*

It isn't my intention to dispose glibly of the fear that society would view vulnerable patients as a liability and would manipulate them to end their lives prematurely. Of course, this concern must be respected, but the risk can be minimized by applying the criteria listed above. Furthermore, this argument assumes that termination of life is invariably an evil against which we must protect vulnerable patients who are poor or otherwise lacking in societal support. But, by definition, we are

137

speaking of patients who desperately wish final release from unrelieved suffering, and poor and vulnerable patients are least able to secure aid in dying if they want it. The well-to-do patient may, with some effort and some good luck, find a physician who is willing to provide covert help; the poor and disenfranchised rarely have access to such assistance in today's world.

Eighth, it is argued that the Netherlands experience proves that societal tolerance of physician-assisted suicide leads to serious abuse. Aside from the fact that the data are subject to varying interpretation depending upon which analysis one believes, the situation in the Netherlands holds few lessons for us, because for many years that country followed the am-

> *"All physicians are bound by the injunction to do no harm, but we must recognize that harm may result . . . from the omission of an act of mercy."*

biguous practice of technically prohibiting but tacitly permitting assisted suicide and euthanasia.

The climate in the United States is different; our regulatory mechanisms would be different (much stricter, of course) and we should expect different outcomes. The experience of Oregon (the only one of our fifty states to permit physician-assisted suicide) is instructive. During the first three years that Oregon's law has been in effect, seventy terminally ill patients took advantage of the opportunity to self-administer medication to end protracted dying. Despite dire warnings, there was no precipitous rush by Oregonians to embrace assisted suicide. The poor and the uninsured weren't victimized; almost all of these seventy patients had health insurance, most were on hospice care, and most were people with at least some college education. There were no untoward complications. The Oregon experience is far more relevant for the United States than the Dutch experience, and it vindicates those who, despite extremely vocal opposition, advocated for the legislation.

Ninth, it has been argued that a society that doesn't assure all its citizens the right to basic health care and protect them against catastrophic health costs has no business considering physician-assisted suicide. I find this an astonishing argument. It says to every patient who seeks ultimate relief from severe suffering that his or her case won't be considered until all of us are assured basic health care and financial protection. These are certainly proper goals for any decent society, but they won't be attained in the United States until it becomes a more generous and responsible nation—and that day seems to be far off. Patients seeking deliverance from unrelieved suffering shouldn't be held hostage pending hoped-for future developments that are not even visible on the distant horizon.

An Act of Mercy Should Not Be a Crime

Finally, it is argued that the status quo is acceptable, that a patient who is determined to end his or her life can find a sympathetic physician who will provide the necessary prescription and that physicians are virtually never prosecuted for such acts. There are at least four reasons to reject the status quo. First, it forces patients and physicians to undertake a clandestine conspiracy to violate the law, thus compromising the integrity of patient, physician, and family. Second, such secret compacts, by their very nature, are subject to faulty implementation with a high risk of failure and consequent tragedy for both patient and family. Third, the assumption that a determined patient can find a sympathetic physician applies, at best, to middle- and upper-income persons who have ongoing relationships with their physicians; the poor, as I've already noted, rarely have such an opportunity. Fourth, covert action places a physician in danger of criminal prosecution or loss of license and, although such penalties are assumed to be unlikely, that risk certainly inhibits some physicians from doing what they believe is proper to help their patients.

I believe that removing the prohibition against physician assistance, rather than opening the flood gates to ill-advised suicides, is likely to reduce the incentive for suicide: patients who fear great suffering in the final stages of illness would have the assurance that help would be available if needed and they would be more inclined to test their own abilities to withstand the trials that lie ahead.

Life is the most precious gift of all, and no sane person wants to part with it, but there are some circumstances where life has lost its value. A competent person who has thoughtfully considered his or her own situation and finds that unrelieved suffering outweighs the value of continued life shouldn't have to starve to death or find other drastic and violent solutions when more merciful means exist. Those physicians who wish to fulfill what they perceive to be their humane responsibilities to their patients shouldn't be forced by legislative prohibition into covert actions.

There is no risk-free solution to these very sensitive problems. However, I believe that reasonable protections can be put in place that will minimize the risk of abuse and that the humanitarian benefits of legalizing physician-assisted suicide outweigh that risk. All physicians are bound by the injunction to do no harm, but we must recognize that harm may result not only from the commission of a wrongful act but also from the omission of an act of mercy. While not every physician will feel comfortable offering help in these tragic situations, many believe it is right to do so and our society should not criminalize such humanitarian acts.

Legalized Physician-Assisted Suicide Has Improved the Care of Terminally Ill Patients

by Linda Ganzini

About the author: *Linda Ganzini is the director of geriatric psychiatry at the Portland, Oregon, VA Hospital, an associate professor at Oregon Health Sciences University, and a faculty scholar of the Open Society Institute's Project on Death in America.*

The Oregon Death with Dignity Act was passed by ballot measure in 1994, and enacted in October 1997. This measure legalized physician-assisted suicide by allowing a physician to prescribe a lethal dose of medication for a mentally competent, terminally ill patient for the purpose of self-administration. Experts predicted that legalized assisted suicide would divert attention and resources from efforts to improve care for dying patients. Several lines of evidence, however, support the contention that care for terminally ill patients in Oregon has improved since the passage of the Death with Dignity Act. For example, more than one third of Oregonians who die are enrolled in a hospice program and two thirds have completed an advance directive before death. Since legalization, death from physician-assisted suicide has been rare, but little is known about the broader effects of the Death with Dignity Act on clinical practice or the perspectives of Oregon physicians on care of the dying.

In 1999, we surveyed all Oregon physicians who were eligible to prescribe under the Death with Dignity Act. Based on responses of 144 physicians (5% of respondents) who had received a request for physician-assisted suicide, we published information on the characteristics and outcomes of requesting patients and the interventions made by physicians other than assisted suicide. These data indicated that 1 in 10 requests for a lethal prescription resulted in assisted suicide. Physicians reported that as a result of palliative interventions, some patients changed their minds about assisted suicide.

This article is based on information submitted by the Oregon physicians who responded to our survey. We report these physicians' attitudes toward the Death with Dignity Act and caring for dying patients, their efforts to improve their ability to care for dying patients, their attitudes, concerns, and sources of information about writing lethal prescriptions, and their discussions and experiences with patients regarding assisted suicide. We compare the characteristics of physicians who received requests for a lethal prescription with those who did not. . . .

> *"Care for terminally ill patients in Oregon has improved since the passage of the Death with Dignity Act."*

Of 4544 physicians on the list from the Oregon Board of Medical Examiners, 212 were in training, 343 were retired or not in practice, and 8 were deceased. Of the remaining 3981, 2641 (66%) returned a survey that was at least two-thirds complete. . . . Seventy-seven percent of responding physicians were men, 61% practiced internal medicine or family practice, and 22% practiced in a town with a population of less than 25,000. Physicians who returned their survey after the third request (with accompanying $25.00 incentive) were more likely to "neither support nor oppose" the Death with Dignity Act and less likely to "support" the act; and more likely to indicate they were "unwilling" to write a lethal prescription compared with respondents "willing" to write a lethal prescription. Otherwise, these 2 groups did not differ on specialty, population of practice, or number of terminally ill patients cared for in the previous year.

Doctors' Knowledge of Palliative Care Improved

In the previous year, 4 of 5 respondents had cared for at least 1 terminally ill patient, more than one third had cared for 6 or more terminally ill patients, and 8% had cared for 21 or more terminally ill patients. Thirty-five percent of physicians (74/213) who cared for 21 or more terminally ill patients per year practiced in the specialties of oncology, radiation oncology, pulmonology, or geriatrics. Twenty-seven percent of all respondents had referred 6 or more patients to hospice in the previous 12 months. Thirty percent of respondents reported that they had increased the number of patients they referred to hospice since 1994, while only 72 (3%) had made fewer hospice referrals. Thirty-three percent of responding physicians perceived that the availability of hospice for their patients had increased since 1994, while less than 1% claimed that hospice was less available.

A high proportion of physicians reported they had made efforts to improve their knowledge of palliative care since 1994. Among the 2094 physicians who cared for at least 1 terminally ill patient in the previous year, 76% reported that they had made efforts to improve their knowledge of the use of pain medications in the terminally ill "somewhat" or "a great deal," 69% reported that they sought to improve their recognition of psychiatric disorders, such as depression, and 79% reported that their confidence in the prescribing of pain medications had improved.

Physicians who had cared for 1 or more dying patients in the previous year were asked about their attitudes toward care of dying patients. In general, these physicians were confident in the care of dying patients, felt competent in communicating with dying patients, and reported that they rarely avoided dying patients. However, 38% reported they found caring for dying patients "not at all" or "only a little" emotionally satisfying, and 46% reported that this type of work was "not at all" or "only a little" intellectually satisfying.

Thirty percent of all physician respondents agreed with a statement that writing a lethal prescription for a patient under the Death with Dignity Act was immoral and/or unethical, 59% disagreed, and 11% neither disagreed nor agreed. A total of 1349 respondents (51%) supported the Death with Dignity Act, 83 (32%) opposed it, and 449 (17%) neither supported nor opposed the law. Four out of 5 claimed they had not changed their views on the law since it passed in 1994. For those who did change their view, almost twice as many reported that they had become more supportive (13%) than more opposed (7%). Fourteen percent of physicians reported that they had become more willing to prescribe a lethal medica-

> *"Many physicians . . . reported they had made efforts to improve their ability to care for terminally ill patients."*

tion since 1994, but 8% were less willing. Overall, one third of respondents were willing to write a lethal prescription under the law, 20% were uncertain, and 46% were unwilling. Fifty-three percent of respondents would consider obtaining a physician's assistance to end their own lives if terminally ill, including 88% of those who were willing to prescribe a lethal medication for a patient.

The Doctor's Position Is Important

Ninety-one percent of respondents were "somewhat" or "a great deal" comfortable discussing their opinion of the Death with Dignity Act with a patient who would ask. Only 18% of physicians agreed with the statement that "since the Death with Dignity Act was enacted, some patients expect me to be available to provide a lethal prescription." One or more patients had asked 949 respondents (36%) if they would potentially be willing to prescribe a lethal medication, including 54% of physicians (513/952) who had cared for 6 or more terminally ill patients in the previous year.

Overall, 21% of physicians reported that at least 1 patient was more positive or comfortable about the physician's care after knowing the physician's position on the Death with Dignity Act. Twenty-eight percent of physicians who were opposed to the law reported that at least 1 patient in their care was more positive knowing the physician's position on the Death with Dignity Act, compared with 21% of physicians who supported the law and 10% who neither supported nor opposed the law. . . .

Death with Dignity Act vs. Federal Drug Laws

Among the 1841 physicians who were not morally opposed to writing a lethal prescription, 58% were at least "a little" concerned about being labeled a "Kevorkian"[1] if they wrote a lethal prescription, 82% were concerned that writing a lethal prescription might violate federal Drug Enforcement [Administration] law, and 65% were concerned that their hospital might sanction them. The Death with Dignity Act allows hospital systems to forbid writing prescriptions under the act on their premises or by physicians they directly employ. Eighteen percent of respondents practiced in a hospital system that has a policy forbidding prescription of lethal medications in accordance with the Death with Dignity Act.

Among the 886 physicians who were willing to prescribe, 23% had received information from a guidebook produced by the Oregon Health Sciences University Center on Ethics in Health Care entitled *The Oregon Death with Dignity Act: A Guidebook for Health Care Providers*, 21% had received information on the Death with Dignity Act from other physicians, 11% had received information from the Oregon Medical Association, 9% from a group that advocates for persons who elect assisted suicide, and 8% from experts or resource persons in their health care system. Fifty-five percent of all physicians who were willing to prescribe, including 15% (11/73) of willing physicians who had actually received a request, had not sought information about the law from any source. Twenty-seven percent of all willing physicians, including 16% (12/73) of willing physicians who had received a request, were "not at all" or "only a little" confident about finding reliable information about what to prescribe for a lethal medication. Thirty-eight percent of willing physicians, including 27% (20/73) of willing physicians who had received a request, were "not at all" or "only a little" confident about their ability to determine when a patient has less than 6 months to live.

The Dying Need Better Care

The passage of the Death with Dignity Act divided Oregon's medical community; however, both proponents and opponents of this law did agree that it underscored the need to improve care of the dying in Oregon. Many physicians who responded to the survey reported they had made efforts to improve their ability to care for terminally ill patients, were more likely to refer these patients to hospice, and believed that hospice is more accessible since passage of the Death with Dignity Act. In 1994, 22% of all deaths in Oregon occurred in persons enrolled in hospice; by 1999, the proportion had increased to 35%. Despite the respondents' perception that hospice had become more available since

1. Dr. Jack Kevorkian is a Michigan physician who assisted in suicides.

1995, the geographic range and capacity of community hospice increased only minimally between 1995 and 1999. This suggests that physicians became more aware of already available services.

In 1999, assisted suicide was the cause of death in 9/10,000 of Oregon deaths and between 1997 and 1999, 5% of Oregon physicians received an explicit request for a prescription for a lethal medication. A much larger proportion of physicians discussed assisted suicide or the Death with Dignity Act with patients. Physicians perceived that more patients found these conversations helpful than upsetting, whether the physicians supported or opposed assisted suicide. In some cases, however, these conversations resulted in a rupture of the relationship, and these ruptures were more likely if the physician opposed assisted suicide. Oregon patients who feel strongly about the right to pursue assisted suicide may prefer to find a physician whose values match theirs early in the course of treatment to avoid having to do so at a later stage of illness. On the other hand, such disruptions may be unnecessary if the physician conveys empathy, respect, and understanding, and clarifies his/her willingness to refer the patient to another physician in a manner that does not communicate abandonment, should the desire for a lethal prescription persist despite palliative care.

> *"Palliative interventions were significantly associated with changes of mind about assisted suicide among dying patients in Oregon."*

In general, patient queries and concerns about assisted suicide as well as explicit requests for lethal medications were especially common for physicians who cared for many terminally ill patients. Each ordinal increase in the number of terminally ill patients cared for increased odds of receiving an explicit request for assistance in suicide between 2 and 7 times. Some commentators have expressed concern, and some studies have supported that requests for assisted suicide may occur in the context of poor care, including physicians' negative attitudes about care of the dying, or lack of physician knowledge about alternatives to assisted suicide. Although our data cannot address all of these concerns, we did find that Oregon physicians who received requests rated themselves more intellectually satisfied by care of dying patients and more likely to have attempted to improve their knowledge of prescribing pain medication for the terminally ill than Oregon physicians who did not receive requests.

Palliative Care Education Must Continue

Other survey findings, however, are of concern. Among physicians who were willing to prescribe and who had received a request for a lethal prescription, 1 in 7 had not obtained information about the Death with Dignity Act from any 1 of several credible sources, 1 in 6 were not confident about finding reliable lethal prescribing information, and 1 in 4 were not confident in determining 6-month life expectancy. Patients who make requests of these physicians may receive a lethal prescription without the comprehensive evaluation currently recommended. We previously demonstrated that palliative interventions were significantly associated with changes of mind about assisted suicide among dying patients in Oregon. These findings underscore that Oregon's extensive efforts at palliative care education must continue if patients are to obtain assisted suicide as only an option of last resort. It also reinforces the need for the second physician consultant (as required in the act) to have expertise in end-of-life care and the act.

There are several limitations in our study. We did not measure actual physician skill in pain and symptom control. One study of oncologists revealed that the physicians' self-assessment of their palliative care skills appeared to exceed their practice as assessed by treatment scenarios. Of concern, one study documents an increase in families' perceptions of pain among Oregon patients who died in acute care hospitals between 1997 and 1998. Respondents were slightly older and less likely to specialize in internal medicine than nonrespondents. Finally, it cannot be concluded that attempts by Oregon physicians to improve their ability to care for terminally ill patients is solely attributable to passage of the Death with Dignity Act. Nationally, there have been extensive efforts to improve physicians' competence in caring for dying patients. Whether the efforts of Oregon physicians differ from the efforts of physicians in other states is unknown, as no comparison is available. Our results are more important in countering concerns that legalized assisted suicide would undermine attempts to enhance care for the dying.

> *"Oregon physicians have made care of the dying a focus for their . . . professional education since 1994 and are more likely to refer patients to hospice."*

Assisted suicide is legal only in the Netherlands and Oregon. Studies from Oregon offer a rare opportunity to examine changes in end-of-life care in the context of legalized assisted suicide. Overall, our findings reinforce that Oregon physicians have made care of the dying a focus for their own professional education since 1994 and are more likely to refer patients to hospice. Many physicians who care for terminally ill patients have had conversations with patients about this issue. Rarely are these conversations upsetting for the patient. A large proportion of physicians, despite not being morally opposed to assisted suicide, have practical concerns about participating in the Death with Dignity Act and only a minority are willing to provide a lethal prescription to a qualified patient. Some physicians who are willing to assist in legalized suicide may lack knowledge necessary to evaluate patients' eligibility. On the other hand, requests are more likely to come to physicians who report that they care for many terminally ill patients, find their care intellectually satisfying, and have attempted to improve their knowledge of pain medications.

Assisted Suicide Will Not Lead to Involuntary Euthanasia

by Daniel E. Lee

About the author: *Daniel E. Lee teaches ethics at Augustana College in Rock Island, Illinois. He is the author of* Navigating Right and Wrong: Ethical Decision Making in a Pluralistic Age.

In the course of the years, my views with respect to the morality of physician-assisted suicide have not wavered one bit. I'm opposed to it. Strongly opposed to it. I agree with Karl Barth that "it is for God and God alone to make an end of human life" and that God gives life to us "as an inalienable loan." I believe that meaning and hope are possible in all of life's situations, even in the midst of suffering. I am very uncomfortable with the idea of physicians, who are trained to preserve life, dispensing lethal drugs to be used to end life.

In recent years, however, as Oregon has legalized physician-assisted suicide and other states have considered doing so, I have found myself wrestling with a very difficult question. Do those of us with deep moral reservations about the morality of physician-assisted suicide have any business using the coercive power of government to try to prevent those who disagree with us from doing what they believe is right? Are there any compelling arguments to justify placing legal roadblocks in the way of terminally ill individuals who wish to end their suffering by ending their lives, provided such decisions are made only after thoughtful, careful deliberation in an environment devoid of social pressure?

When what some might do poses a significant risk to the health and well being of others, a strong case can be made for intervention. But does a rationale based on protection of those who might be harmed work in the case of physician-assisted suicide? Protecting vulnerable individuals from threats posed by others is one matter. But what if the consequences of the act are born primarily by the perpetrator of the act?

Daniel E. Lee, "Physician-Assisted Suicide: A Conservative Critique of Intervention," *Hastings Center Report*, vol. 33, January 2003. Copyright © 2003 by The Hastings Center. Reproduced by permission.

Chapter 3

The Paternalism Argument

One of the most frequent arguments made by those opposed to legalization—an argument with strong overtones of paternalism—holds that we always ought to intervene to prevent self-destructive behavior. But do we have either the right or the wisdom to decide what is best for other people in situations in which they are perfectly capable of making their own decisions? In *On Liberty*, John Stuart Mill cautions, "A person should be free to do as he likes in his own concerns, but he ought not be free to do as he likes in acting for another, under the pretext that the affairs of the other are his own affairs."

A distinction is often made between hard (or strong) paternalism, which would permit intervening because of a belief that those doing the intervening know what is best for others, and soft (or weak) paternalism, which would permit intervening to secure an outcome consistent with the values held by those who are being coerced. Because of deficiencies in our decision making processes or failures of the will, we sometimes act in ways at odds with our own deeply held values and desires, or fail to do things mandated by these values. In such cases, coercive intervention can have the salutary effect of forcing us to do what in fact we really want to do.

In a thoughtful little book [*Social Philosophy*] published three decades ago, Joel Feinberg, commenting on John Stuart Mill's strong defense of individual liberty, observes, "Nevertheless, there are some actions that create a powerful presumption that an actor in his right mind would not choose them." The stronger the presumption, "the more elaborate and fastidious should be the legal paraphernalia required, and the stricter the standards of evidence," if that presumption is to be overridden. And what of suicide? Feinberg comments, "The desire to commit suicide must always be presumed to be both nonvoluntary and harmful to others until shown otherwise. (Of course, in some cases it can be shown otherwise.)"

There is a good deal of wisdom in Feinberg's approach. Suicide and attempted suicide often are acts of desperation by individuals who, as a result of mental illness or other distorting factors, are not in full command of their senses. In such cases, an ethic that values life and affirms the dignity of each person mandates intervention to prevent self-destruction.

But as Feinberg allows, it is also possible that in some cases suicide really is a freely chosen course of action by individuals in full command of their senses. In advocating "elaborate and fastidious" legal procedures

> *"Provisions of the Oregon law ... make it very clear to those contemplating ending their lives that they are under no pressure to do so."*

to assess situations such as these, he emphasizes that "the point of the procedure would not be to evaluate the wisdom or worthiness of a person's choice, but rather to determine whether the choice really is his."

Rigorous Standards Provide Protection

The Oregon Death with Dignity Act specifies an elaborate procedure consistent with the most rigorous standards of voluntariness. Requirements include two oral requests for lethal medication separated by at least fifteen days, a written request witnessed by two people followed by a fifteen-day waiting period, a determination that the patient is capable of making health care decisions, and the opportunity to rescind the request at any time. Before prescribing lethal medications, the prescribing physician must inform the terminally ill individual of alternatives to suicide and explicitly give the terminally ill individual an opportunity to rescind the request at the end of the fifteen-day waiting period.

Some fear that allowing physician-assisted suicide could result in social pressures compelling the aged and the infirm to exercise this option. In an article that appeared in *Christianity Today* shortly after Oregon legalized physician-assisted suicide, Peter J. Bernardi warned that "the right to die may become the duty to die." He argued, "Radical autonomy is a deadly deception. Proponents of mercy killing argue for the right of mentally competent, terminally ill adults to receive a physician's assistance to commit suicide. The reality is that such autonomous requests will be subtly or not so subtly influenced by others."

> *"Rigorous safeguards ... can prevent nonvoluntary euthanasia by ensuring that euthanasia occurs only at the request of the suffering individual."*

But is this necessarily the case? Various provisions of the Oregon law are intended to make it very clear to those contemplating ending their lives that they are under no pressure to do so. For example, the requirement that physicians, prior to prescribing lethal medications, must inform terminally ill individuals requesting such medications about hospice care and other alternatives is a way of saying, "Look, you don't have to do this. There are other options." And the requirement that there be multiple opportunities to rescind the request, including an explicitly stated opportunity at the end of the fifteen-day waiting period, is a way of saying, "Are you sure you really want to do this?" In short, if physician-assisted suicide is presented as an option that no one need exercise, it remains a matter of individual choice, rather than a decision forced or helped along by social pressure.

Also commonplace is the "slippery slope" argument, which warns that allowing voluntary physician-assisted suicide invites abuses, such as physicians taking it upon themselves to end the lives of terminally ill patients. Daniel Callahan has reported that in the Netherlands, where physician-assisted suicide has been practiced for a number of years, "there are a substantial number of cases of nonvoluntary euthanasia, that is, euthanasia undertaken without the explicit permission of the person being killed."

Like many others, I find nonvoluntary euthanasia morally reprehensible. But does physician-assisted suicide inevitably lead in this direction? Supporters of legalizing physician-assisted suicide frequently contend that rigorous safeguards, such as those incorporated in the Oregon law, can prevent nonvoluntary euthanasia by ensuring that euthanasia occurs only at the request of the suffering individual. Their arguments have considerable merit.

> *"If physicians . . . and others are prohibited from administering lethal drugs to terminally ill patients . . . nonvoluntary euthanasia is precluded."*

There is another firewall—one that is also built into the Oregon law—that might be even more significant. This is the requirement that lethal drugs be self-administered, rather than administered by the prescribing physician or anyone else. If physicians, family members, and others are prohibited from administering lethal drugs to terminally ill patients, and that restriction is rigorously enforced, nonvoluntary euthanasia is precluded.

The Dutch Experience

As for the Dutch experience, it should be noted that until the Dutch Parliament legalized physician-assisted suicide in April 2001, all forms of active euthanasia were technically illegal in the Netherlands, even though legal authorities often looked the other way when physicians prescribed lethal medications for terminally ill patients. A widespread practice that functions outside of the law is by its very nature difficult to regulate and inevitably invites abuse. In short, legalizing physician-assisted suicide and carefully regulating its practice might be a more effective way of preventing a slide down a slippery slope leading to nonvoluntary active euthanasia than continuing the legal prohibition on physician-assisted suicide.

Finally, it is significant that the Oregon experience to date in no way suggests that a slide down a slippery slope is imminent. The option allowed by Oregon's Death with Dignity Act has been used very sparingly. In 2001 (the most recent year for which statistics are available as this article goes to press), twenty-one Oregonians chose to end their lives by ingesting a lethal dose of medication prescribed by a physician, accounting for 0.33 percent of the 6,365 Oregon deaths from similar diseases. During 2000, the number was twenty-seven (0.38 percent) of the 6,964 deaths from similar diseases. The number of Oregonians opting for physician-assisted suicide has remained fairly stable, ranging from sixteen in 1998, the first year the law was in effect, to twenty-seven in both 1999 and 2000. Clearly, there is no landslide in the making.

When all things are considered, the arguments in favor of continued prohibition of physician-assisted suicide are not particularly compelling. This is not to suggest that those of us with deep moral reservations about physician-assisted suicide should swallow our scruples and spearhead legalization campaigns. But it does suggest that we should not stand in the way of thoughtful individuals such as Timothy Quill and Marcia Angell who favor legalization.

Those of us opposed to physician-assisted suicide would do well to focus our efforts on helping others discover the meaning and hope that are possible in life, even in the midst of suffering. We can accomplish far more by reaching out in a loving, caring manner to those experiencing great suffering, instead of sitting around moralizing about what they should or should not do and threatening physicians with legal penalties if they act in ways at odds with values we hold dear. If we were to do a better job of responding to suffering individuals in a loving, caring manner, physician-assisted suicide would in all likelihood be an option rarely, if ever, chosen.

Chapter 4

How Does the World View Assisted Suicide?

Chapter Preface

Debates about assisted suicide occur everywhere in the world. Even when the practice is legalized in a nation, arguments about it do not stop. Switzerland is an example of this fact. Laws in nations where assisted suicide is legal, such as the Netherlands and Belgium, typically require a physician's intense involvement in and often presence during assisted suicide. This requirement is regarded as a necessary safeguard to confirm the terminal nature of the patient's disease and ensure that the desire for suicide is not the result of temporary depression. The Swiss, however, take a different approach to the involvement of doctors in assisted suicide. Assisted suicide is well accepted in Switzerland and has been legal for over sixty years, but the practice is considered at odds with the physician's duty to heal and save lives. Doctors may, if they choose, be involved in an assisted suicide, but they are discouraged from doing so. According to the ethical recommendations of the Swiss Academy of Medical Sciences, assisted suicide is "not part of the physician's activity." The Swiss view— unique in the world—is that assisted suicide, while acceptable, should not be linked to or dependent on physicians.

According to Article 115 of the Swiss penal code, assisting in a suicide is not considered a crime if the assistor's motive is an unselfish one, such as bringing an end to unbearable pain or suffering. Thus, it is legal for anyone with altruistic motives to assist in a suicide. This fact of Swiss law combined with the disassociation of assisted suicide from the medical profession (including hospitals) has led to the rise of private right-to-die societies such as EXIT. EXIT claims over fifty thousand members who help Swiss citizens to die peacefully. The EXIT helper makes all the arrangements for the assisted suicide and may even hand the patient the lethal dose of barbiturate. Liberal laws that permit suicide assistance by lay people have protected the Swiss medical profession from the threats to its professional integrity. However, many argue that the lack of professional control over this lethal procedure invites abuse.

Andreas Frei, a doctor at Psychiatriezentrum Luzern, Switzerland, writes in *Swiss Medical Weekly*, "We feel the danger can not be ruled out that this lay-organisation [EXIT] . . . still offers a radical, oversimplified solution, not only for people suffering from serious medical problems but from difficult social conditions, as well." Critics also claim that so-called suicide tourists, ill foreigners who come to Switzerland to take advantage of its right-to-die societies, are an unintended consequence of liberal, lay-assisted suicide laws. Dorle Vallender, a member of the Swiss Parliament, proposed a bill that may be voted on in 2004 that would regulate right-to-die groups and make the rules that surround assisted suicide for foreigners more complex.

Dissuading medical personnel from becoming involved in assisted suicide makes Switzerland unique. Not rare is the vociferous debate over euthanasia found throughout the world. Authors in the following chapter explore how people in Canada, England, and the Netherlands view the risks and benefits of assisted suicide.

Worldwide Approval for Assisted Suicide Is Increasing

by Gerald A. Larue

About the author: *Gerald A. Larue is emeritus professor of religion and adjunct professor of gerontology at the University of Southern California. He is a Humanist Laureate serving on the Secretariat of the International Academy of Humanism.*

Longevity has become a global reality. The benefits of modern health research, the conquest of childhood diseases, improved sanitation, new medications, and technical procedures have raised the projected life span for newborns and contributed to dramatic increases in world population. Unfortunately, not all long-lived individuals die peacefully. Some die painful, torturous deaths. When life is without quality, when pain and discomfort rob life of its significance, some persons cry out for release through death—a good death through euthanasia. Euthanasia has become a complex global issue for the 21st century, with different cultures wrestling with the variety of ethical, religious and legal factors involved in helping someone to die legally. This essay touches on some of the humanistic ethical dimensions involved in efforts to legalize euthanasia.

It can be assumed that, given a choice, most human beings would choose a gentle or easy death devoid of pain or suffering and without loss of dignity, identity, autonomy, or the ability to reason. Unfortunately, most patients, including the elderly, do not enjoy the privilege of making such a choice. For some, dying involves a long, distressful process, characterized by misery, feelings of nausea or suffocation, with intubations, debilitation, and degeneration. Efforts to control pain with drugs are not always successful and the attempts often render the patient insensible and in danger of severe brain injury. "Euthanasia," which can be simply defined as "a good death" or perhaps "a beneficent death," has emerged as a global end-of-life issue that has special relevance for the elderly, although the term embraces all ages.

Dramatic increases in human longevity, made during the twentieth century, have transformed the expected life span at birth in developed countries from 47 years in 1900 to the late '70s today and in developing countries to just over 60 years of age today. It is anticipated that by the year 2020, the elderly will constitute about 25 percent of the world population. Obviously, the issue of death-with-dignity will become increasingly important.

The Medical Factor and Death with Dignity

As medical expertise and technology continue to spread throughout the world, moral, ethical, social, and legal health issues arise, each related, in one way or another, to the prolongation of life and to the ways in which many individuals, particularly the elderly, end their lives. Today, life can be sustained indefinitely by the use of machinery and intubations. In some cases, patients, who have suffered severe brain damage and have entered a persistent vegetative state in which they are cognitively unaware, are kept alive for years. Efforts to prolong life have produced instances where terminally ill patients suffer horrific deaths despite efforts to control pain. The question arises: how do individuals who are being kept alive achieve "a death with dignity?"

The Euthanasia Issue

Euthanasia has acquired a number of different labels. For example, euthanasia can be voluntary or involuntary, passive or active. Passive voluntary euthanasia occurs when, in accord with a terminally ill patient's expressed wish, life-supports are removed and the patient is permitted to die "naturally" or "as a consequence of the disease." Some patients die immediately; others linger on for hours or days finally dying from dehydration and starvation. Involuntary euthanasia—that is the bringing about of a person's death without the consent of the person—is almost always treated as homicide, even when the act can be recognized as producing a "merciful death."

Active voluntary euthanasia (often termed "aid-in-dying") refers to death caused, in response to the terminally ill patient's expressed will, through direct intervention by someone other than the patient. Death may be induced by the administration of lethal medications or by lethal injection.

There is debate as to whether there is really any difference between active and passive euthanasia. In the minds of some, the removal of life-supports, or passive euthanasia, is to be differentiated from active euthanasia, which is defined as "doing something to terminate life." On the other hand, for many ethicists, "passive euthanasia" has become a "weasel term" serving only to deny responsibility and perhaps to exonerate the medical staff and the doctor

> *"Euthanasia has become a complex global issue for the 21st century."*

from being accused of having "done" something to cause the patient's death.

Recently, the phrase "doctor-assisted-suicide" has been added to the euthanasia vocabulary. Acting in accord with the patient's wishes, a physician provides the terminally ill individual with lethal medication. The patient decides when to take the medication, so that the physician does not participate directly in the death. Of course, rational, but severely handicapped patients, such as those in the final stages of ALS (Amyotrophic Lateral Sclerosis), are automatically eliminated from this mode of dying because they are not able to take medication without assistance. In countries where suicide and assisted suicide are against the law, doctor-assisted-suicide would not be tolerated.

> *"Euthanasia . . . has emerged as a global end-of-life issue that has special relevance for the elderly, although the term embraces all ages."*

Recently, plastic-bag-death has received some publicity. Plastic-bag-death permits a terminally ill patient to commit suicide without incriminating others. The patient is supplied with sleeping pills, perhaps a glass of alcohol, such as vodka, to enhance the effectiveness of the sleeping potions, an airtight plastic bag large enough to fit comfortably over the head, a dust mask, and an elastic band. The provider leaves the premises. The patient, now alone, swallows the sleeping tablets, drinks the alcohol, dons the dust mask (to keep the plastic from adhering to the mouth and nose), pulls the plastic bag over the head and secures it with the elastic band around the neck. Any temporary breathing discomfort can be alleviated by extending the rubber band to permit air to enter. Ultimately, the patient falls asleep and dies quietly by asphyxiation.

Global Euthanasia Laws

In the global community, because euthanasia is often loosely defined, the determination of the ways in which different legal systems handle the subject becomes too complex to explicate simply. It is possible to state that, throughout the world, passive voluntary euthanasia for the terminally ill is not often treated as illegal. The abandonment of so-called "heroic measures" and the removal of life-sustaining equipment including feeding tubes is not equated with the abandonment of the patient. Rather, the recognition of the principle of futility and the acknowledgment that "the disease has won" refocuses treatment from efforts to cure to palliative care.

In those instances where the patient is not able to communicate wishes or where the patient has not provided advanced directives stipulating the conditions under which life-support is to be abandoned, medical staff and family are faced with a dilemma. The family may seek to exercise substituted judgment and, on the basis of statements the dying person made in the past, request the withdrawal of life support. In the absence of such statements, the medical staff and the family may seek to act in "the best interests" of the patient and seek to have life-support removed. Or, the patient may be placed in a hospice environment where efforts are made to control pain and to provide an easy death.

Active voluntary euthanasia and doctor-assisted-suicide are illegal in every country throughout the world except Colombia. In Holland, the Dutch government does not prosecute physicians who, in accord with a terminally ill patient's request, provide lethal medications or give lethal injections. However, Dutch physicians must follow an established protocol. Euthanasia was voted into law in Northwest Australia but the enactment of the law is being held up and debated in law courts. In the state of Oregon in the USA, strong efforts to overturn the will of the people who voted for Ballot Measure 16, which legalized doctor-assisted suicide, were made by the Roman Catholic Church and some fundamentalist Protestant groups. The millions of dollars that were poured into the anti-freedom-of-choice legislation caused the issue to be placed on the ballot a second time where it was approved by an overwhelming majority. At the time of writing, new efforts are being made to find legal loopholes to thwart the will of the people.

In Canada, aid-in-dying and physician-assisted suicide are against the law. Doctors who participate in helping patients to die face possible imprisonment of up to 14 years.

In 1962, a high court in Nagoya, Japan, declared euthanasia legal under special circumstances and specified that it should be performed by a medical doctor. A 1990 survey of members of the Japan Medical Society revealed that 87 percent of its members would honor a patient's desire "to die with dignity." However, any euthanasia performed without patient consent is against the law.

In Mexico, Italy, and South Africa, euthanasia is treated as murder. Although no cases have been reported in Mexico, in Italy, when physician aid-in-dying comes to light, the law usually interprets the act as a physician responding to extenuating situations and sentences are meted out accordingly. In 1975, in South Africa, a medical doctor who gave his cancer-stricken father an overdose of Pentothal, received a suspended sentence and had his medical license suspended for two years.

> *"By the year 2020, the elderly will constitute about 25 percent of the world population. . . . The issue of death-with-dignity will become increasingly important."*

In Britain, groups supporting euthanasia have been active for decades but both euthanasia and physician-assisted suicide are treated as homicide. Unofficial estimates suggest that the number of unreported cases run in the thousands annually.

France treats euthanasia as homicide, but at the same time the actions of French doctors who specialize in what is termed "helping patients to die" are regarded as easing a patient's suffering and pain rather than deliberately causing death.

In Germany, the term "death-help" is substituted for "euthanasia" to avoid any comparison with the genocide that occurred during the Nazi regime. Both euthanasia and doctor-assisted-suicide are illegal and punishable by up to five years in prison.

Although euthanasia is not legal in Israel, the courts acknowledge that there are situations in which a doctor may take into consideration a patient's expressed wish not to have life prolonged by artificial means. In other words, passive voluntary euthanasia can be tolerated under certain circumstances.

Physician Support Is Widespread

Although survey after survey reveals that many medical doctors support the right of terminally ill patients to request aid-in-dying and have expressed a willingness to comply with these requests, there are also many doctors who oppose active voluntary euthanasia and their opposition is supported by law. Physicians, who support and honor the right of terminally ill patients to choose the time and mode of their demise, may participate surreptitiously in the patient's death. The medical mode of ending the patient's life in accord with the patient's will

> *"Throughout the world, passive voluntary euthanasia for the terminally ill is not often treated as illegal."*

is by increasing morphine dosage under the guise of seeking to control pain. Of course the physician knows that the morphine will have a "double effect" and kill the patient, but it is assumed that doctor's intent was not to kill but to ease suffering. Therefore, when frail, elderly, terminally ill, individuals request euthanasia, some medical personnel will cooperate by increasing the morphine dosage in the assurance that they will be protected from litigation by the "double effect" argument. These physicians believe that to prolong the life of a terminally ill and suffering person by drug therapy, blood transfusions or surgical intervention is unethical.

In response to worldwide pleas for euthanasia from the terminally ill, and for compassionate and merciful release from prolonged and useless suffering, "right-to-die" societies have been formed in countries throughout the world. Discussion, debate and dialogue involve members of the healing community, philosophers, ethicists, psychologists, and representatives of major religious bodies which have taken pro or con stands on the issues involved. In their efforts to legitimize active euthanasia for the terminally ill, these right-to-die advocates argue that, in certain circumstances, a strong legal and moral case for voluntary euthanasia can be made on the basis of compassion and recognition of human rights. . . .

Right-to-die societies insist that both passive and active euthanasia must be rigidly controlled by laws that establish procedures, protocols and safeguards designed to regulate the careful application of euthanasia to certain qualified, terminally ill persons. Such laws would serve to protect the elderly from being coerced or exploited or devalued on the basis of age or handicaps or costs of treatment.

Ethical Issues

Moral, ethical and religious issues pertaining to euthanasia embrace subjects as diverse as "patient autonomy," "quality of life," "sanctity of life," "death with dignity," "patient's rights," and "playing God." Medical personnel and their patients, both old and young, wrestle with problems associated with treatment futility, informed choice, right-to-die, autonomy versus paternalism, beneficence versus maleficence, and so on, each of which impacts, either directly or indirectly, on the issue of euthanasia.

What is most important in any discussion of global euthanasia is the recognition of the varied ethnic, national and religious differences to be found and respected in communities throughout the world. At the same time, the ethical issues that are raised by the subject of euthanasia are all embracing and include the following:

Patient Autonomy

In democratic countries, where individual freedom to choose is accepted as a civil right, end-of-life decisions should be made, primarily, by the patient. Self-determinism pays respect to an individual's personal values and enables the individual to be responsible for his or her own life. To deny competent individuals, and in particular elderly persons, the right to choose not only denies respect for their lifetimes of decision making but smacks of medical paternalism. Obviously, attitudes towards the process of dying will vary. Religious and cultural traditions including local customs will tend to dictate patterns to be followed. However, the empowerment of the elder and recognition of the elder's personal values must not be denied. In most countries, however, elderly patients who wish to exercise their autonomy and choose immediate death over lingering death, are denied their right to choose.

In developed countries, a Living Will, drawn up by a competent individual, provides a legally recognized means for the expression of personal end-of-life wishes. A second document, often titled "The Durable Power of Attorney for Health Care," enables an individual to select a trusted person and to give that individual the power of attorney for health care, thereby

> *"In response to worldwide pleas for euthanasia from the terminally ill . . . 'right-to-die' societies have been formed . . . throughout the world."*

ensuring that a patient, no longer able to communicate wishes, will still be given a voice regarding treatment. Beyond the importance of legal protection for the terminally ill, respect for the personhood of the terminally ill should be expressed through loving, supportive care.

Voluntary passive euthanasia, which is provided in response to the expressed wish of terminally ill patients who do not want to be "kept alive" on machines, is given wide support by ethicists and the medical personnel. The patient's expressed wish may be a witnessed verbal statement or be provided in written form as in a Living Will or through an appointed attorney for health care. Problems arise when an otherwise healthy person has entered a persistent vegetative state without having expressed their wishes or intentions concerning end-of-life treatment. Such persons can be kept alive by medications and gastric tube feeding for many years.

In cases where medical personnel are ready to admit that continuing treatment is futile, and where there is no way of ascertaining the wishes of the patient, involuntary passive euthanasia may be practiced on the basis of what is known as "substituted judgment." Relatives or other involved individuals seek to act according to "what the patient would choose" or in "the best interests" of the patient. Some hospitals have established "ethics committees" to provide guidance.

> *"What is most important in any discussion of global euthanasia is the recognition of . . . ethnic, national and religious differences . . . throughout the world."*

Informed Choice, Informed Consent.

Patient autonomy automatically includes the right to full information concerning the nature and development of the terminal illness, the choices for treatment that remain, the anticipated consequences of each form of treatment, and what will occur if the patient refuses treatment. Such information is often withheld from the elderly person. Paternalistic physicians may seek to shield the elderly patient from the truth or from a full evaluation of a terminal disease in the belief that the elderly are less able than younger persons to handle troublesome information. When medical personnel conclude that further treatment is futile and that nothing can be done to stop the progress of the disease, all competent patients, including elderly patients, need to be fully informed. Only then can the informed patient make an informed choice between alternate treatments and comprehend the consequences of choosing no treatment. Informed choice also provides the terminally ill patient with time and opportunity to make closure with those who matter most.

Informed choice immediately raises the issue of the patient's capacity to make a medical decision.

Playing God: Sanctity of Life, Quality of Life

For some, the sanctity-of-life thesis rests upon the theological argument that life is a gift or a loan from God and that only God should determine when that gift or loan should be returned. Those who seek to end their life are, therefore, "playing God." The thesis has been challenged for not every person will accept a theological interpretation of life. . . .

Modern medicine has been accused of "playing God" by keeping alive those who would, without technological support, die. It is at this point that sanctity of life doctrine clashes with "quality of life" experiences. Arguments claiming theological merit in suffering may encourage some to choose not to accept euthanasia, but the theology of one group cannot be sanctioned as acceptable for all.

The Hospice Alternative

Pressures—emotional, physical, psychological, and spiritual—placed on the terminally ill and on their caregivers have given rise to an ever-expanding hospice movement. By accepting the fact that a disease cannot be overcome and that the life of the patient will probably end within a six-month period, hospice organizations provide palliative care for the patient and supportive care for the family. No effort is made to prolong life and no medications are provided to fight the disease. Pain control and patient comfort are primary. Hospice facilities offer 24-hour care. Familial in-home care is supported by hospice volunteers, who aid in alleviating burdens and stress associated with caring for a terminally ill individual. Although hospice care varies in quality from place to place, the end result is the enhancement of the significance of the life of the terminally ill elder and the easing of stress among care-givers—both of which also benefits the dying patient.

It is important to recognize that some pain is intractable and cannot be controlled, even in a hospice setting.

Can the Rights of the Terminally Ill Be Protected by Law?

The deep concern underlying this question is that, for the elderly, the right to die will become a duty to die. There is fear that elderly patients might be pressured by family, friends, the government, health care providers, social workers or by the example of other terminally ill patients, to choose euthanasia, even though that choice may not be in accord with their personal values. In other words, the implication is that those to whom the terminally ill elder would ordinarily look for succor, strength and support, now become life-opposers seeking, for the sake of economy, inheritance, weariness, or other reasons, to terminate the life of the elder.

> *"To deny competent individuals, and in particular elderly persons, the right to choose not only denies respect for their . . . decision making but smacks of medical paternalism."*

The idea of the right to die becoming the duty to die is, of course, an abstract concern. There will always be greedy relatives who would prefer to have a terminally ill elder die sooner than later. However, under law, such persons will have to convince physicians and, perhaps, also hospital personnel, that the elder's life should be ended because of greed or some other malicious reason, rather than because of the ravages of the disease. To seek to pressure the terminally ill elder to ask for assistance in dying would be to aid and abet a suicide, which is punishable by law and which will remain a crime even after euthanasia laws are passed.

Could family members who are weary of caring for a frail terminally ill elder or who, because medical costs are reducing a possible inheritance from the elder, subtly or perhaps not so subtly, encourage the patient to request an early death? One can only acknowledge that such a scenario could occur. The best safeguard against such a situation would be the questions asked by a competent physician or counselor. Any violation of legalized euthanasia protocol would be subject to prosecution like any other violation of law.

"In most countries . . . elderly patients who wish to exercise their autonomy and choose immediate death over lingering death, are denied their right to choose."

No matter what potential dangers may be conjured up in protest, the legalization of active euthanasia or doctor-assisted suicide can provide terminally ill elders with a personal choice regarding how and when they will die. Such choice enhances autonomy and respects the personal values.

It is generally accepted that active euthanasia must be legalized to protect those, particularly health professionals, who aid in the death of the terminally ill from litigation. Those who oppose active euthanasia argue that any legislation that affords such protection can become a slippery slope whereby elderly persons who are not terminally ill might be euthanized, and the extended list of those who would be at risk includes the frail and the physically or mentally handicapped. Efforts to use what occurred in the death camps in Nazi Germany overlook the difference between a totalitarian state and a democratic government. A careful examination of every piece of proposed euthanasia legislation makes it absolutely clear that the proposed programs include only the terminally ill who request euthanasia. It is also clear that the number of terminally-ill elderly who would be affected by proposed right-to-die legislation will be small. The use of "fright techniques" and dishonesty employed by those opposed to the rights of the terminally ill to choose euthanasia have been labeled "unethical" and "shameful."

Fears have been expressed that a terminally ill individual, particularly an elderly person, who is not in intractable pain may, simply because of depression, request aid in dying. Again, most legislative proposals recognize this fact and call for examination and diagnosis by a psychiatrist or other mental health expert.

Would Doctor-Patient Relationships Be Weakened?

Opponents of doctor-assisted death argue that, if doctors are given the right to assist in the ending of their patients' lives, patients will no longer trust their doctors. They claim that legalization of doctor-assisted death would destroy the relationship between the physician and patient. The doctor will no longer be viewed solely as one dedicated to fighting of disease and preserving of life; now the doctor will have a second role as the one who causes death, thereby clouding the doctor's healing role. On the other hand, patients may view the doctor as a rescuer from a lingering death marked by intractable pain. Euthanasia, in any form, must be based on patient choice; the doctor can only become involved if invited to do so by the patient. For the doctor to recommend euthanasia would constitute a violation of physician responsibility which could result in litigation.

It has been pointed out that many doctors on graduation take the Hippocratic oath which prescribes beneficence and specifically outlaws medically assisted death (. . . To please no one will I prescribe a deadly drug, nor give advice which may cause his death). In response, it has been pointed out that many doctors have never taken the oath and further, that many who do, simply repeat it as an ancient formula without any belief in the deities who are called upon to witness the oath (Apollo, Aesculepius, Hygeia, Panacea). Students, teachers, and administrators in some hospitals have created their own formulas as part of graduation ceremonies. Further, the prohibition of abortion in the Hippocratic code dates the oath and renders it out-of-touch with medical practice in those countries where abortion is not illegal.

A Global Concern

What concerns us in this issue is the maximizing and empowering of the individual, particularly the terminally ill elderly person, so that, in accordance with their beliefs, their values, their associations, and their commitments, they may feel free to choose the manner of their dying. Their choice must be an informed choice which rests on the physician sharing all aspects of the development of their illness or disease, the presentation of all alternative approaches to the termination of life, and patients' right to choose the way in which they will die.

It is abundantly clear, that as the population of the world increases and the numbers of those facing terminal illness grow in proportion, the issue of euthanasia will become more important. This [viewpoint] can only serve as a brief introduction to a global concern. The position of freethought groups has been expressed over and over again since 1973 when, together with prominent lawyers, physicians, philosophers, psychiatrists, Nobel-prize winners and clergy, representatives of the American Humanist Association and Ethical Culture Societies signed "A Plea For Beneficent Euthanasia." Their support for the terminally ill individual's right to choose euthanasia has been reaffirmed in more recent statements.

Most Dutch Physicians Endorse Assisted Suicide

by Bregje D. Onwuteaka-Philipsen et al.

About the author: *Bregje D. Onwuteaka-Philipsen is a researcher in the Department of Social Medicine, Institute for Research in Extramural Medicine, Vrije Universiteit, Amsterdam.*

Empirical data on the rate of euthanasia, physician-assisted suicide, and other end-of-life decisions have greatly contributed to the debate about the role of such practices in modern health care. In the Netherlands, the continuing debate about whether and when physician-assisted dying is acceptable seems to be resulting in a gradual stabilisation of end-of-life practices. . . .

In the Netherlands, euthanasia, physician-assisted suicide, and other medical end-of-life decisions have been discussed for several decades in the medical profession, by legal and ethics specialists, in public debates, and in the national parliament. The first quantitative studies of the rate and major characteristics of these practices were done in 1990. Those studies provided a reliable overview of end-of-life decision-making practices in the Netherlands and had an important impact on the national and international debate. End-of-life decision making became recognised as a part of modern health care for many patients who are approaching death; about 39% of all deaths seemed to be preceded by a medical decision that probably or certainly hastened death. The deliberate hastening of death by administration of lethal drugs was rare, but was most frequently used at the explicit request of the patient. However, this decision was also made in about 1000 cases per year without an explicit request. Alleviation of severe pain and symptoms by use of opioids or similar drugs in high doses, while taking into account hastening of death as a possible but not intended side-effect, seemed to be a frequent practice, as were decisions to withhold or withdraw potentially life-prolonging treatments.

The hastening of death by administration of lethal drugs is an act at the border of accepted medical practice, and, therefore, some form of control was deemed necessary by the Dutch parliament. Since 1991, Dutch physicians have had to report all cases in which they administered or supplied drugs with the explicit intention of hastening a patient's death, to enable legal assessment by the Public Prosecutor. This notification procedure was assessed in 1995, and developments in end-of-life decision-making practices were simultaneously monitored by replicating the 1990 incidence studies. The rate of euthanasia had significantly increased during this 5-year period, but the rate of physician-assisted suicide and ending of life without a patient's explicit request had remained virtually unchanged. After the 1995 study, the notification procedure was revised, and came into force in 1998. Cases were assessed by the Public Prosecutor only after being advised by a multidisciplinary committee of medical, ethics, and legal specialists. The renewed notification procedure was assessed in 2001–02, in combination with another rate study.

> *"End-of-life decision making became recognised as a part of modern health care for many patients who are approaching death."*

We present new data on the rate in 2001 of euthanasia, physician-assisted suicide, and other end-of-life decisions in the Netherlands, and a longitudinal analysis of decision-making practices since 1990. We investigated also physicians' attitudes towards end-of-life decision making during the period 1990–2001.

We studied end-of-life decision-making practices and attitudes in 1990, 1995, and 2001. All studies consisted of physician interviews and death-certificate studies. Details of the 1990 and 1995 studies have been described elsewhere. The questions and study designs that were used to collect the data were identical in all years. . . .

Frequency of Requests Increases

The total annual number of deaths in the Netherlands increased by 5.3% between 1990 and 1995, and by 3.5% between 1995 and 2001. The number of explicit requests for euthanasia or assisted suicide rose from 8900 in 1990 to 9700 in 1995, which is an increase of 9.0%. Between 1995 and 2001, the number remained stable at 9700.

The death-certificate studies showed the rate of euthanasia increased from 1.7% of all deaths in 1990 to 2.4% in 1995, and further to 2.6% in 2001. In the interview studies, no further increase was found in 2001. The frequency of physician-assisted suicide and the ending of life without the patient's explicit request remained virtually unchanged during all years. The lessening of pain or other symptoms while taking into account or appreciating a possible life-shortening effect occurred in 18.8% of all deaths in 1990, 19.1% in 1995, and in 20.1% in 2001. The incidence of non-treatment decisions rose between 1990 and 1995, but remained stable in 2001.

In 2001, the proportion of physicians who ever in their working career had performed euthanasia or assisted in suicide was 57%. Family physicians were more frequently involved in this practice than clinical specialists and nursing-home physicians. The increase in number of physicians who had ever performed euthanasia or assisted in suicide between 1995 and 2001 was among family physicians (1995 63%, 2001 71%) and nursing-home physicians (1995 21%, 2001 36%), but not clinical specialists (1995 37%, 2001 37%). For physicians who would never perform euthanasia, the proportion fell consistently: 4% in 1990, 3% in 1995, and 1% in 2001.

The proportion of physicians who were ever engaged in the ending of life without a patient's explicit request decreased from 27% in 1990 to 23% in 1995, and further to 13% in 2001. Furthermore, physicians' unwillingness to ever do so increased, especially after 1995, from 45% in 1995 to 71% in 2001. We saw the decrease in willingness mainly among family physicians and clinical specialists; nursing-home physicians were already quite reluctant in 1995. . . .

During the whole study period, euthanasia and physician-assisted suicide were relatively uncommon among patients dying at the age of 80 years or older. In 1995, the rate of euthanasia had increased especially among people aged 80 years or younger. Euthanasia was more frequent among male than female patients in 1990, but not in 1995 and 2001. Euthanasia and physician-assisted suicide were mainly performed among patients dying of cancer. The rise in the rate of euthanasia was also largest among cancer patients, and remained invariably low among patients with circulatory diseases. Euthanasia and physician-assisted suicide were mainly performed by family physicians, who frequently care for patients dying at home. The proportion of euthanasia cases among patients dying while being cared for by a nursing-home physician had stabilised, but the absolute number of cases among nursing-home patients had grown because of the increased involvement of nursing-home physicians in death.

> *"In 2001, the proportion of physicians who ever in their working career had performed euthanasia or assisted in suicide was 57%."*

Ending of life without a patient's explicit request occurred most frequently among people dying at age younger than 65 years. Among these patients the incidence decreased between 1990 and 1995 from 1.6% to 1.1%, but in 2001, it had remained virtually unchanged at 1.0%. Ending of life without a patient's explicit request occurred somewhat more frequently among male than among female patients in 1990, but the proportions were equal for both sexes in 1995 and 2001. This practice frequently involved patients with cancer, and was performed most commonly by clinical specialists.

Physicians' Attitudes Have Changed Little

Alleviation of pain or symptoms while taking into account or appreciating a life-shortening effect occurred in about one in five cases in all age-groups. This practice occurred more frequently among female than male patients, frequently involved cancer patients, and was practised most commonly by nursing-home physicians. This practice increased most among people aged 80 years and older, and among patients with diseases other than cancer. Decisions to withhold or withdraw potentially life-prolonging treatment were most frequently made for elderly patients. The increase in non-treatment decisions for elderly patients we noted in 1995, did not continue to 2001. The high frequency of such decisions among female patients is explained partly by the fact that women generally die at older ages than do men. Whereas other end-of-life decisions were especially evoked by having cancer, non-treatment decisions commonly involved other diagnoses as well.

Physicians' attitudes towards people's rights in end-of-life decision making have altered only slightly during the period 1990–2001. In 1990 and 1995, 64% of all physicians thought that people have the right to decide about their own life and death; in 2001 this proportion was slightly lower. Fewer than half thought that patients would be less inclined to ask for euthanasia if they knew that their physician is willing to perform it if needed. About a third thought that euthanasia could be avoided by providing adequate palliative care to terminal patients, but in 1995 and 2001, this proportion seems to be lower than in 1990. There seems to be a slightly increasing anxiety among physicians that economic measures are going to affect end-of-life decision making. In 2001, physicians more frequently reported having become more restrictive about euthanasia and less frequently permissive.

Rates Have Stabilised

The rate of euthanasia and explicit requests by patients for physicians' assistance in dying in the Netherlands seems to have stabilised, and physicians seem to have become somewhat more restrictive in their use. Euthanasia remains mainly restricted to groups other than patients with cancer, people younger than 80 years, and patients cared for by family physicians, who were already frequently involved in 1990. The continuing debate on whether and when physician-assistance in dying may be acceptable and on procedures to ensure transparency and quality assurance seems to have contributed to this stabilisation.

The rate of physician-assisted suicide remains remarkably low compared with that for euthanasia, despite recommendations of leading authorities such as the Royal Dutch Medical Association to choose physician-assisted suicide if possible. There is

> *In 1990 and 1995, 64% of all physicians thought that people have the right to decide about their own life and death."*

an argument that patients' autonomy and responsibility in end-of-life decision making are more articulated in assisting with suicide than in providing euthanasia. Such features might, however, be overruled by the physicians', and probably the patients', need to control the act and to have medical assistance available in case of unforeseen difficulties. Euthanasia is also frequently preferred over assisted suicide because of physical weakness or incapacity of patients.

The combination of a decreasing proportion of physicians who have ever engaged in ending of life without a patient's explicit request and a stable number of such cases could be partly explained by the rise in the number of physicians in the Netherlands. Furthermore, physicians who are still willing to end life without a patient's explicit request may be engaging in these practices frequently. In previous studies, we have noted that the explicit intention of hastening death is similar to that with which euthanasia is performed. Other characteristics of these cases, however, such as the frequent use of morphine or other opioids, are frequently more similar to the alleviation of symptoms in which hastening of death was not an explicit intention. Such alleviation of symptoms precedes death in about 20% of all cases, and was the only end-of-life decision that had clearly increased in 2001, especially for nursing-home patients. In addition to a growing interest in palliative care at the end of life, reports in which the life-shortening potential of opioids is limited and evidence that the quality of terminal care is commonly less than optimum may have contributed to a diminished reluctance to use opioids in palliative care for terminal patients.

> *"The current frequency of end-of-life decisions may represent a stable number . . . in a . . . society in which end-of-life decision making is . . . openly discussed."*

Death Is Part of Medical Decision Making

We find the absence of a rise in the proportion of non-treatment decisions after 1995 surprising. Advances in medical technology increase the number of possible interventions to treat seriously ill patients and the health-care costs for such interventions also increase, especially in the elderly age-groups. A growing number of interventions might also involve a growing number of decisions not to apply them, but this hypothesis is not reflected in our findings. Non-treatment decisions concern many different interventions in various situations. To refrain from potentially life-prolonging treatment might not always be perceived as an end-of-life decision, especially when such abstinence is inspired mainly by medical motives or involves low-grade technology.

Our study has some obvious limitations. First, it is limited to the experiences and attitudes of physicians. Views of patients, their family, and other caregivers were not studied. Furthermore, no inferences can be made from our data on the quality of end-of-life care. We asked physicians what they did (or did not) do and why they did it (or not), but avoided any reference to a moral assessment of their practices. The high participation rates in all studies and the coherence of the data between different studies and different years supports the idea that our findings are a reliable overview of end-of-life decision-making practices in the Netherlands.

Death and dying have become increasingly part of medical decision making, and health care is currently attributed much responsibility for the quality of the dying process. There is a growing awareness that end-of-life care should aim at improving the quality of life of patients and their families through the prevention and relief of pain and symptoms. The current frequency of end-of-life decisions may represent a stable number of cases that can be expected in a modern Western society in which end-of-life decision making is frequently and openly discussed and, under specified circumstances, accepted. Advances in medicine may further improve the importance and impact of end-of-life decision making.

Dutch Physicians Increasingly Oppose Assisted Suicide

by F.P. Tros

About the author: *F.P. Tros is a former Master of English in Dutch secondary and higher education.*

In the Netherlands, a remarkable development appears to be taking place. At the exact moment that the new law on euthanasia and assisted suicide is due to come into effect—and just as our Belgian neighbors are getting ready to enact a similar law—many Dutch physicians are recoiling from the success of their struggles to bring this about. Secularized as the Dutch may have become, their missionary zeal has never left them. But it now seems that, in running with this ideal of preventing end-of-life suffering, they have become too big for their wooden shoes.

It all began some two decades ago when the judiciary decided to take a lenient view of what were, from the sentimental point of view, mercy killings; and so the thin end of the wedge was deftly inserted. Gradually, the authorities became uncomfortable with an unofficial policy in which the Ministry of Justice decided not to prosecute euthanasia if committed under certain conditions. They sought to regularize the situation, and legal euthanasia is now about to become the law of the land. If ever hard cases have proved to make bad law, it is here. The law now regulating what has so far been a practice that existed on sufferance is a product of modern secular Holland: turning a blind-eye to felonies. The permissiveness of the sixties has become official policy in this nation of formerly staid and sober people.

Charges of Intolerance

The principled opposition in Parliament, which came mostly from the Christian Democrats and the smaller orthodox-Protestant parties, was met by charges

F.P. Tros, "Too Big for Their Wooden Shoes," *Human Life Review*, vol. 27, Fall 2001, pp. 53–56.

of intolerance and an undemocratic attempt to bend the majority to the will of a stiffnecked minority beset by outmoded prejudices. A fundamental ethical discourse is practically impossible in a country where the media are the preserve of the liberal elite, and where the limits of the philosophical range of the pro-euthanasia party are best exemplified by the Minister of Health's stock reply to whether euthanasia is morally acceptable: she emphasizes the great care with which the decisions to euthanize are reached and executed; she addresses the moral question not at all. One wonders what her reaction

> *"Many Dutch physicians are recoiling from the success of their struggles to bring [a new law on euthanasia and assisted suicide] about."*

would be to the argument of a proponent of the death-penalty that, after all, the executions are carried out with the best technical means available.

In the November 10th [2001] Saturday supplement of the liberal newspaper *NRC Handelsblad*, there appeared an interview with four members of the team for Euthanasia Consultation and Support in Amsterdam. This group and similar ones around the country frequently provide the second opinion required for euthanasia to be exempted from prosecution (up till now) or to be lawful (as soon as the new law comes into effect). Consequently the four family doctors on the Amsterdam team have a long and varied experience of euthanasia in practice. The average general practitioner may engage in euthanasia once or twice a year; these physicians are—in addition to their own cases—intimately involved in some fifteen to twenty of their colleagues' cases each year.

The members of this team felt the need to convene regularly to discuss their cases, and, as they say banteringly, "to have a good cry over things." The *Handelsblad* reporter had some difficulty in gaining admittance to one of their quarterly meetings: it was unprecedented to have an outsider present, and she was warned that the discussions tended to get rather emotional. She had expected to find that the avant-garde of Dutch euthanasia would again be extending the frontiers of physician-assisted self-destruction. But she was wrong.

One member had decided to give up her work on the team on the grounds that she could no longer in conscience accept responsibility for euthanasia as it was being practiced. "The law requires us to explore all avenues before we carry out euthanasia. But I see now that this happens only too infrequently."

A Misguided Approach

A general feeling among the team members was that they had initially approached euthanasia from the wrong side: why hadn't they concentrated on palliation first and euthanasia second, instead of the other way around? It is illustrative of this new awareness that peer groups for palliative care have recently been established within the teams for Euthanasia Consultation and Support. These groups are now studying other methods for relieving the suffering of terminal patients. "Ignorance and lack of awareness have caused people to be flushed into the euthanasia procedure to whom a whole lot of life quality could have been offered," one of the group members said. And, most telling with regard to what happens once a culture of death has become accepted: "When one has been so intently focused on euthanasia, one develops a blind spot for other possibilities." Further: "There are some (of my own patients) who died through euthanasia that now make me realize that, with my present knowledge of things, we would have gone a very different way." And (one can imagine a bitter "I told you so!" from opponents to euthanasia) one member mentioned that: "We have been reproached abroad with following the reverse road in having a tiptop regulation for euthanasia and letting other ways of relieving pain go by the board." This remark called forth from a colleague: "It is of course a matter of what is the thing at a given moment, too. We are followers of fashion like anybody else."

A wholly unforeseen consequence of the euthanasia policy is that it evolved from a physician's last resort to a patient's right: death on demand. "You can now get landed," one physician said, "in a situation of parleying with your patient: 'We can do this now, can't we?' This does make me think now and then: My god, yes, you are dying, but why should I deliver death two weeks in advance?" Another doctor calls the whole set-up a "vending machine": "Slip in your money, out pops your hot dog—make your request, out pops your euthanasia."

> *"Ignorance and lack of awareness [about palliative care] have caused people to be flushed into the euthanasia procedure."*

One of the due-care requirements is that the physician, together with the patient, must be convinced that there is no other reasonable solution. But here is the rub, says one of the participants: "One cannot judge of the patient's facing interminable and unendurable suffering, without sufficient knowledge of the means to relieve suffering. It seems doubtful to me whether general practitioners are in a position to make that judgment." Another doctor related how she used to feel it her duty to mention euthanasia to an incurable patient who was beyond the help of traditional medication, "for fear they wouldn't dare to bring up the subject." Since her immersion in the subject of palliation, she has deliberately avoided the E-word, and what does she see? "Nobody ever asks for it now."

"A physician and a patient must never decide for euthanasia, when the physician is insufficiently informed about the possibilities offered by palliative care," the Minister of Health, Dr. E. Borst, said as early as 1996. "But how can doctors improve their knowledge beyond the point that prescribing a sufficient number of Vesperax sleeping-tablets will help patients kick the bucket as a matter of course?" Palliative care was hardly part of the family doctor's training until a year ago. Only last September [2002] was a motion introduced in Parliament to promote palliative-care training. (An earlier Christian-Democratic motion had been defeated.)

"Drion's Pill"

Even as some of the erstwhile enthusiasts for euthanasia now lament the consequences, others have gone beyond seeking release from terrible pain and are focusing now on aid for people who are simply tired of living. The Minister of Health gave it as her opinion, the day after the new euthanasia bill was passed by the First Chamber, that a next step should be the provision of what is called—after the auctor intellectualis [originator of the idea]—"Drion's Pill."[1] 'This future, so far fictitious, pill would be distributed to those who might need it—naturally, with great wisdom and great care and under strict safeguards. A first category of recipients would be the old and ailing, who could thus, at their own convenience and at a self-determined and freely chosen moment, decide to get out. Also on the list would be the very old who are not really ill or suffering but who have simply become bored with life.

This culture of death that has grown so enormously over the past twenty years evidently found a fertile soil in the secularized minds of the Dutch people. It is perhaps indicative of the estrangement from the nation's Christian heritage that the Minister of Health could triumphantly greet—unwittingly no doubt, and no offense meant—the new law's passing on April 20th (a week after Good Friday) with Christ's words from the Cross: It is finished.

What then—against this backdrop of shallow humanism, sloppy thinking, and cheap triumphalism among the lawgiving classes—can be expected to result from the apparent change of heart among the vanguard of those who have the widest experience in this field? We should not be over-optimistic about the chances for an immediate change in the moral attitude of the nation as a whole and the progressist elite in particular. The Minister of Health lost no time after the publication of the disturbing *Handelsblad* interview in emphasizing that however good the care given in the terminal phase, euthanasia remains a worthy way of coping. Letters to the editor betrayed shocked concern lest one of the chief attainments of our days should be lost, and tried to belittle the new position of the interviewees by saying it results from their over-involvement with euthanasia—a kind of oversensitiveness that one never hears of in the case of gynecologists who have delivered their hundredth (or thousandth) human child, or of surgeons who have performed their umpteenth appendectomy. Although *Handelsblad* published the interview, its lead article summed up with "But the crucial concern also of this new law remains the right of individual self-determination of the suffering person."

No, we should be grateful that, in a great and growing number of physicians,

---

1. This was a pill that the elderly could take to voluntarily end their lives. It was named for Dr. Huib Drion, the Dutch professor who first wrote about it in 1991.

humaneness is winning over a frigid intellectualism that reduces a supreme human act, the act of dying, to a medical procedure to be got over with as painlessly and as quickly as possible. What we may hope for, and pray for, is that not humanism but humaneness will win the day. "No man is an Iland, intire of it selfe; every man is a peece of the Continent, a part of the maine; if a Clod bee washed away by the Sea, Europe is the lesse, as well as a Promontorie were, as well as a Mannor of thy friends or of thine owne were; any mans death diminishes me, because I am involved in Mankinde."

Most Canadians Want Physician-Assisted Suicide Legalized

by Bob Lane

About the author: *Bob Lane is the founding director of the Institute of Practical Philosophy at Malaspina University-College in British Columbia, Canada, and a teacher of philosophy and religious studies there.*

I started to write "the Sue Rodriguez case[1] has reminded us all. . . ." and then I realized how wrong that is. It is not the Sue Rodriguez "case"—it is Sue Rodriguez who has reminded us all of our own mortality and our need to think carefully about the kind of society we want to live and to die in. I knew Sue Rodriguez only through the media, heard her speak so eloquently and painfully in support of what she believed in, watched as her strength was sapped by the devastating disease (amyotrophic lateral sclerosis), and was moved by her clear thought and her bravery as a person facing death. Here was a woman who acted on her beliefs with courage and tenacity and whose grace has enriched us all.

She challenged us to think about the difference between what our law of the land says and what our people say. Her death, and her life, say to us "think carefully about these matters of life and death for they are not academic and distant but are a necessary part of everyone's existence."

"A Gentle and Easy Death"

In this [viewpoint] I want to focus on the controversial and difficult issue of assisted suicide or euthanasia. First some ground clearing and preparation: "euthanasia" means "a gentle and easy death" and has come to mean "the good death of another" or "mercy killing." It is controversial because it brings into

---

1. Sue Rodriguez petitioned the Canadian Supreme Court to allow a physician to assist her in suicide. Her petition was denied.

focus and conflict some very powerful and competing values. Certainly one of society's traditional attitudes, expressed morally, legally, philosophically, and religiously is that human life merits special protection. In fact, some claim that human life is an absolute value. For them the taking of human life then becomes a wrong even in the case of voluntary euthanasia. And for some this perceived moral wrong should be prohibited by the full force of the law. The clash here is between protection of human life and the right to decisional autonomy, and as well raises the question of the extent to which the criminal law should be used to

> *"The clash . . . is between protection of human life and the right to decisional autonomy."*

enforce particular moral positions. And the conflict is one of absolutism versus consequentialism. Are some acts absolutely morally prohibited, or do we assess the goodness or badness of acts based upon their consequences?

More ground clearing: one of the bad arguments sometimes used against euthanasia comes from an oft-cited article written in 1949 by Leo Alexander. Alexander was a judge at the Nuremberg trials after World War II who employed a classic slippery slope argument (a fallacy that occurs when the conclusion of an argument rests upon the claim that a certain event will set off a chain reaction leading in the end to some undesirable consequence, and there is not sufficient reason to think that the chain reaction will actually take place) to suggest that any act of mercy killing inevitably will lead to the mass killings of unwanted persons. He wrote: "The beginnings at first were a subtle shifting in the basic attitude of the physicians. It started with the acceptance of the attitude, basic in the euthanasia movement, that there is such a thing as life not worthy to be lived. This attitude in its early stages concerned itself merely with the severely and chronically sick. Gradually, the sphere of those to be included in this category was enlarged to encompass the socially unproductive, the ideologically unwanted, the racially unwanted and finally all non-Germans." Critics of this position point to the fact that there is no relation at all between the Nazi "euthanasia" program and modern debates about euthanasia. The Nazis, after all, used the word "euthanasia" to camouflage mass murder. All victims died involuntarily, and no documented case exists where a terminal patient was voluntarily killed. The program was carried out in the closest of secrecy and under a dictatorship. One of the lessons that we should learn from this experience is that secrecy is not in the public interest.

Scientific Advances

Advances in medical science have also had a stunning effect on social policy. Medical advances and technology have made it possible, for example, for us to cure pneumonia in a person suffering from terminal cancer by administering antibiotics; before this discovery that patient would have died of pneumonia.

Cardiac arrest and kidney failure are no longer fatal with the appropriate technological intervention. AIDS has intensified the debate over assisted suicide. Palliative care has improved, and it is rare now to find a physician who is worried about giving too much of a painkilling narcotic to a suffering patient on the grounds that it may be habit forming. In the midst of all these changes in the art of medicine and care-giving there remains the moral question of, not what can be done, but what should be done?

Euthanasia is discussed in churches, philosophy classes, pubs, street corners, homes, medical societies, nursing classes, hospices, journals, and in legislative assemblies across the land. There is no shortage of information and opinion. Anyone interested in obtaining more information will find an abundance of books and articles in the Malaspina University-College library. I suggest that you start with the *Law Reform Commission of Canada's Working Paper 28* (euthanasia, aiding suicide and cessation of treatment) from 1982. This paper reviews the relevant issues of law, medicine, religion, and societal attitudes in a readable format, and after reviewing the situation makes several recommendations. Though [twenty-two] years old now, it still provides an excellent overview of the arguments.

Here is the question: is it possible for us as a society to recognize and assert the fundamental importance of life while at the same time recognizing and asserting the right of a terminally ill patient to die with dignity?

> *"In the midst of . . . changes in . . . medicine and care-giving there remains the moral question of, not what can be done, but what should be done?"*

"There is no record in Canadian case-law of a single conviction of a doctor for having shortened the life of one of his or her terminal patients by administering massive doses of pain-killing drugs." (*Law Reform Commission*, 1982) [A news report on June 22, 1996, reads "Toronto Dr. Maurice Genereux . . . became the first doctor in Canada to be charged with assisting a suicide" *The Weekend Sun, Vancouver*].

Changing the Law

Given that there have been few problems in case law, why should we consider changing the law?

One reason for considering change is that prosecution is possible for anyone assisting another in committing suicide, and the Criminal Code of Canada has a penalty of up to fourteen years for the act. There is, as it stands, no degree of predictability for patients or physicians in how the courts will rule on the general rules established in the Criminal Code. Yet another concern is that according to recent polls (1989) some 77% of Canadians disagree with the law against assisted suicide. And yet another reason for considering legal changes to the Code is that many people believe that assisted suicides are being carried out now on humanitarian grounds even though the law forbids such action. It is often the case that laws lag behind society's attitudes, beliefs, and moral arguments. . . .

A more basic problem however has to do with the use of criminal law to enforce moral positions held by some members of society. The challenge for us in Canada today is to allow for sometimes competing and strongly held moral principles in the euthanasia debate. On the one hand we should value autonomy and on the other we should value life. The Law Reform Commission Working paper of 1982 puts it this way: "Law must also recognize, as it now does implicitly, the principle of personal autonomy and self-determination, the right of every human being to have his [her] wishes respected in decisions involving his [her] own body. It is essential to recognize that every human being is, in principle, master of his [her] own destiny. He [She] may, of course, for moral or religious reasons, impose restrictions or limits on his [her] own right of self-determination. However, these limits must not be imposed on him [her] by the law except in cases where the exercise of this right is likely to affect public order or the rights of others."

In 1972, for example, the criminal offense of attempted suicide was repealed. Laws should, in general, allow for the maximum expression of individual moral and religious beliefs, and should not be used to restrict or limit individual autonomy as long as that expression of autonomy is not harmful to others. Thus, even if one is religiously opposed to euthanasia, it does not follow that one has a right to insist, through the criminal law, that others follow one's religious beliefs. Dr. Gifford-Jones, writing in *The Ottawa Citizen*, October 6, 1989, puts this point strongly: "I'm sure Canadian physicians will find a host of moral, ethical and religious reasons to damn . . . active euthanasia. Some would agree with it in the privacy of the doctors' lounge. But publicly they will not have the courage to say so. Current attitudes on ethical issues in this country worry me and they should concern others who believe in personal privacy and freedom of choice. I'm tired of listening to moralists who believe they have a profound understanding that the rest of us don't. And that their moral code, having the stamp of the Almighty, is beyond reproach."

Death Is Evil

James Rachels, an American philosopher, in an influential paper titled "Active and Passive Euthanasia" writes: "Fixing the cause of death may be very important from a legal point of view, for it may determine whether criminal charges are brought against the doctor. But I do not think that this notion can be used to show a moral difference between active and passive euthanasia. The reason why it is considered bad to be the cause of someone's death is that death is regarded as an evil—and so it is. However, if it has been decided that euthanasia—even passive euthanasia—is desirable in a given case, it has also been decided that in this instance death is no greater an evil than the patient's continued existence. And if this is true, the usual reasons for not wanting to be the cause of someone's death simply do not apply."

Is there a difference, do you think, between a person who, at a dying person's request, prepares a poison and leaves it on the bedside for her to take, and a person who helps the patient to drink it or who administers it directly at the request of a dying person who is unable to take it herself? Is there, in short, a real distinction between killing and letting die?

> *"Some 77% of Canadians disagree with the law against assisted suicide."*

Sue Rodriguez and Karen Ann Quinlan have done more than ethicists, doctors, and moralists to rivet public attention on the legal and moral aspects of euthanasia. In 1994 Sue Rodriguez chose to die. In 1975 Karen Ann Quinlan, for reasons still unknown, ceased breathing for several minutes. Failing to respond to mouth-to mouth resuscitation by friends she was taken by ambulance to a hospital in New Jersey. Physicians who examined her described her as being in "a chronic, persistent, vegetative state," and later it was judged that no form of treatment could restore her to cognitive life. Her father asked to be appointed her legal guardian with the expressed purpose of discontinuing the respirator which kept Karen alive. After some delay the Supreme Court of New Jersey granted the request. The respirator was turned off. Karen Ann Quinlan remained alive but comatose until June 11, 1985, when she died at the age of 31.

These cases and others like them demand that we think carefully through a number of conceptual issues. *What is a person?* What is death? How does the difference between active and passive function in arguments for and against euthanasia? Is there any difference between killing and letting die?

Killing and Letting Die

The question of personhood bears on euthanasia as on abortion debates. What criteria should be used to determine personhood? Is it just a matter of species? That is, are all and only biological humans persons? That does not seem right because for the theist, it must be the case that God or gods, angels and so forth are also persons in the moral sense. Further, if we do discover some alien race on a distant planet would their lack of a certain DNA string be sufficient to say that they were not persons, capable of making decisions and acting on them? And in fact, here on our own planet is there not a strong argument for treating the Great Apes as persons, as a recent book advocates? The importance of this conceptual issue is just that if we could establish the criteria for personhood then those qualifying enjoy the same rights as any other patient. It seems right to say, for example, that the person Karen Ann Quinlan died sometime in 1975 though her body survived until 1985.

It used to be that death meant the termination of breathing. Later physicians defined death as a total stoppage of the circulation of blood. This definition served well until recent technology made it possible to sustain respiration and heartbeat indefinitely, even when there is no brain activity. The need for still viable organs for transplantation has resulted in a refined definition based on brain wave activity.

It has long been held that the distinction between active and passive euthanasia is crucial for medical ethics. The idea is that although it may be permissible in some cases to withhold treatment and allow a patient to die, it is never permissible to take any direct action to bring about that death. North American Medical Associations base their ethical conduct on this distinction, as in this statement by the American Medical Association: "The intentional termination of the life of one human being by another . . . is contrary to that for which the medical profession stands . . . The cessation of the employment of extraordinary means to prolong the life of the body when there is irrefutable evidence that biological death is imminent is the decision of the patient and/or his immediate family."

Active vs. Passive Euthanasia

This so-called distinction between active and passive was challenged by the philosopher James Rachels in a paper first published in 1975 in the *New England Journal of Medicine*. In that paper Rachels challenges both the use and moral significance of that distinction for several reasons. First, he argues, active euthanasia is in many cases more humane than passive; second, the doctrine leads to decisions concerning life and death being made on irrelevant grounds; and third, the doctrine rests on a distinction between killing and letting die that itself has no moral significance. Rachels urges doctors to reconsider their views. He writes: "To begin with a familiar type of situation, a patient who is dying of incurable cancer of the throat is in terrible pain, which can no longer be satisfactorily alleviated. He is certain to die within a few days, even if present treatment is continued, but he does not want to go on living for those days since the pain is unbearable. So he asks the doctor for an end to it, and his family joins in this request."

> *"If one is religiously opposed to euthanasia, it does not follow that one has a right to insist, through criminal law, that others follow one's religious beliefs."*

"Suppose the doctor agrees to withhold treatment . . . The justification for his doing so is that the patient is in terrible agony, and since he is going to die anyway, it would be wrong to prolong his suffering needlessly. But now notice this. If one simply withholds treatment, it may take the patient longer to die, and so he may suffer more than he would if more direct action were taken and a lethal injection given. This fact provides strong reason for thinking that, once the initial decision not to prolong his agony has been made, active euthanasia is actually preferable to passive euthanasia, rather than the reverse."

Is killing someone worse than letting them die? Rachels asks us to consider these two cases: In the first Smith will gain a large inheritance if anything should happen to his young cousin. One evening while the youngster is taking a bath, Smith sneaks into the bathroom and drowns the child, and then arranges things so it will look like an accident. In the second parallel case, Jones will gain a large inheritance and plans to drown his cousin, but as he enters the bathroom Jones sees the child slip and hit his head and fall face down in the water. Jones watches and does nothing.

> *"It has long been held that the distinction between active and passive euthanasia is crucial for medical ethics."*

Now, Smith killed the child while Jones "merely" let the child die.

Rachels' question: did either man behave better, from a moral point of view? "If the difference between killing and letting die were in itself a morally important matter, one should say that Jones's behavior was less reprehensible than Smith's. But does one really want to say that?"

Living Wills

If the crucial issue in the euthanasia debate is the intentional termination of the life of one human being by another, then how can it be consistent to forbid mercy killing and yet deny that the cessation of treatment is the intentional termination of a life? What is the cessation of treatment if it is not the "intentional termination of the life of one human being by another"? The so-called distinction between active and passive does not provide a useful moral distinction.

Courts in the United States and Canada have upheld the right of competent adult patients to refuse life-preserving medical treatment. The famous *Cruzan v. Missouri Health Services* case went to the United States Supreme Court in 1990, and the court ruled that even if the patient is not competent to make the decision to stop treatment it may be made by a surrogate acting according to the patient's wishes. One consequence of such rulings is the increased interest in so-called Living Wills.

Living Wills as yet have no legal status in Canada, but efforts are being made to allow for people to express their wishes in the form of advance directives to physician, next of kin, and lawyer as to the treatment desired when the situation arises.

In the meantime, we need to consider carefully the arguments for and against voluntary active euthanasia. And after that deliberation is complete, the second part of the debate will centre on what we want the law to allow or prohibit. Euthanasia raises two basic moral issues that should be distinguished: the morality of euthanasia, and following that, the morality of euthanasia legislation.

Arguments for Euthanasia

- Individuals have the right to decide about their own lives and deaths.
- Denying terminally ill patients the right to die with dignity is unfair and cruel.

181

• The golden rule requires that we allow active euthanasia for terminally ill patients who request it in certain situations.

• People have the right to die with dignity and lucidity.

The words of two recent letter writers (*Vancouver Sun*, Feb. 23, [2004]) add another dimension to the discussion, reminding us again of the human dimension, the personal, lived, existential component of the decision. Gayle Stelter writes, "For almost seven years I have been living with cancer, mostly joyously and gratefully, but gradually seeing the disease encroaching relentlessly on my once healthy body. Throughout these years, I have thought long and hard about death and I've discovered that it's not the prospect of death itself that is so frightening, but the process of dying. So to give myself courage, I have held an option in reserve. When I can see no quality ahead, when I am capable of bidding my loved ones a coherent farewell, when I am still in control of my resources, I will enlist someone's help to speed me on my journey. . . . For those of us who may choose to leave while there is still an element of control, of coherence, may we be fortunate to have a friend, a loved one, a health professional who will use their gifts in order that we may be excused. To deny such expert guidance in this last rite would be both heartless and inhuman."

> *"How can it be consistent to forbid mercy killing and yet deny that the cessation of treatment is the intentional termination of a life?"*

Or, listen to Susan Hess from Vancouver, "I have multiple myeloma . . . a rare bone marrow cancer . . . [that] destroys the blood, bones, immune system, kidneys and sometimes liver and spleen. The worst of it is the disintegration of the skeleton. . . . Unless one is lucky enough to die of sepsis first, the death is long and agonizing. The act of sitting up can fracture the vertebrae and lifting the dinner tray can fracture both forearms. Who deserves that? For what principle?"

Arguments Against Euthanasia

• Active euthanasia is the deliberate taking of a human life.

• We cannot be sure that consent is voluntary.

• Allowing active euthanasia will lead to abuses.

• There is always the possibility of mistaken diagnosis, a new cure, or spontaneous remission.

The philosopher J. Gay-Williams has argued against euthanasia in this way: "I hope that I have succeeded in showing why the benevolence that inclines us to give approval of euthanasia is misplaced. Euthanasia is inherently wrong because it violates the nature and dignity of human beings. But even those who are not convinced by this must be persuaded that the potential personal and social dangers inherent in euthanasia are sufficient to forbid our approving it either as a personal proactive or as a public policy." ("The Wrongfullness of Euthanasia," 1979).

Everyone has heard of the Netherlands experiment with legalized euthanasia, and I recommend Barney Sneiderman's paper "Euthanasia in the Netherlands: A Model for Canada?" published in *Humane Medicine*, April, 1992, for a sensitive and intelligent review of the Dutch approach. Sneiderman argues that we must provide the best care, the best pain control, but when the patient is still plagued by unbearable and unrelievable suffering and asks for release then "we will abide by your request because there is no other way that we can show you our compassion."

I believe that there are some circumstances when euthanasia is the morally correct action. I also understand that there are real concerns about legalizing euthanasia because of fear of misuse and/or overuse and the fear of the slippery slope leading to a loss of respect for the value of life. We do need to proceed with caution. We need full and open discussion, improvements in research, the best palliative care available, and above all we need to think about the topic together. Our best approach at this time may be to modify homicide laws to include motivational factors as a legitimate defense. Just as homicide is acceptable in cases of self-defense, it could be considered acceptable if the motive is mercy. Obviously, strict parameters would have to be established that would include patients' request and approval, or, in the case of incompetent patients, advance directives in the form of a living will or family and court approval.

Euthanasia is homicide. Some homicides are justified.

Canadian Doctors Reject Physician-Assisted Suicide

by Richard A. MacLachlan and Philip C. Hébert

About the author: *Richard A. MacLachlan is chair and Philip C. Hébert is a member of the College of Family Physicians of Canada's Ethics Committee.*

The Ethics Committee of the College of Family Physicians of Canada (CFPC) introduces a new statement endorsed by the National Board of the CFPC on December 8, 1999, regarding assisted suicide and active euthanasia. This statement is a complete reworking of a 1990 statement entitled "The Dying Patient: Ethical Considerations for Canadian Family Physicians." This new statement has gone through numerous revisions and received suggestions from a variety of committees and individuals inside and outside the CFPC. We believe it fairly represents the current ethical consensus regarding assisted suicide and active euthanasia. It cannot be the last word on these subjects because the debate concerning these practices continues to evolve. The CFPC issues this statement both to guide Canadian physicians and to promote dialogue and debate about ethically sensitive matters.

This new statement simply says that, at this time, certain medical practices for dying patients are relatively uncontroversial ethically and others are more morally contentious. Palliative care and decisions to forgo life-sustaining care are, with appropriate provisions and safeguards, ethically and legally acceptable. The more morally contentious practices are, of course, assisted suicide and active euthanasia, and physicians in Canada ought to avoid these practices at this time.

The committee believed it important to distinguish between these end-of-life practices to help guide and support front-line physicians caring for the dying and the critically ill. It reminds physicians not to abandon patients who are dying but to provide comfort to them, even if such measures might hasten death. Palliative care physicians know all too well, however, that the purported danger of "overdosing" a dying patient with drugs such as morphine is exaggerated and causes some physicians to undermedicate patients. Family physicians face very few professional hazards in this area, as long as the palliative treatment is proportionate to the patient's suffering; is not intended to directly cause death; and uses appropriate, symptom-directed, escalating doses of drugs.

Explore Requests for Death

Faced with implicit or explicit requests for assisted suicide and active euthanasia, physicians are encouraged to explore such requests with patients and their families and care providers. Often requests to accelerate death—and this can equally apply to requests to withdraw or not to provide life-sustaining care—are born out of patient suffering, loneliness, and despair. Not all of these patients are easy to treat, but sometimes they can tolerate the seemingly intolerable if they know someone *cares* for them. This means taking time to explore with patients the meaning of requests for death and what, if anything, can be done to help manage the whole spectrum of a patient's suffering.

Too readily acquiescing to requests for assistance to die (as such requests might arise out of temporary despair and reversible depression) can send a subtle message to patients: "You can't be helped because I cannot help you. Unfortunately, it is your time to die." Therapeutic nihilism regarding end-of-life care ought to be strenuously resisted, as a great deal can be done to improve care at the end of life. Clinicians need to recognize that requests to accelerate death are often cries for more help, not genuine requests to end life. Physicians who fail to provide appropriate medical treatment to critically ill patients might face professional or legal sanctions. (A physician in Toronto, [Ontario,] was . . . jailed for providing a lethal dose of drugs to a suicidal nonterminally ill patient.)

The committee recognizes that death is not the worst fate for some patients; there are conditions of unrelieved suffering and imminent death that call for reducing treatment. Hippocrates recommended that physicians ought to cease treatment for patients "overmastered by their disease." Just when this point is reached is a matter of clinical judgment that is made more difficult because of the new technology of medicine. Results of the SUPPORT [Study to Understand Prognoses and Preferences for Outcomes and Risks of Treatment] study have shown how challenging it is to

> *"Canada ought to avoid these practices."*

change end-of-life care. Because we can do so much more in medicine these days, it is difficult to recognize when "enough is enough." Clinicians, patients, and families can, unfortunately, sometimes collude in overtreatment.

Difficult Decisions

Decision making at the end of life is difficult and unlikely to get easier. But maybe that is how it should be. If decisions to limit care or to allow patients to die were ever to become easy or routine, we should all worry about medicine.

This statement does not, and cannot, resolve the ethical debate over whether assisted suicide and active euthanasia could *ever* be a morally appropriate response to suffering. Oregon has legalized physician-assisted suicide and some empirical data are available on that experience. That article joins an already rich literature on medical practices and attitudes in various countries regarding physician-assisted suicide. Physicians are encouraged to contribute to the ongoing debate on how best to manage end-of-life care.

Statement Concerning Euthanasia and Physician-Assisted Suicide

The College of Family Physicians of Canada (CFPC) distinguishes palliative care and appropriate decisions to forgo life-sustaining treatment from acts of assisted suicide and active euthanasia. Specifically:

• The CFPC *does not* support assisted suicide and active euthanasia, as they are illegal and controversial acts.

• The CFPC *does* support and recommend guidelines on appropriate end-of-life care and ongoing societal discussion of these issues by members of the CFPC, physicians generally, other health care professionals, patients, their families, and, indeed, all citizens in our society.

1. The goals of medicine are not only to cure disease and decrease suffering but also to provide the best possible end-of-life care, when cure is no longer possible.

2. Patients and families are due effective, comprehensive, and competent palliative care. Such care strives to meet physical, psychological, social, and spiritual expectations and needs of those living with illness.

> *"The CFPC [College of Family Physicians of Canada]* **does not** *support assisted suicide and active euthanasia, as they are illegal and controversial acts."*

3. Patients have the right to participate in decisions about their care. This includes the right to appropriate medical care as well as the right to forgo life-sustaining measures.

4. A decision to withhold or withdraw certain treatments might result in the earlier death of a patient, but this consequence is ethically acceptable and legally permissible if carefully and thoughtfully made. Where a patient's wishes to have specific treatment withheld or care withdrawn run counter to the physician's own values and an impasse is reached, the physician must seek to transfer the patient to another physician who might accommodate the patient.

5. Substitute decision makers for an incapable patient should make decisions for the patient in accordance with the patient's prior expressed wishes or, if such wishes are unknown or not applicable, shall act in the incapable person's best interests (taking into consideration the patient's prior wishes, beliefs, and values, and the treatment's effect upon the patient's well-being and its balance of benefits and harms).

Advance Care Planning

6. Physicians ought to seek clarification of a patient's views about care at the end of life by providing counseling and assistance in the area of advance care planning (living wills, mandates for health care, powers of attorney for personal care, proxy decision making). The goal of advance care planning is to encourage physicians, patients, and their significant others to discuss issues concerning death and dying; such discussions can better prepare patients for serious illness and encourage realistic end-of-life care.

7. It is sometimes claimed that treatment aimed at alleviating suffering might occasionally hasten a patient's death. This concern, especially pertaining to opioids, has been overstated. The reality is that the suffering of many dying patients is undertreated.

8. All care aimed at alleviating symptoms due to advanced, terminal disease is ethically acceptable and legally permissible if administered to relieve the patient's suffering, if it is commensurate with that suffering, and if it is not a deliberate infliction of death.

9. Acts intentionally causing a patient's death either by a physician (active euthanasia) or with a physician's help (assisted suicide) are to be distinguished from the appropriate practice of withholding or withdrawing life-sustaining care. Even if done out of best possible compassionate motives, the former practices are ethically controversial and illegal under the Criminal Code of Canada.

10. A patient's request for the deliberate infliction of death by a physician or with a physician's help ought not to be agreed to and calls for urgent attention by the physician. Such requests are often prompted by depression, poor palliation, isolation, and fear of abandonment. Input and consultation might be required from other health care professionals (such as a palliative care specialist, a social worker, an ethicist, a psychiatrist) for help in clarifying the patient's needs and exploring alternative ways of helping the patient.

Assisted Suicide Should Be Legalized in England

by Mary Warnock

About the author: *Mary Warnock is a British moral philosopher and author of the* Intelligent Person's Guide to Morals.

A House of Lords select committee is about to be set up to consider the issue of assisted suicide. [In 1993] I sat on a committee that was concerned with the more general concept of euthanasia. At that time we concluded that the law should not be changed and that assisted death should remain a criminal offence unless a decision should be made in court making it permissible for the patient to die in very particular circumstances, such as when someone is in a persistent vegetative state and needs a life-support machine to be turned off.

A great deal was made at that time of the distinction between killing and allowing to die, neither doctors nor nurses being prepared to contemplate killing when the whole ethos of their professions demanded that they attempt to keep people alive.

This seemed to me a wholly bogus distinction. The committee also considered the case of terminally ill patients. It was alleged that a doctor could never be sure that a patient was in fact terminally ill nor that an extra dose of morphine, for example, would hasten death. This seemed an odd argument for doctors to use.

I was a member of that committee and I went along with its conclusions, conscious nevertheless that the arguments leading to the conclusions were suspect and therefore that the conclusions were not to be regarded as written in stone.

I believed that at some time or other the medical and nursing professions would have to face the fact that being alive was, in certain circumstances, contrary both to a person's wishes and his interests, and that palliative care, even if available, would not render his suffering endurable.

The establishment of the new euthanasia committee is the outcome of a private member's bill,[1] introduced into the House of Lords by Lord [Joel] Joffe, a highly intelligent, sensitive and humane man.

It is a bill of extremely limited scope. It proposes that those who are terminally ill and within sight of death and who are suffering severely, but who are of sound mind and who have expressed a wish to die before their condition becomes yet more unbearable, may be assisted to die, without the risk that whoever assisted them should be charged with murder.

There has been one recent case, that of Diane Pretty, that caused widespread pity and partly motivated these proposals.

She was an intelligent person who knew exactly how her paralysis from motor neurone disease [ALS] would progress until in the end she would die of suffocation. She was physically incapable of committing suicide herself, but she knew that if her doctor or her husband helped her they would be liable to a charge of mur-

> *"Being alive was, in certain circumstances, contrary both to a person's wishes and his interests."*

der. Her appeal for assisted death was turned down by courts in Britain and by the European Court of Human Rights and in the end she died of suffocation, just as she had feared.

Like many others I was moved by Diane Pretty's case. In a less traumatic way my husband suffered similarly. He had a progressive and incurable lung disease called fibrosing alveolitis. Like Diane Pretty, he had a horror of suffocation and knew this would be the manner of his death. After the consultant at the Brompton hospital could do no more for him he was in the hands of our GP [general practitioner], a trusted friend.

When my husband confessed to him his terror of suffocating, the doctor said: "We will not let it happen, I promise," and after that, I suppose, increased the dose of morphine.

Death came and not too horribly. But this doctor was putting himself at risk. I am certain that what he did was right. He was acting from compassion, surely the deep motive of the medical profession at its best. I support Lord Joffe's bill because I cannot believe that what happened to Diane Pretty was justifiable.

More than One Doctor Must Agree

We are told that hard cases make bad law. But if cases are very hard then I believe it is time to look at the law again. The new bill seeks to legitimise assisted suicide only for the perhaps smallish category of people who are known to be near death, who are suffering and who are mentally competent and of course who have expressed a wish to die.

It is essential to recognise these limits. It would provide, too, that more than

---

1. As this volume went to press, Joffe's bill had not been passed.

one doctor would have to agree that the conditions were all satisfied.

There are those who would oppose the bill on absolute grounds, generally derived from the religious belief that deliberately to end a life at whatever stage is contrary to God's commands.

For such believers, arguments turning on the patient's suffering or his wishes will carry no weight. They will never regard assisted suicide as acceptable, whatever the law permits.

I think I understand this dogmatic belief though I do not share it. But the law cannot be determined by a particular religious belief. There must exist moral considerations behind the law separate from religion (even if influenced by it) deriving their authority from an idea of the common good.

I am therefore more interested in the arguments against the bill put forward by those of no dogmatic faith. These often take the form of the so-called slippery slope argument.

If the admittedly small group targeted in Joffe's bill are allowed to be helped to their death, who will be next? Won't there be a gradual erosion of our abhorrence of murder, until in the end we think it's all right to kill off anyone who expresses a wish to die or anyone who is incurably ill or in pain or who is terminally ill but mentally incompetent to express a wish? Is that the sort of society we wish to live in?

Many of those who deploy such arguments add that palliative medicine can ease the suffering of the dying and that if we concentrate on improving such care and ensuring that it is accessible, then the bill will be unnecessary. On this point there is evidence that some suffering cannot be alleviated by medicine, however skilled the treatment.

As for the slippery slope, the whole point of legislation is to place an immovable barrier to prevent our slipping further down it. On one side of the barrier is assisted suicide for those who genuinely want it and who anyway are on the verge of death, imposed by one person on another who has expressed a wish to die.

If Joffe's bill proposed a new category of such death called mercy killing then I could see the force of the slippery slope argument and would oppose the bill. But it does not do this. Assisted suicide is a different thing. We should trust the medical profession to observe the criteria laid down in the bill. If they did not they could be prosecuted.

There are other objections based on the difficulty of ensuring that the criteria are indeed satisfied. What is the definition of terminal illness, for example? How do we ascertain that someone is really competent to make a decision to die?

In some cases it might be difficult to determine such matters. But this difficulty should not be used to prevent relief for the clear-cut cases, for Diane Pretty and others like her. I am not arguing that anyone has a right to assisted suicide: I am arguing rather that sometimes compassion demands that they be allowed it. Doctors, unless their religion forbids it, should come to accept this as part of their duty.

British Physicians Oppose Assisted Suicide

by Right to Life UK

About the author: *Right to Life UK is a British pro-life organization committed to upholding the dignity of human life from conception to its natural end.*

Almost three out of four doctors (74%) in Great Britain would refuse to perform assisted suicide if it were legalised. A clear majority (56%) also consider that it would be impossible to set safe bounds to euthanasia as compared to 37% who disagree. In addition there are marked differences in attitudes to hospice and geriatric care between doctors opposed to euthanasia and those who support such a policy.

These facts emerge from a major survey completed by 986 doctors by the Opinion Research Business (ORB) over a two-week period—March 26-April 9, 2003. To ensure impartiality, ORB had the final decision on all questions. The survey was administered by the foremost medical internet company in the UK, Doctors.Net.UK, who contacted 9,000 doctors and medical specialists, including those in palliative care, oncology, psychiatry, geriatrics, general surgery and general practice. There was an 11% response which is typical for an internet survey of this nature.

The survey was commissioned by Right To Life and the initial results were launched at a press conference held by the All-Party Parliamentary Pro-Life Group in the House of Commons on Tuesday, May 13, 2003, Chairman of the parliamentary group, Jim Dobbin MP (member of Parliament) (Labour—Heywood & Middleton) said:

"We welcome these initial results. They are very much in keeping with a survey published in *Hospital Doctor* (13th March, 2003) which showed that 57% of doctors were opposed to the law in Britain being changed to allow euthanasia. In the ORB survey, Doctors were also invited to make comments and we have been amazed by the response. They have provided a wealth of information and demonstrate that a clear majority of doctors are opposed to the Lord Joel Joffe

Bill—The Patient (Assisted Dying) Bill—which aims to legalise assisted suicide and is to have its Second Reading in the House of Lords in June [2003]."

Most Doctors Disagree with Assisted Suicide

"We intend to present additional data (together with doctors' comments) from the survey to parliamentary officers in the Lord Chancellor's Office and the Department of Health. The validity of doctors' concerns about the difficulties of setting safe bounds to euthanasia can be seen when we consider the manner in which we have been stampeded in the last few weeks from the tragedy of the late Mr Reginald Crew who had Motor Neurone Disease, followed by the second tragedy of Robert and Jennifer Stokes, neither of whom was terminally ill. Yet, all three went to Switzerland for assisted suicide and there is no doubt that all three cases could be covered by Lord Joffe's Bill which has the complete support of the Voluntary Euthanasia Society."

To the question "As a doctor do you agree with assisted suicide?" 25% agreed, 60% disagreed and 13% were undecided.

The number who rejected euthanasia was higher—61% as compared with 22% in favour and 14% undecided.

However, the numbers of those rejecting both euthanasia and assisted suicide rose steeply when doctors were asked would they actually take part in such procedures. 26% said they were willing actually to practice assisted suicide as compared with 74% who would refuse.

The number who would refuse to practice positive euthanasia if made legal was even higher at 76% in comparison with 23% who would do so.

Not one palliative care doctor who responded to the survey would practice either euthanasia or assisted suicide.

In response to a question on the British Medical Association (BMA) policy which opposes the legalisation of euthanasia/assisted suicide, a majority (59%) felt it should not change. In comparison 28% felt it should alter, while 13% were undecided. More than four out of five (82%) doctors who reject euthanasia/assisted suicide support the BMA policy as compared with only 9% of those doctors who favour euthanasia.

Throughout the survey there were marked differences in the attitudes of doctors who support euthanasia/assisted suicide and those who are opposed. This was particularly significant on the BMA, on setting safe limits to euthanasia and on the development of hospice and geriatric care.

> *"Almost three out of four doctors (74%) . . . would refuse to perform assisted suicide if it were legalised."*

Overall 56% of doctors agreed with the House of Lords Select Committee on Medical Ethics which considered that it would be impossible to set safe bounds on euthanasia, 37% did not agree and 7% did not know. However, the number who agreed with the Lords Committee was very much lower (only 7%) among doctors who support euthanasia/assisted suicide compared with 75% of doctors who reject euthanasia.

Doctors Favour Palliative Care

Most doctors evidently support greater developments in both hospice and geriatric care. The survey revealed that overall 66% of doctors considered that the pressure for euthanasia would be lessened if there were more resources for the hospice movement, whereas 22% did not agree and 12% were undecided. However, less than half (48%) of those who support euthanasia/assisted suicide felt that developments in the hospice movement would have any effect, compared with almost three in four (72%) of doctors opposed to these practices. Palliative care doctors were the most supportive of increased resources for hospices.

A majority of doctors (55%) also felt that pressure would be reduced if greater resources were allocated to geriatric care. 30% disagreed and 15% did not know. The comparative figures for doctors opposed to euthanasia/assisted suicide with those in support were 61% as compared to 35%.

The survey explodes the idea that many people are clamouring for euthanasia. The experiences of doctors reveal otherwise.

In response to a question asking how many patients had requested euthanasia during the past three years nearly half (48%) of the doctors said not one. 37% quoted less than five; 11% gave numbers between 5 and 10 patients; only 2% gave figures of more than ten. In their comments

"To the question, 'As a doctor do you agree with assisted suicide?' 25% agreed, 60% disagreed, and 13% were undecided."

doctors said that in their experience requests for euthanasia were often "cries for help that have been resolved with good symptom control . . . they almost invariably want relief from distress."

The number of relatives requesting euthanasia was even lower than from patients themselves. 68% of doctors said that none had approached them in the last three years; 22% quoted less than five such experiences; 5% quoted figures between 5 and 10; and 1% gave numbers of more than ten. 3% said they did not know or that the question was not applicable to them.

Nonetheless, a substantial minority of doctors were concerned about possible pressures from families and colleagues if euthanasia and assisted suicide were legalised. Nearly half (47%) felt that if euthanasia and assisted suicide were made legal they would not be confident of being able to exercise their judgment without pressure from relatives. 29% were confident and 24% did not know.

On the other hand over half of doctors (58%) were confident of being able to exercise their judgment free from beneficiaries. 29% were not confident and 12% did not know. A disturbing figure was that relating to pressure from colleagues. Overall 43% were not confident that they would be able to exercise their judgment free from pressure from medical and nursing colleagues. 28% were confident and a further 28% did not know.

A majority of doctors (57%) felt that they could withstand pressures resulting from NHS [National Health Service] resources. In comparison 28% were not confident and 15% did not know. Palliative care doctors showed the most concern on this issue.

Although a majority of doctors were confident that they would be able to detect whether a request for assisted suicide was part of a depressive illness—10% very confident and 53% quite confident—a substantial minority lacked such confidence. 30% said they were not very confident and 7% not at all confident.

Not surprisingly, psychiatrists were the most confident (86%) as compared with 63% of general practitioners.

Organizations to Contact

The editors have compiled the following list of organizations concerned with the issues debated in this book. The descriptions are derived from materials provided by the organizations. All have publications or information available for interested readers. The list was compiled on the date of publication of the present volume; the information provided here may change. Be aware that many organizations take several weeks or longer to respond to inquiries, so allow as much time as possible.

American Civil Liberties Union (ACLU)
125 Broad St., 18th Fl., New York, NY 10004
(212) 549-2585
e-mail: aclu@aclu.org • Web site: www.aclu.org

The ACLU champions the rights of individuals in right-to-die and euthanasia cases as well as in many other civil rights issues. The foundation of the ACLU provides legal defense, research, and education. The organization publishes the quarterly *Civil Liberties* and various pamphlets, books, and position papers.

American Foundation for Suicide Prevention (AFSP)
120 Wall St., 22nd Fl., New York, NY 10005
(212) 363-3500 • fax: (212) 363-6237
e-mail: mtomecki@afsp.org • Web site: www.afsp.org

Formerly known as the American Suicide Foundation, AFSP supports scientific research on depression and suicide, educates the public and mental health professionals on how to recognize and treat depressed and suicidal individuals, and provides support programs for those coping with the loss of a loved one to suicide. It opposes the legalization of physician-assisted suicide. AFSP publishes a policy statement on physician-assisted suicide, the newsletter *Crisis*, and the quarterly *Lifesavers*.

American Life League (ALL)
PO Box 1350, Stafford, VA 22555
(540) 659-4171
Web site: www.all.org

ALL is a pro-life organization that provides information and educational materials to organizations opposed to physician-assisted suicide and abortion. Its publications include pamphlets, reports, the monthly newsletter *ALL About Issues*, and books such as *Choice in Matters of Life and Death* and *The Living Will*.

American Medical Association (AMA)
515 N. State St., Chicago, IL 60610
(312) 464-4818 • fax: (312) 464-4184
Web site: www.ama-assn.org

Founded in 1847, the AMA is the primary professional association of physicians in the United States. It disseminates information concerning medical breakthroughs, medical and health legislation, educational standards for physicians, and other issues concerning medicine and health care. It opposes physician-assisted suicide. The AMA operates a library and offers many publications, including its weekly journal *JAMA*, the weekly newspaper *American Medical News*, and journals covering specific types of medical specialties.

American Society of Law, Medicine, and Ethics (ASLME)
765 Commonwealth Ave., 16th Fl., Boston, MA 02215
(617) 262-4990 • fax: (617) 437-7596
e-mail: aslme@bu.edu • Web site: www.aslme.org

The society's members include physicians, attorneys, health care administrators, and others interested in the relationship between law, medicine, and ethics. The organization has an information clearinghouse and a library, and it acts as a forum for discussion of issues such as euthanasia and assisted suicide. It publishes the quarterlies *American Journal of Law and Medicine* and *Journal of Law, Medicine, and Ethics;* the newsletter *ASLME Briefings;* and books such as *Legal and Ethical Aspects of Treating Critically and Terminally Ill Patients.*

Center for the Rights of the Terminally Ill
PO Box 54246, Hurst, TX 76054
(817) 656-5143

The center opposes euthanasia and assisted suicide and maintains that these practices threaten the rights of the elderly, handicapped, sick, and dying. Its publications include pamphlets such as *Living Wills: Unnecessary, Counterproductive, Dangerous* and *Patient Self-Determination Act of 1990: Problematic, Dangerous.*

Compassion In Dying
6312 SW Capitol Hwy., Suite 415, Portland, OR 97239
(503) 221-9556 • fax: (503) 228-9160
Web site: www.compassionindying.org

Compassion In Dying believes that terminally ill adults who are mentally competent have the right to choose to die without pain and suffering. The organization does not promote or encourage suicide, but it does offer moral support to those who choose to intentionally hasten death. It publishes the quarterly newsletter *Compassion in Dying.*

Death With Dignity National Center
520 S. El Camino Real, Suite 710K, San Mateo, CA 94402-1702
(650) DIGNITY (344-6489) • fax: (650) 344-8100
e-mail: ddec@aol.com • Web site: www.deathwithdignity.org

The goal of the Death With Dignity National Center is to promote a comprehensive, humane, responsive system of care for terminally ill patients. It publishes a variety of information, including the pamphlet *Making Choices at the End of Life.*

Dying With Dignity
802-55 Eglinton Ave. E, Suite 802, Toronto, ON M4P IG8 Canada
(800) 495-6156 • fax: (416) 486-5562
e-mail: info@dyingwithdignity.ca • Web site: www.dyingwithdignity.ca

Dying With Dignity seeks to improve the quality of dying for all Canadians. It educates Canadians about their end-of-life health care options and provides counseling when requested. In addition, the organization offers living wills, works to legalize advanced directives in Canada, and seeks public support to legally permit voluntary physician-assisted dying. It publishes a quarterly newsletter, *Dying with Dignity*, and the pamphlet *Dying with Dignity.*

End-of-Life Choices
PO Box 101810, Denver, CO 80246
(800) 247-7421 • fax: (303) 639-1224
e-mail: info@endoflifechoices.org • Web site: www.endoflifechoices.org

Founded as The Hemlock Society in 1980, End-of-Life Choices has one core goal: to assure freedom of choice at the end of life. The organization advocates for the right of terminally ill, mentally competent adults to hasten death under careful safeguards. End-of-Life Choices creates, promotes, and supports legislation to maximize end-of-life options throughout the United States. It provides education, information, and advice about choices at the end of life and options available to the terminally ill. Their Web site provides helpful links, and they offer a variety of books and literature for sale online.

Euthanasia Research and Guidance Organization (ERGO)
24829 Norris Ln., Junction City, OR 97448-9559
(541) 998-1873 • fax: (541) 998-1873
e-mail: ergo@efn.org • Web site: www.finalexit.org

ERGO advocates the passage of laws permitting physician-assisted suicide for the advanced terminally ill and the irreversibly ill who are suffering unbearably. To accomplish its goals, ERGO offers research data, works to increase public awareness, and helps to raise campaign funds. The organization also provides the manual *Final Exit*, drug information, technique advice, and moral support to terminally ill individuals contemplating suicide.

Hastings Center
21 Malcolm Gordon Rd., Garrison, NY 10524-5555
(914) 424-4040 • fax: (914) 424-4545
e-mail: mail@thehastingscenter.org • Web site: www.thehastingscenter.org

Since its founding in 1969, the center has played a central role in responding to advances in medicine, the biological sciences, and the social sciences by raising ethical questions related to such advances. It conducts research and provides consultations on ethical issues. The Hastings Center does not take a position on issues such as euthanasia and assisted suicide, but it offers a forum for exploration and debate. The center publishes books, papers, guidelines, and the bimonthly *Hastings Center Report*.

Human Life International (HLI)
4 Family Life, Front Royal, VA 22630
(540) 635-7884 • fax: (540) 622-2838
e-mail: hli@hli.org • Web site: www.hli.org

The pro-life Human Life International is a research, educational, and service organization. It opposes euthanasia, infant euthanasia, and assisted suicide. It publishes the monthly newsletter *HLI Reports*, the monthly dispatch *Special Report*, and the monthly report *HLI Update*.

International Anti-Euthanasia Task Force (IAETF)
PO Box 760, Steubenville, OH 43952
(614) 282-3810 • fax: (614) 282-0769
e-mail: info@iaetf.org • Web site: www.iaetf.org

IAETF opposes death-with-dignity laws. It maintains an extensive and up-to-date library devoted solely to the issues surrounding euthanasia. IAETF publishes position papers and fact sheets on euthanasia-related topics, as well as the bimonthly *IAETF Update* and the report *When Death Is Sought*.

National Hospice and Palliative Care Organization
1700 Diagonal Rd., Suite 625, Alexandria, VA 22314
(703) 837-1500 • (800) 658-8898 • fax: (703) 837-1233
e-mail: info@nhpco.org • Web site: www.nho.org

The organization works to educate the public and health care professionals about the benefits of hospice care for the terminally ill and their families. It promotes the idea that, with proper care and pain medication, the terminally ill can live out their lives comfortably and in the company of their families. The organization opposes euthanasia and assisted suicide. It publishes the quarterlies *Hospice Journal* and *Hospice Magazine*, as well as books and monographs.

National Right to Life
512 Tenth St. NW, Washington, DC 20004
(202) 626-8800 • fax: (202) 737-9189
e-mail: nrlc@aol.com • Web site: www.nrlc.org

National Right to Life opposes euthanasia, physician-assisted suicide, and abortion because it believes these practices disregard the value of human life. It launches educational campaigns and publishes educational materials to help inform the public about issues such as abortion, euthanasia, and physician-assisted suicide. Its *National Right to Life News* is published twice each month.

Park Ridge Center
205 W. Touchy Ave., Suite 203, Park Ridge, IL 60068-4202
(847) 384-3504 • fax: (847) 384-3557
e-mail: al.hurd@advocatehealth.org • Web site: www.parkridgecenter.org

The Park Ridge Center explores the relationship between health care, religious faith, and ethics. It also facilitates discussion and debate about topics such as euthanasia and assisted suicide. The center publishes monographs, including *Active Euthanasia, Religion, and the Public Debate*, and the quarterly journal *Second Opinion*.

Right to Die Society of Canada
PO Box 39018, Victoria, BC V8V 4X8 Canada
(416) 535-0690 • fax: (604) 386-3800
e-mail: right@freenet.victoria.bc.ca
Web site: http://ncf.davintech.ca/freeport/social.services/rt-die/menu

The society respects the right of any mature individual who is chronically or terminally ill to choose the time, place, and means of his or her death. It helps patients throughout the dying process. It publishes informational pamphlets, brochures, and the periodic serial *Last Rights*.

Bibliography

Books

Kumar Amarasekara et al.	*Euthanasia, Morality, and the Law.* New York: Peter Lang Publishing, 2003.
Margaret P. Battin, ed.	*Death, Dying and the Ending of Life.* Hampshire,UK: Ashgate Publishing, 2003.
Mark Blochner	*The Right to Die? Caring Alternatives to Euthanasia.* Chicago: Moody Publishers, 1999.
Seamus Caven	*Euthanasia, the Debate over the Right to Die.* New York: Rosen Publishing Group, 2000.
Raphael Cohen-Almagor	*The Right to Die with Dignity: An Argument in Ethics, Medicine, and Law.* Piscataway, NJ: Rutgers University Press, 2001.
William H. Colby	*Long Goodbye: The Deaths of Nancy Cruzan.* Carlsbad, CA: Hay House, 2003.
Miriam Cosic	*The Right to Die: An Examination of the Euthanasia Debate.* London: New Holland Publishers, 2003.
Karen J. Donnelly	*Cruzan v. Missouri: The Right to Die.* New York: Rosen Publishing Group, 2003.
Jocelyn Downie	*Dying Justice: A Case for Decriminalizing Euthanasia and Assisted Suicide in Canada.* Toronto: University of Toronto Press, 2004.
Kathleen M. Foley and Herbert Hendin, eds.	*The Case Against Assisted Suicide: For the Right to End-of-Life Care.* Baltimore: Johns Hopkins University Press, 2002.
Elaine Fox et al.	*Come Lovely and Soothing Death: The Right to Die Movement in the United States.* Farmington Hills, MI: Gale Group, 1999.
Elizabeth Atwood Gailey	*Write to Death: News Framing the Right to Die Conflict from Quinlan's Coma to Kevorkian's Conviction.* Westport, CT: Praeger Publishers, 2003.

Daniel Hillyard and John Dombrink	*Dying Right: The Death with Dignity Movement.* New York: Routledge, 2001.
Robert C. Horn, ed.	*Who's Right (Whose Right?): Seeking Answers and Dignity in the Debate over the Right to Die.* Sanford, FL: DC Press, 2001.
Derek Humphry	*Final Exit: The Practicalities of Self-Deliverance and Assisted Suicide for the Dying.* New York: Dell Publishing, 2002.
Derek Humphry and Mary Clement	*Freedom to Die: People, Politics, and the Right-to-Die Movement.* Irvine, CA: Griffin Publishing, 2000.
Kalman J. Kaplan, ed.	*Right to Die Versus Sacredness of Life.* Amityville, NY: Baywood Publishing, 2000.
Loretta M. Koppleman and Kenneth Allen DeVille, eds.	*Physician-Assisted Suicide: What Are the Issues?* New York: Kluwer Academic Publishing, 2001.
Shai Joshua Lavi	*The Modern Art of Dying: The History of Euthanasia in the U.S.* Princeton, NJ: Princeton University Press, 2004.
Barbara Coombs Lee and Barbara Roberts, eds.	*Compassion in Dying: Stories of Dignity and Choice.* Troutdale, OR: New Sage Press, 2003.
Roger S. Magnusson	*Angels of Death: Exploring the Euthanasia Underground.* New Haven, CT: Yale University Press, 2002.
William F. May	*Testing the Medical Covenant: Active Euthanasia and Health Care Reform.* Grand Rapids, MI: Wm. B. Eerdmans Publishing, 2004.
Gary E. McCuen, ed.	*Doctor-Assisted Suicide and the Euthanasia Movement.* Hudson, WI: G.E McCuen Publications, 1999.
Charles F. McKhann	*A Time to Die: The Place for Physician Assistance.* New Haven, CT: Yale University Press, 1999.
Alan Meisel	*Right to Die, 2002 Cumulative Supplement.* New York: Aspen Publishers, 2002.
Georges Minois	*History of Suicide: Voluntary Death in Western Culture.* Lydia G. Cochrane, trans. Baltimore: Johns Hopkins University Press, 1999.
Suzanne Ost	*An Analytical Study of the Legal, Moral, and Ethical Aspects of the Living Phenomenon of Euthanasia.* Lewiston, NY: Edwin Mellen Press, 2003.
Phillip H. Robinson	*Euthanasia and Assisted Suicide.* South Bend, IN: Linacre Centre, 2004.
Barry Rosenfeld	*Assisted Suicide and the Right to Die: The Interface of Social Science, Public Policy, and Medical Ethics.* Washington, DC: American Psychological Association, 2004.

Bibliography

J. Donald Smith	*Right-to-Die Policies in the American States: Judicial and Legislative Innovation.* Levittown, PA: LBF Scholarly Publications, 2002.
Robert S. Wood	*Peaceful Passing: Die When You Choose with Dignity and Ease.* Sedona, AZ: In Print Publishing, 2000.
Sue Woodman	*Last Rights: The Struggle over the Right to Die.* New York: Perseus Publishing, 2001.
Xibi Xu et al.	*The Right to Die.* London: Minerva Press, 1999.
Marjorie B. Zucker	*The Right to Die Debate: A Documentary History.* Westport, CT: Greenwood Publishing Group, 1999.

Periodicals

Thomas Bowden	"Assisted Suicide: A Moral Right," Ayn Rand Institute, April 1, 2002. www.aynrand.org.
British Medical Journal	"Death in a Consumer Society," February 1, 2003.
Linda Ganzini et al.	"Physicians' Experiences with the Oregon Death with Dignity Act," *New England Journal of Medicine*, February 24, 2000. www.nejm.org.
Wayne J. Guglielmo	"Assisted Suicide? Pain Control? Where's the Line?" *Medical Economics*, October 11, 2002.
Brian Johnston	"Assisted Suicide in Oregon: Deaths More Widespread," *National Right to Life News*, April 2003.
John Keown	"Death by Another's Hand a Slippery Slope: The Diane Pretty Case," *The Times*, May 7, 2002.
James D. Moore	"One Year Down: Oregon's Assisted-Suicide Law," *Commonweal*, March 12, 1999.
Jennifer A. Parks	"Why Gender Matters to the Euthanasia Debate," *Hastings Center Report*, January 2000.
John Pipe	"Assisted Suicide and the Quality of Life of Persons with Disabilities: A Study Document," National Council of Churches Committee on Disabilities, January 2000. www.ncccusa.org
Diane Raymond	"Fatal Practices: A Feminist Analysis of Physician-Assisted Suicide and Euthanasia," *Hypatia*, Spring 1999.
Amanda Ripley	"Has the Movement Gone Too Far?" *Time International*, April 28, 2003.
Betty Rollin	"My Mother Died in Peace When She Was Ready," *Los Angeles Times*, November 8, 2001.
Lawrence Rudden	"Death and the Law," *World and I*, May 2003.
Wesley J. Smith	"Australia's Dr. Death Spreading the Assisted-Suicide Gospel," *National Right to Life News*, December 2002.

Wesley J. Smith — "Continent Death," *National Review Online*, December 23, 2003. www.nationalreview.com.

Lois Snyder et al. — "Assisted Suicide: Finding Common Ground," *Annals of Internal Medicine*, March 21, 2000.

Jacob Sullum — "Deadly Medicine: The Real Problem with Physician-Assisted Suicide," *Reason Online*, April 19, 2002. www.reason.com.

Keith Taylor — "Was Dr. Kevorkian Right? Why Cling to Life Without Savor? *Free Inquiry*, Spring 2003.

Agnes van der Heide et al. — "End-of-Life Decision-Making in Six European Countries: Descriptive Study," *Lancet*, August 2, 2003.

Cathy Young — "More Abuses of Federal Power," *Boston Globe*, October 14, 2002.

Index

France, prohibition of euthanasia in, 157
Frank, Ray, 29
Freedom to Die (Humphry and Clement),
  128
Frei, Andreas, 152
Fry, Prem S., 31

Gallup poll, 35, 36
Ganzini, Linda, 140
Gay-Williams, J., 182
Germany
  euthanasia in, under Nazis, 38
    was camouflage for mass murder, 176
  prohibition of euthanasia in, 158
Girsh, Faye, 12
Golden, Marilyn, 113
Goodwin, Peter A., 82
Greene, Rex, 115
Gunning, Karl, 38–39

health maintenance organizations. *See*
  managed health care
Hébert, Philip C., 184
Hemlock Society, 10, 11–12
Hendin, Herbert, 116, 119–20
Hentoff, Nat, 39
Hess, Susan, 182
Hippocrates, 185
Hippocratic Oath, 40, 102
  assisted suicide is compatible with, 134
  is out of touch with modern medical
    practice, 163
Hogan, Michael R., 30, 50, 89
Hook, Christopher, 95
hospice care, 161
  is alternative to assisted suicide, 41
    con, 21
Hospital Doctor (journal), 191
Hull, Richard T., 25
Humane Medicine (journal), 183
human life protections, threats to, 89–94
Humphry, Derek, 10–11, 12, 36–37, 87,
  128
Humphry, Jean, 10
Hyde, Henry J., 60

In Defense of Life (Fournier and
  Watkins), 38
International Task Force on Euthanasia
  and Assisted Suicide, 76
Italy, prohibition of euthanasia in, 157

Japan, legalization of euthanasia in, 157

Jean's Way (Derek Humphry), 10
Joffe, Joel, 189, 191
Johnson, Harriet McBryde, 14
Joint Commission on Accreditation of
  Healthcare Organizations (JCAHO), 41
Jones, Robert E., 51, 54, 56, 72, 74, 86

Kass, Leon R., 102
Kevorkian, Jack, 36, 70
  most clients of, were women, 48

Lancet (journal), 40
Lane, Bob, 175
Larue, Gerald A., 10, 154
Lee, Daniel E., 146
Lee v. Oregon (1997), 122, 123
Lethal Drug Use Prevention Act
  (proposed), 60
Let Me Die Before I Wake (Derek
  Humphry), 10
Lewis, C.S., 36
living wills, 22, 159, 160
  lack legal status in Canada, 181
Longmore, Paul, 115
Lund, Nelson, 62

MacLachlan, Richard A., 184
Madison, James, 67–68
Madorsky, Julie G., 14
managed health care, 114–16, 126–27
Matheny, Pat, 45, 124
Mead, Margaret, 98–99
Medical Journal of Australia, 40
medical profession, physician-assisted
  suicide would undermine, 107
medical science advances, effects of
  on death and dying, 20
  on social policy, 176–77
Meditation XVII (Donne), 174
Meier, Diane, 107
Mexico, prohibition of euthanasia in, 157
Mill, John Stuart, 147
More, Thomas, 17

National Review (magazine), 37
National Right to Life Committee, 86
Nazi Germany, euthanasia in, 38, 97
  was camouflage for mass murder, 176
Netherlands, 17–18, 38–39
  euthanasia rates have stabilized in,
  · 167–68
  euthanasia without consent in, 98, 110,
  166

Swiss Academy of Medical Sciences,
152
Swiss Medical Weekly (journal), 152
Switzerland, assisted suicide law in,
152–53

terminal illness/terminally ill
assisted suicide would harm care of,
103–12
con, 133–39, 140–45
creates no exemption to drug laws, 91
laws can protect rights of, 161–62
Tocqueville, Alexis de, 68
treatment withdrawal. *See*
refusal/withdrawal of treatment
Tros, F.P., 169
Tucker, Kathryn, 82

United States v. Rutherford (1979), 79
USA Today (newspaper), 35
Usery v. Turner Elkhorn Mining Co.
(1976), 61

Vacco v. Quill (1997), 25, 82
Vallender, Dorle, 152
Vancouver Sun (newspaper), 182
Van Den Haag, Ernest, 37

Walker, David F., 12
Wallace, Marian, 35
Warnock, Mary, 187
Washington v. Glucksberg (1997), 52,
55, 57, 82, 91, 92, 122–23, 130
Watkins, William, 38
Weekend Sun, Vancouver (newspaper),
177
Wernow, Jerome R., 43
Wertham, Fredric, 38
Whatever Happened to the Human Race
(Schaeffer), 37
Wickett, Ann, 10
women, assisted suicide would harm,
47–48, 111–12

Young, Robert, 16